THE HUM OF THE WHEELS THE ROAR OF THE CROWD

Dr Harry Irwin is Emeritus Professor (Communication), Western Sydney University.

THE HUM OF THE WHEELS THE ROAR OF THE CROWD

Five Cycling Shaw Brothers from Woolloomooloo

HARRY IRWIN

Australian Scholarly

First published 2018 by
Australian Scholarly Publishing Pty Ltd
7 Lt Lothian St Nth, North Melbourne, Vic 3051
Tel: 03 9329 6963 / Fax: 03 9329 5452
enquiry@scholarly.info / www.scholarly.info

ISBN 978-1-925801-52-1

Cover design: Wayne Saunders

Front cover: Fred Shaw on the track, from Ayer's Sarsaparilla advertisement.
Sydney Mail, 20 July 1901

Back cover: Bicycle racing under lights at the Sydney Cricket Ground, c.1903.
Australian Town and Country Journal, 14 January 1903

Dedicated in Memory of William Shaw and his wife Mary Anne Inch, their daughter Mary Amelia Shaw and her husband Brice Heber Thomas.

Contents

Acknowledgements ix

1. Backstories: Bicycling, the Shaw Family and Woolloomooloo 1

Bicycling in Australia in the 1880s and 1890s

Crazy about bicycling – High wheelers (penny farthings) and safety bicycles (safeties) – Women on wheels – Clubbing – Whirling wheels and coloured jackets – 'Diamonds flash from his ties' v cash cycling – A mug's game: gambling and corruption – The cycling news

The Shaw Family of Woolloomooloo

The family of William and Mary Anne Shaw – The grocer and the grocer's wife

The 'Loo in the Late 1800s

At first a 'pretty place', then docks, pubs, brothels and billiard rooms – Fishing boats and sailboats on Woolloomooloo Bay

2. On Your Marks: William Nathaniel Shaw 36

Road racing in Sydney – From road to track racing – Lillie Bridge – Life after bicycle racing

3. 'One of the Fastest Sprinters': Samuel Robinson Shaw 51

Off and away – The 'surprise packet' – 'One of the three best amateur riders in the colony' – Goulburn calling – Beating Megson on New Year's Day – Spills and wins – League of New South Wales Wheelmen – The Paddington Bicycle Club – Shaw Brothers, boot importers – Motorcycles and motorcycle sport – Donald (Don) Samuel Ewart Shaw

4. Soldiering On: Henry Tait Shaw 81

Joining the wheelers for one-mile racing – Changing tack? – Back on the saddle – The Megson–Lewis benefit and the motocycle – Marriage, a hawker's licence, a ball, a business and bankruptcy – Private Henry Tait Shaw, ANZAC veteran

5. 'A Man of Great Determination': Frederick Ewart Shaw 97

Pedestrianism – Following his brothers into bicycle racing – Goulburn to Sydney road race, 1896 – A smoke concert and back to the path – Winning the 1897 Newcastle Wheel Race – Rumours of a visit to England – Getting about – North to Brisbane, and beyond – Dinghy sailboating, a new interest – Cycling and sailing – Challenge racing – Texas Jack v. Fred Shaw, Horseman v. Cyclist – Spruiking Ayer's Sarsaparilla – More cycling, more sailing – Building bicycles at Newtown, Sydney – Shaw Brothers, boot and shoe importers and retailers – The Bicycle Depot, Camden and Fred Shaw's Etna brand bicycles – 'Camden to Queensland by Motor' – Marriage, and Etna motorcycles – The Camden Motor Garage – Return to Sydney and the end of the road

6. Long-Distance Road Racer: Thomas John Shaw 155

In Brisbane with brother Fred – Tom's South Brisbane Bicycle Agency, marriage, the loss of twin sons and insolvency – The Warrnambool to Melbourne road race (The Dunlop Road Race) – Tom's trouble with the law, and his mother-in-law – Sojourn in Camden, and a Camden to Sydney Road Race – Goulburn to Sydney Road Race – Family matters, a bicycle business at Granville, bankruptcy and the T. J. S. bicycle

7. The Brother-in-Law: Brice Heber Thomas 172

'To Mary from Brice' – Brice and his bicycles – 40 races at Lillie Bridge – The Young Harry *and the* Regina *– A gold medal from a win at Goulburn? – Marriage, a family, tailoring, managing, a mixed business and an Etna connection*

Notes 187

Select Bibliography 212

Index 216

Acknowledgements

I am indebted to many people for their encouragement and generous assistance in the writing of this book, among them Nick Walker, Anastasia Buryak, Helen Latemore and Wayne Saunders from Australian Scholarly Publishing, Rick Nelson (with whom, over many years, I have enjoyed countless conversations about the outcomes of his Shaw family research, and who made helpful comments on my first draft), Ian Irwin, Kelley Videbeck, Judy Healey, Betty Nelson, Margaret Leask, Alan Leask, Jennifer Williams, Jann Shaw, Phil Shaw, Roy Everett, Christine Shinn, Kath Young, Kate Boyd, Alison Irwin, Pam Shaw, Margaret Parker, Peter Kable, Kate Risely, Rod Charles, Craig Fry, George Nelson, Janet Macdonald, Ashleigh Ward, Dr Ian Willis, Dr Ian Hoskins, John Wrigley, Julie Wrigley, Dr Marc Rerceretnam, Rene Rem, Melody McDonald and Janice Johnson.

I also thank the staff and officers of State Archives and Records NSW, National Archives of Australia, Queensland State Archives, Powerhouse Museum (Sydney), Museum of Australia, Camden Museum, Sydney Cricket Ground Museum, Australian National Maritime Museum, Historical Atlas of Sydney, Dictionary of Sydney, National Library of Australia, State Library of New South Wales, Mitchell Library, State Library of Queensland, State Library of Victoria, State Library of South Australia, Stanton Library (North Sydney), Western Sydney University Library, Society of Australian Genealogists, Australian Defence Force Academy (University of New South Wales), Australian War Memorial,

Camden Library, Warrnambool Historical Society, Geelong Heritage Centre and Camden Historical Society.

That leads me to my final word of thanks: to my wife Bebz, who I admire (among many other reasons!) for her interest, support, encouragement and assistance, for critically reading my drafts, assisting me remedy my IT blunders and for offering many suggestions that have improved my telling of this story of turn-of-the-20th-century bicycle racing. As I have so often said, she is a treasure.

CHAPTER 1

Backstories: Bicycling, the Shaw Family and Woolloomooloo

BICYCLING IN AUSTRALIA IN THE 1880s AND 1890s

Crazy about bicycling

Australia's first bicycle craze occurred in the 1880s and 1890s. While there had been precursors to the bicycle that attracted public attention, real and sustained interest came with the development of high wheeler cycles in the late 1870s and then, from the mid-to-late-1880s and strongly into the 1890s, the so-called safety bicycles. Large numbers of young men, and later young women, found the 'newfangled' human-powered transportation machines irresistible and rushed to capture their share of the mobility, excitement and standing that the purchase of a bicycle would confer upon them.

Noted Australian cycling historian Jim Fitzpatrick has argued that the idea of 'bicycling' is fundamental to understanding the appeal of the new technology:

> A cyclist is not a person on wheels, but a person with wheels. There is an immense difference. While 'riding a bicycle' is the

> usual image, bicycling is essentially a man-machine operation that allows mode to be matched to terrain, optimising the use of wheel and foot. When sand, mud, obstacles, high winds, or a steep incline make pedalling difficult, the rider can get off and walk. The cycle can be pushed, carried, lifted over fences and floated across rivers. Heavy loads and bulky weight can be transported on it. Moreover, man and machine can be readily carried on wagons, trucks, cars, boats, or trains. It was that combination that radically altered the human travel equation in the 1890s.[1]

It was quickly recognised that bicycles would revolutionise the way people moved to and from work and social engagements, how they would be able to extend their exploration of cities and the countryside, and how they would conduct their businesses. Just as quickly, it was recognised that bicycle racing on existing roads and on flat track circuits would appeal to competitors, bicycle manufacturers, retailers and spectators and that bicycle racing would provide a welcome new avenue for wagering. And from 1890 to 1894, when all of the Australian colonies were in the grip of a severe depression, and for the remainder of that decade when the depression's consequences continued to be felt, relatively cheap and accessible bicycling offered interest, excitement and scope for achievement among aspirational members of the working classes.

At first, bicycles were imported from England, where they were manufactured in large numbers in the well-established engineering city of Coventry and surrounding towns, and from the United States, Canada and France. Imports of completed cycles, along with successive imports of constantly improved versions, were available to Australian buyers soon after they were marketed in their country of origin. Transport by steamships delivered bicycles to the hungry Australian colonial markets within two months of them leaving the distant factories where they were manufactured. Gradually some small-scale manufacturing, using mainly imported components, appeared in the colonies.[2]

Across the Australian colonies, bicycle dealerships sprung up in the cities and larger country towns. New machines could be bought on terms for as little as five shillings a week, or approximately one sixth of the earnings of the average working man. In the 1890s, 200,000 new bicycles were sold in Australia,[3] with many of these finding multiple owners as a robust second-hand market developed. By 1897, close to 150 makes or brands of bicycle were available on the Australian market[4] and small-scale Australian manufacturing had commenced with locally fabricated frames and imported components such as wheels, cranks, chains and saddles.

High wheelers (penny farthings) and safety bicycles (safeties)

The first high wheeler, high rider or 'ordinary' bicycle to reach Australia was imported to Melbourne in 1875.[5] Others followed and Melbourne became the initial centre of the bicycling craze.

The term 'ordinary' that came into everyday use to describe the high wheeler was chosen to convey that these new machines were being used 'as a vehicle, as an *ordinary* means of transport'.[6] Ordinariness was thought of as 'a quality meeting the everyday need to personal mobility across and beyond the expanding urban environs'.[7] Retrospectively, the high wheeler or ordinary was nicknamed the 'penny farthing', a catchy name that has stuck because the bicycle's dramatically different sized wheels looked like the large penny and the small farthing (one quarter of a penny) coins positioned alongside one another.

Ordinaries came in numerous wheel sizes. The largest of the big wheels was up to 60 inches in diameter for tall riders and wheels down to 50 inches accommodated the varying heights of others. Smaller versions were made for children. Ordinaries also came with varying mechanical configurations (especially for pedals and crank) but common to (almost) all was that the pedals propelled the large front wheel by means of direct drive and without a driveshaft or chain. Steering, of course, was also carried out via the front wheel. The much smaller rear wheel was simply a trailing wheel to assist balance.[8]

High wheelers, it has been said,[9] were not for the faint-hearted. They required practice to mount and dismount, had a high centre of gravity not always conducive to stability, were uncomfortable because of their solid rubber tyres and were not suited to rough road surfaces. A not uncommon occurrence, particularly on poor surfaces, was for a rider, without any protective headgear, to 'take a header' over the handlebars and tall front wheel. Riders who 'took a header', or otherwise parted company with their machines, were often said to have 'come a cropper', a term apparently inherited from horse riding sports and one that remains in frequent use in cycling circles today.

It was clear by the mid-1880s that, although ordinaries had captured the public's imagination, a safer bicycle was demanded. Manufacturers delivered, unsurprisingly with the generic name of the 'safety' bicycle, or simply the 'safety'. The safety, 'with equal-sized, wire-spoked wheels mounted on ball bearings, the rear wheel being driven by pedals and a chain from a central axle, and with pneumatic tyres and a diamond-shaped frame of tubular steel, then developed swiftly to become the standard bicycle for the next century'[10] – and to the present day.

Safeties had much lower centres of gravity than ordinaries because their identically or similarly sized wheels were much smaller than the high wheeler's front wheel. Without a large front wheel to dictate a high saddle, riders were much closer to the ground so that mounting and dismounting were easier and falls from machines were less common and less harmful. The new safeties were much friendlier towards older men, women and children.

They were also more technically sophisticated. One writer, emphasising the technical advances made with the safety bicycle, commented:

> That lightweight, deceptively delicate-looking mechanism, embodying several ingenious technological innovations (the roller bearing, chain, tangential-spoked wheels, tubular frame, and pneumatic tyre) permitted a unique man-machine

interaction … It was, in essence, a machine with a human engine.[11]

Safety bicycles weighed about 25–30 pounds, about half the weight of some ordinaries. They were strong and reliable and required little maintenance.[12] Their rubber cushion tyres were a vast improvement, in terms of rider comfort, over the thin, solid tyres of ordinaries. Subsequent development of pneumatic tyres carried tyre technology a step further.

High wheelers (ordinaries) racing at the Brisbane Exhibition Ground in the 1880s. State Library of Queensland

Safeties did not replace ordinaries overnight. During the early years of the safety bicycle, which escalated in numbers from around 1885, buyers had a choice of new machines. Increasingly they chose the safety over the ordinary and by 1892–3 ordinaries were all but obsolete and increasingly regarded as something of a novelty. The ordinary was ordinary no more.

While clearly the design and efficiency of bicycles over the 130 years or so since the appearance of the safety (for example, lightweight frames, variable gearing and braking technology) has steadily evolved, the design influence of the safeties is readily apparent in bicycles manufactured right up until the present day.

The arrival of the safety bicycle did a great service to cycling and to the emerging multi-layered bicycle industry. Safeties re-energised and dramatically boosted the cycling craze that had commenced a decade earlier with the high wheeler.

Women on wheels

In the earliest days of Australian cycling women largely went without wheels. The overwhelming majority did not ever ride a bicycle. The high and heavy penny farthings were incompatible with women's Victorian-era dress and the churches, along with many individuals (both women and men), saw the bicycle as a moral threat. Numerous articles appeared in the press, some by noted medical men who, without offering any supporting scientific evidence, opposed women taking to the roads on bicycles on medical grounds – including 'hygiene' and that bicycle riding might lead to reproductive malfunction.

Those early attitudes to women on wheels changed quite dramatically by the late 1890s, although the chapter on cycling for women in a book by H. Graves and George Lacey Hillier, published in London in 1898, was clearly an afterthought.[13] That final chapter of the book, written by the Countess of Malmesbury, amounted to just six pages! In the same year as this book was published, Mademoiselle Serpolette, who had been match racing other women in Europe for over three years, visited Australia to promote Gladiator brand bicycles. While on her widely publicised tour in Australia she offered to race any woman on equal terms. There were no takers.

Writing about Australian women and competitive cycling, one cycling historian has stressed that several thousand 'middle- and upper-class' women were involved in cycling in the 1890s. Women 'cyclistes' were involved in competitive endurance riding,[14] including Century Runs (100-mile events) and Melbourne to Sydney runs. Often the same women participated in adventure touring, where the competition was to explore new country in remote areas.[15] Particularly in Melbourne, there were also a small number (compared with those for men) of 'ladies' races' despite a disapproving public and despite cycle racing bodies not permitting women to compete in the many carnivals and events they organised.[16]

Written and photographic accounts of cycling race meetings in the 1890s tell of, and show, many women present. At the larger meetings conducted at the Sydney Cricket Ground many had at their disposal the facilities of the Members Pavilion and the grand Ladies Pavilion that was opened in 1896.[17]

Women asserted their right to ride, even if not riding to race. Commenting on influences on Australian women cyclists, Fiona Kinsey has argued that class-consciousness and fashion influenced the development of promenading, club cycling and charity riding among women in the 1890s. At the same time men were attracted by a strong sense of adventure to touring, endurance (often long distance overland riding over thousands of miles) riding and racing.[18] With respect to an interest by some women in promenading she said:

> During the 1890s cycling craze, socialites and other women wanting to be fashionable promenaded on the prominent streets in their fashionable best. Not only did women 'do the block' on a bicycle, but it also became popular for women to have their photographic portrait taken posed with a bicycle, either in a studio photograph or in a snapshot.[19]

Cycling journals, aimed primarily at a male readership were, however, also helpful in encouraging interest from women. In November 1896, for example, the very first issue of the *Cycling Gazette*, the official organ of the New South Wales Cyclists' Touring Union, featured an article about a prominent female cyclist, the Secretary of the Ladies Bicycle Club,[20] and initiated a ladies' page that continued in later issues.[21] Other issues of the journal carried display advertisements from the Cycling School, Sydney, showing women enjoying riding bicycles.[22]

Cyclists with their safety bicycles rambling in South Australia, c.1900.
State Library of South Australia

Clubbing

The arrival of bicycles in Australia and the bicycling craze that immediately followed was accompanied by the formation of bicycling clubs. As early as 1878 the Melbourne Bicycle Club was formed for high wheelers. The Sydney Bicycle Club was formed a year later.[23] Other colonies were not far behind: a Tasmanian Club was inaugurated in 1880, South Australian and Queensland clubs in 1881 and the Western Australian Cycling Club was established in 1891. Some larger rural towns established cycling clubs, for example at Dubbo, New South Wales in 1866.[24]

Cycling clubs proliferated in the cities. Some represented particular suburban areas, some were primarily social clubs built around a variety of cycling activities, some had origins within a church body and others were focussed on weekend and public holiday 'runs' into the near countryside, sometimes known as 'rambling' or touring. As bicycles became more accepted, ladies only clubs were formed. Other clubs were formed for the express purpose of fostering road and track racing, although generally these also offered social activities sometimes for men only but on other occasions involving wives and lady friends of members.

In Sydney, the Suburban Bicycle Club was formed in May 1882, the Redfern Bicycle Club in September of the same year, the Balmain Bicycle Club in April 1883, the Crusaders' Bicycle Club in 1887, the League of New South Wales Wheelmen in 1893, the Sydney Ladies Bicycle Club in February 1895 (at first with just nine members) and the Waratah Rovers Cycling Club (for Presbyterian cyclists) in March 1896.[25] A meeting called to establish an 'upper crust' or society club, the Hampden Cycling, Riding and Driving Club, in May 1896, to be based in a pavilion the organisers hoped the government would construct for them in Centennial Park, sought 'to bring together the nicest people in the nicest possible way'. This elitist proposal met with opposition from many who thought the 'toffs' were seeking special advantages. Objectors gate-crashed the first club outing at Centennial Park. The government did not build the hoped-for pavilion and the club bought two grand eastern suburbs houses for use as clubrooms.[26]

Clubrooms were not often as grand as those finally settled upon by the Hampden Club. Many clubs held their early meetings, sometimes as frequently as weekly, in spaces provided by eager city hotels or coffee houses. As their finances improved, a few of the larger clubs rented space in city buildings for their club meetings and some of their social events and to provide facilities, such as change room, for members. By 1897, the League of New South Wales Wheelmen had moved its clubrooms from George Street to much larger premises in Wynyard Lane that allowed an expansion of facilities to include a books and newspapers reading room, a billiard room, a gymnasium, a piano and a telephone.[27] In 1899 the Sydney Bicycle Club maintained a library of books and magazines.[28]

Men-only social activities included 'smoke concerts' and 'rinking nights'. Smoke concerts, held in the evenings at clubrooms of city and country town hotels, were often scheduled after a day's racing or a multi-day racing carnival. Usually concerts were chaired by the club's president. Toasts and speeches were in abundance. Cups, medals and cash prizes from recent racing events were presented. Entertainment was in the form of musical items, recitations and comedy skits presented by members and/or outsiders contracted for the event. The atmosphere was akin to that of the music hall. Plenty of opportunity existed, inside and outside the venue, for the pipe smoking that was an almost universal male bonding ritual of the times. Smoke concerts were jolly social evenings. Rinking nights were held at ice skating rinks popular in the 1880s and 1890s. Some skated. Others, no doubt, smoked and talked. One such event was the Summer Hill Bicycle Club's Grand Cyclists' Rinking Night held at the Sydney Elite Skating Rink on Monday 17 September 1888.[29] That rinking night was organised in honour of the visit of inter-colonial cyclists. Smoke concerts and rinking nights were marked by high levels of camaraderie. They fostered club loyalty, friendship, morale building and solidarity. As one cycling historian has argued, bicycle clubs became a focus for fellowship.[30]

In 1890, the Speedwell Bicycle Club, with 53 active members and 18 honorary members, conducted a range of events all of which appear to have been for men. Among the events were an opening run of the season to Coogee that attracted 175 cyclists, two open handicap road races (one from Parramatta to Penrith, the other from the city to Homebush), a four-day tour through the Illawarra district, a race meeting at the Association Cricket Ground (now the Sydney Cricket Ground) with the Sydney Harriers Club, two smoke concerts, a rinking event at the Crystal Palace Skating Academy and a cricket match against the Redfern Bicycle Club.[31]

The Sydney Bicycle Club conducted a wide range of activities in 1899 that included a number in which women were involved. Apart from the racing, a camp at Jenolan Caves, smoke concerts, billiard tournaments, Saturday afternoon runs to popular beaches and cricket matches for the men, the club also held an annual picnic, an annual ball, a harbour excursion, a theatre party and singing and dancing socials at the club's rooms.[32]

Other club social activities were designed to be more inclusive and embrace women and children. Several cycling clubs held annual balls as, for example, that of the League of New South Wales Wheelmen that set down its Fifth Annual Ball for Friday 5 August 1895 at the Paddington Town Hall,[33] one of the city's largest ballrooms. Two hundred people attended.[34] Harbour excursions were another favourite and inclusive event with, again for example, the League of New South Wales Wheelmen arranging a family day out to celebrate their 1896 Winter Cycling Carnival. Invitation cards told that the excursion would take place on Sunday 23 August, with the chartered steamer *Baldrock* leaving the Erskine Street, Darling Harbour, wharf at 10am.[35]

Some cycling bodies also accepted civic responsibilities and lobbied authorities in an effort to improve conditions for cyclists. For example, in 1894 the newly formed League of Victorian Wheelmen, in a move that significantly boosted the local manufacture of bicycles, successively lobbied the government to reduce customs duties on imported bicycle parts from 25% to 10%.[36] In 1899 the New South Wales Cyclists' Union spoke out about the need for a 'North Shore Bridge' (the Sydney Harbour Bridge as it would be named when opened in 1932), street watering, city traffic as it affected cyclists, the right of the road and planning for public cycle paths.[37] That Union's Touring Branch also produced a handbook to enable cyclists to plan cycling tours that included road maps, directions, distances, medical information and accommodation details.[38]

Whirling wheels and coloured jackets

While the often-made claim that bicycle racing probably began about five minutes after the world's second bicycle was manufactured exaggerates to capture attention, racing by one man and his machine against another certainly began very early in the history of cycling. The first races were on-the-spot challenges on city streets by young men who engaged in what was called 'scorching'. 'Scorchers', as they soon came to be known, often raced one another with little regard for public safety and quickly became thought of as wild and reckless, as menaces.[39] They were thought of as larrikins of the wheel.[40] The police set out to be 'stoppers' to reckless riding in the streets with a device that could puncture up to 20 holes in the tyres.[41] One observer wrote, 'Notwithstanding the eternal crusade against this undesirable class of rider, he is still in our midst, and a walk down George Street [Sydney] at any hour will reveal him in all his recklessness and ungainly attitude'.[42] Scorching was an early form of street racing.

Cycle racing soon became an organised activity (although scorching continued) and moved from city streets to involve both road racing on the established, but rough, roads of the day and track racing. Track, or 'path' racing first took place on agricultural showground arenas and cricket fields, both of which readily allowed oval or circular tracks to be marked out, were grassed and possessed spectator facilities. Over time some of the more central of these tracks, the forerunners of velodromes, were modified, for example by the provision of safer, sealed (with cinders, concrete or asphalt, the latter sometimes painted white) surfaces, banking and gas or electric lighting to allow night time race meetings. So popular was bicycle racing that venue administrators often earned more in a year by making them available to cycle racing clubs than they did from cricket or football.

So-called scratch races, where all competitors started simultaneously in one line, were vastly outnumbered in Australia by handicap races. Competitors began handicap races at intervals determined by race officials known as handicappers. The strongest riders, based on judgements about past performances, 'form' and the nature of the track or road, were 'scratch men', the last to start. Weaker riders were given head starts of a stated number of yards for track races or minutes for the cross-country road races. Those who were flagged away first were known as the 'front men', 'front markers' or 'limit men'. Following them were the other starters right down to the 'rear markers' and scratch men at the pre-determined distance or time intervals.

The stated objective of handicapping usually was that it gave every rider a fair chance of winning or taking out a place. Just as important, in terms of attracting paying crowds and creating betting opportunities, was ensuring close and exciting race finishes. The best riders began their race at a disadvantage they had to overcome in order to win. Weaker riders had to maintain the advantage of their handicap if they were to succeed. On occasions, especially in the longer road races, a prize – often a substantial one – was awarded to the rider who covered the distance in the fastest time. Handicaps for each rider were published in newspapers in the days prior to a race. That often led to withdrawals when riders decided the handicap they had been allocated meant they had little chance of success and might better put their efforts into another race.

Among the more notable road races was Victoria's annual 165-mile (265 km) Warrnambool to Melbourne race. In Sydney there were short road races from the city south to Botany and return, while elsewhere in New South Wales races were run between, for example, Goulburn and Sydney and Camden and Sydney. Long distance road races required quite sophisticated organisation to ensure riders' cycles were available to them at the start (carriage of cycles and competitors by train from Melbourne or Sydney had to work smoothly), riders had to be fed and watered during races that could occupy up to ten hours (longer for the stragglers), and provision had to be made to assist injured riders and those whose cycles required repairs. The management and considerable costs of the exercise were usually borne by the Dunlop Rubber Company, manufacturers of bicycle tyres, who sponsored road race events and reaped associated publicity advantages.

In Sydney, small clubs conducted track races at suburban parks such as those at Redfern, St Leonards and North Sydney. Much of the earliest Sydney racing was conducted at the privately owned Lillie Bridge Grounds, close to the city in Forest Lodge (Glebe). These races were often conducted as a minor part of a programme of pony racing and pedestrian (running and walking) races. It is not surprising that, in those circumstances, bicycle racing attracted the interest of bookmakers and punters. Bets could be placed at the grounds or (illegally) on the special trams that conveyed people to these largely evening events.

The practice of conducting cycling events to contribute to the programmes of more broadly based 'sports days' was not uncommon. Early on, it helped introduce cycling sports to sports-minded spectators who may not have considered attending a meeting entirely given over to cycling events. The practice lent variety to the programmes of other sporting events and attracted paying spectators eager to witness the sporting side of the bicycling craze. Sometimes only a single cycle race was part of these programmes, as when an event was staged during the half-time interval of major football matches. And, at the first Sports Meeting of the Darlinghurst Harriers Amateur Athletics Club in 1891, just one three-mile mixed bicycle race (mixed in the sense that riders on both ordinaries and safeties could compete) was included with running and walking races and a football game.[43] At other times cycle races formed part of the programme of sports and other activities at highland gatherings, charity days that sought to raise funds to support hospitals or for poor relief, and at similar days held by friendly societies and Freemasons' lodges. All such meetings were characterised by a carnival atmosphere that was inclusive of women and children and helped build a healthy image of cycling.

As the sport grew and its capacity to draw large crowds increased, and as a large part of Sydney cycle racing came to be dominated by the League of New South Wales Wheelmen, race meetings were held at the Agricultural Ground and what was to become the Sydney Cricket Ground. In Victoria, the League of Victorian Wheelmen found the Melbourne Cricket Ground to be a popular and accessible venue and the Adelaide Oval found favour for South Australian meetings. And in Queensland the League of Queensland Wheelmen made Brisbane's Cricket Ground at Woolloongabba (the 'Gabba') the home of competitive cycling.

As early as July 1869, 10,000 spectators (all men – it was a men only event) turned our to watch velocipedes, forerunners of penny farthing bicycles, race at the Melbourne Cricket Ground.[44] In later years, crowds of this size were commonplace and often considerably exceeded. A two-day carnival of the League of New South Wales Wheelmen in Sydney in 1895 drew 60,000 spectators, partly because the visiting American champion Arthur Zimmerman was competing. Attendances at race meetings hosted by the Australian Natives' Association (ANA)[45] in Melbourne in 1898 and 1899 drew crowds of 50,000 and 65,000.[46]

Cyclist being paced by a motorcycle, Melbourne Exhibition Track, Carlton, 1903. State Library of Victoria

Track and road racing took many forms, one of which was paced riding. The idea was simple, the practice less so. Competitors rode close behind another bicycle ridden by a non-competitor, whose task it was to set the pace for his man and shelter him to allow higher speeds to be attained. In effect, the pacer acted as a windbreak and reduced drag. Of course, this complicated the running of events, made them more dangerous, added to the excitement and made the racing more difficult for spectators to follow. Over time the pacing bikes evolved into tandems and further into machines with three, four, five and even six riders. In the closing years of the 1890s motorised bicycles and then specially built motorcycles were developed as pacing machines and what were termed motorpace bicycle races were conducted. The pace machines, with elongated swept back handlebars, seated the rider back and high so he could almost stand to offer further protection to the event competitor, known as a pace follower, riding behind.

Cycling clubs adopted uniforms and colours and firmly enforced adherence to them. When it was formed in 1878, the Melbourne Bicycle Club determined that 'the club uniform consist of myrtle green coat, knickerbockers, stockings and cap, and silver badge. Members are requested to wear the same at Club meetings and when touring. White straw hats with club ribbon (green and gold) to be worn in summer'.[47] Interestingly, the club appointed Collins Street costumiers Alston & Brown as outfitters to members. Tellingly, members were warned not to wear their uniform or badges on Sundays. The churches were not all behind the development of cycling. As late as 1897, for example, Melbourne's Presbyterian General Assembly condemned the bicycle as 'evil' for its 'desecration of the Sabbath'.[48]

One insight into the dress and the racing colours of cycle racing competitors' silk jackets is provided by the programme for an 1888 meeting of the Sydney High School Amateur Athletic Club at the Association Cricket Ground that listed club colours for a three miles bicycle handicap (students, ex-students and 'strangers' were eligible to race). The rules specified that 'all competitors must appear in University costume (i.e. sleeved Jerseys and Knee trousers)' and their club colours.[49] Those colours were listed as red and black (New South Wales Cyclists' Union), red and white (Crusaders' Bicycle Club), black and white (Rovers Bicycle Club), brown and rose (Suburban Bicycle Club), cerise and blue (St Leonards Bicycle Club), Oxford and Cambridge Blue (Summer Hill Bicycle Club), brick red (Sydney Bicycle Club). One rider not affiliated with any club rode in pink and black, another in maroon and gold.[50] It is easy to appreciate how one commentator became excited about the spectacle of track racing, describing it as 'whirling wheels and coloured jackets'.[51] Another equally enthusiastic commentator wrote of the 'electrical effect' upon spectators as the men swept by with a whirr 'and a rustle of silk'.[52]

An 1895 advertisement placed in the *Sydney Wheelman* by David Braham & Co., 'tailors by appointment to the Leading Cycling Clubs for the past 9 years', and 'importers of every Requisite for Training and Racing' revealed an array of clothing for cyclists and something of the colour of the sport.[53] Bicycle suits, 'to measure on the shortest notice' were two guineas, well in excess of a working-man's weekly wage. More modestly priced at twelve shillings and six pence were cashmere bicycle suits, jersey and pants, available in navy, black, brown, cardinal and pale blue, with jersey and pants supplied in different colours if required. Cellular cycling shirts and matching caps were available. Cellular bicycle stockings were offered in navy, black and grey and cellular three-quarter cycling hose in heather mixture, grey, navy and black. Special colours could be made to measure. And those wanting cycling gauntlets and gloves, sashes, hats, ribbons and ties would not have been disappointed.

The League of New South Wales Wheelmen enforced dress and colour regulations. By January 1897, at which time a review was under way, the League stated that silk or satin caps were to be worn by all competitors and that every rider was to wear long sleeves, plain black knickerbockers, and black socks. Also obligatory for all riders competing under the rules of the League were long-sleeved woollen jerseys, in the colours registered with the Colour Steward, to be worn sweater fashion over the knickerbockers, with the colours on both jersey and knickers.[54]

Uniforms were often required for club outings. The Redfern Bicycle Club specified that its colours be blue and gold and that 'the uniform be brown coat and navy blue stockings, and caps be optional at moonlight runs' and that 'Members shall wear same at all Club Runs'.[55]

Racing cyclists who came a cropper could be quite badly injured. The dangers of riding in Melbourne's Austral Wheel Race were summed up in an oft-quoted anonymous poem:

After the Austral's over,
After the track is clear –
Straighten my nose and shoulders,
Help them to find my ear.[56]

With the ever-present threat of spills and resultant injuries in mind, larger clubs like the League of New South Wales Wheelmen formed and equipped what they termed 'ambulance corps'.

'Diamonds flash from his ties' v cash cycling

Much early Australian racing was amateur racing with no cash prizes awarded. Competitors rode for prizes such as silver cups, trophies and gold and silver medals, some with precious stones attached. Race sponsors then expanded the range of prizes to include silver trays, tankards, clocks and items of jewellery such as gold necklaces, bracelets and brooches. Winners of these spoils were not permitted to sell their prizes or in any way convert them into cash. To do so meant they lost their amateur status. Riders were expected to compete for the glory of the sport, to build trophy cabinet collections and to win jewellery for wives or mothers or to impress the ladies. In an apparent reference to expensive tiepins, one cycling historian noted that jewellery was sometimes for the rider himself and 'diamonds flash from his ties'.[57]

Two photographs captioned 'A Bird's-eye View of the Trophies Won by Con on the Wheel', preserved in an album of cycling memorabilia by the State Library of New South Wales,[58] illustrate the extent and variety of valuable prizes won by an amateur. Con Dwyer, a 'noted flyer' and Champion of Victoria and Amateur Champion of Australia in the late 1880s, displayed his prizes on and in front of a piano. So many were they that the piano had to be dressed twice to display the total winnings, and two photographs resulted. Among the prizes evident were at least half a dozen elaborate clocks, a large boxed cutlery setting, and an array of silverware trays, platters, teapots, and bowls along with a variety cut-glass spirits-storage bottles and tableware. As well, the display exhibited an extensive collection of what appear to be watches and jewellery. The piano on which the two displays were arranged was also a cycling prize. Newspaper articles of the day tell that Con Dwyer won the high-quality Ronisch piano, imported from Dresden, Germany, for his win in the Melbourne Bicycle Club's three-mile bicycle race in 1886. The piano was valued at 84 guineas (£88) at a time when average annual male earnings were about that same amount. Second prize in that three-mile race was a 30 guineas Waltham watch and third prize was a trophy worth twelve guineas. Con's piano was not the most expensive piano ever offered as a prize. Also in 1886, first prize for Melbourne's first Austral Wheel Race, a three-mile handicap, was a grand piano valued at £200.[59]

While Con Dwyer's trophy photographs dramatically illustrate the motivation and rewards for amateur racing, they also drive home a realisation of why so many riders became dissatisfied with their amateur status and the strict rules concerning their winnings. Successful riders, the 'cracks', could win many hundreds of pounds worth of glittering prizes but they could only look at them or give them away and not convert them to cash or barter them.

To make matters more difficult for cash strapped amateurs, the Australian Cycling Union prohibited amateurs, on penalty of suspension, from competing for money, teaching, training or coaching as a livelihood, pace making for a professional or using a professional as a pacemaker, or 'backing himself, or allowing himself to be backed, either in a public or private race'.[60]

The time was right for professional cycling, commonly known as cash cycling, where the prizes were paid in cash, albeit sometimes supplemented by a gold medal. The League of New South Wales Wheelmen, established in late 1893, followed by the League of Victorian Wheelmen and similar leagues subsequently formed in the other colonies, gave great impetus to Australian professional or cash cycling. Although the value of their cash prizes was often topped by their Victorian colleagues, in 1895 the League of New South Wales Wheelmen was offering rich cash prizes. In an advertisement in the *Sydney Wheelman* for its forthcoming Monster Racing Carnival to be held at the Sydney Cricket Ground on Saturdays 16 and 23 November, the League trumpeted that total prize money offered would be £375.[61] Five events (with numerous heats) were set down for the first day of the carnival and four events (again with numerous heats) for the second day.

The big money event on the first day was the Sydney Wheel Race over two miles. Ten shillings was charged to submit an entry for the race and another ten shillings if the entry was accepted. Of the 130 sovereigns (each equivalent to a pound sterling) prize money offered for this race, first prize was 100 sovereigns, second fifteen and third five. Those placed first and second in heats were to win 30 shillings and ten shillings respectively. On the second day, the one-mile Metropolitan Handicap offered identical prize money. The half-mile League Cup offered 20 sovereigns to the winner, five to the second placegetter and only one to the rider coming home third. The half-mile Championship of Australia on day one offered ten sovereigns and a gold medal worth five sovereigns to the winner and three and two sovereigns for second and third place. The five-miles Championship of New South Wales on the second day made available similar winnings, including the gold medal for the winner. What must have been obvious to the men racing was that in each of the nine races the prize money on offer was heavily skewed towards first place. They would have to ride to win.

Generous cash prize money appealed to many previously amateur riders, who turned professional and switched to cash cycling in droves. And the League of New South Wales Wheelmen, now with access to venues with large spectator capacities, grew quickly in size and power. By 1895 the League, headquartered in Sydney, had established thirteen country branches: at Maitland, Goulburn, Parramatta, Newcastle, Bathurst, Albury, Young, Dubbo, Singleton, Ballina, Lismore, Bega and Bombala.[62] A year later the League boasted 40 country branches, although some, for example Temora with nine members, had very few enrolled.[63] Another measure of the League's rapid growth and success was that in its first year of operation its income was £5,757,[64] a very large sum of money for the day. The League had instantly become a large sports business.

To build cycling interest within regional centres, and to encourage city-based riders to travel and compete there, from time to time the League advertised forthcoming provincial events by distributing cards at its city headquarters and city race meetings. One such card, printed for the Newcastle branch in February/March, promoted a ten-event racing programme to be conducted on Easter Saturday and Easter Monday in April 1898.[65] The card headlined the £76 prize money allocated for the meeting and the branch's claim that Newcastle had the 'best banked track in the colony' (a claim widely accepted at the time and a special attraction to riders because it guaranteed higher speeds) and set out, for each race, the distance, entry fee, total prize money and how it was to be distributed among the placegetters. One event, a one-mile roadster race, was for the League's Northern District riders only. The event offering the greatest prize money, a two-mile scratch race, also paid a five-shillings prize for each lap. Other events were open handicaps of half, one and two miles, multicycle handicaps over two and three miles, a second- and third-class handicap for up-and-coming riders, a half mile scratch race and a youth's race for boys aged under fourteen. Competitors travelling to Newcastle by rail for the weekend were enticed by having to pay only a single fare for a double journey.

The town of Bourke on the Darling River in far western New South Wales was typical of country centres that enjoyed a programme of bicycle racing sponsored by the League in 1898. On the afternoon of Good Friday, the newly formed Bourke branch of the League of New South Wales Wheelmen hosted what they billed as a 'Bicycle Carnival' at the Bourke Showground. The programme commenced with a one-mile Novice Bicycle Race (£4, £1) and continued with an Open Handicap Bicycle Race, also over one mile (£4, £1, 10s). The highlight of the afternoon's racing was the Bourke Wheel Race over two miles (£7, £2, £1). The fourth event was the Ladies' Bracelet Bicycle Race, a title that referred to the prize for first prize rather than suggesting women riders would compete. Run over half a mile, the first placegetter had the choice of a ladies' bracelet or £4. The rider placed second received £1. A condition of entry was that only ladies could nominate competitors. In addition to the four bicycle races, a foot race and a tug of war, the latter between twelve cyclists and twelve pedestrians (foot racers), were included on the programme.[66] A programme footnote added that 'Second and Third Prizes are only approximately correct, and are subject to slight alteration'. Two years later, the League branch at the even more remote opal mining settlement of White Cliffs offered £60 prize money at a race meeting. The principal event was the Opal Wheel Race, for which £30 was allocated.[67]

Other rewards accrued to successful cyclists, especially the cracks. Cycle dealers were among the first to realise that a win on Saturday translated into sales on Monday. Dealers and manufacturers often gave separate rewards in cash or kind to successful professional riders of their machines. Tyre importers did the same. And, although betting by competitors was often banned it was commonplace and led to numerous money-making practices, including the fraudulent fixing of races. Many racing men supplemented their race earnings with endorsements for cycles, tyres, patent medicines and pick-me-ups. Professional riders were simply those who rode for cash: they were not full-time race cyclists earning an income from cycle racing and they were always on the lookout for ways to supplement prize money. The better riders did very well. As the Australian cycling historian Jim Fitzpatrick observes, 'cycle racing was a good candidate for being the most lucrative sporting activity an individual could attempt throughout the 1890s'.[68]

Printed programmes, sold at the gates for sixpence in the 1890s, were a common, almost universal, feature of bicycle race meetings. Printed on cheap paper and listing officials (clerk of the course, referees, judges, starters, handicappers, timekeepers and laptakers), events, distances, start times, riders who had been accepted, handicaps and the prize money on offer, they were throw away items usually discarded on leaving the ground. From the vast numbers printed, few have survived[69] and some of those that have survived are elusive.[70] Surviving programmes are sometimes annotated to show details like non-starters, the winner and placegetters and the winning time.

It was common for bicycle race meeting programmes to include advertisements, usually of full-page size. For example, the programme for the Grand Amateur Race Meeting of the Suburban Bicycle Club held at the Association Cricket Ground, Moore Park on Saturday 17 May 1890[71] included numerous display type (illustrated) advertisements. Some were placed by tailors and cyclists' outfitters such as Harold Mutton of Oxford Street, Braham and Mutch of King Street, who offered 'Bicycle Suits to Order' and 'Special Dressing Rooms and Lavatories for Cyclists', and J. Pearson of King Street, the 'Cyclists' Tailor'. Coplands of George Street made known they were agents for 'the famous Robinson and Price Safety Bicycles', W. Kerr, 'Practical Jeweller', drew attention to his specialty in club badges and trophies and Bruce and Massey advertised their piano warehouse. Myers and Solomon offered a reminder they stocked fireworks for the Queen's Birthday, the Adams Cafe of George Street, with its four-table billiard room, promoted itself as 'for cyclists and athletes' and Penfold

& Co, who remain in business today in Sydney as stationers, and who had printed this programme for the Suburban Bicycle Club in 1890, made known their expertise as 'account book makers'.

Dymocks, still the largest bookseller in the Sydney CBD, advertised 'one million books' in the programme for the Speedwell Bicycle Club's Grand Amateur Autumn Race Meeting at the Lillie Bridge Ground on 30 May 1891.[72] In the same programme Freeman and Co. advertised their photography business and Braham and Mutch let it be known they were 'Cyclists and Athletes Outfitters by Special Appointment to NSW Clubs'. A year earlier an advertisement by a dealer in Bathurst, in the programme for a meeting of the local Occidental Bicycle Club, stated that he had 'Racing Machines on Hire'.[73] That advertisement, revealing as it did that a man need not own a racing bicycle to enter a race, revealed another commercial aspect of the developing sport.

By 1899 the range of products advertised in race programme booklets had grown, The programme for the first day of the League of New South Wales Wheelmen's Monster Carnival in October, for example, carried advertisements for Japanners and enamellers, aerated water, an engraver, cutlery, Farmer's Ladies' Floating Baths at the Domain, bicycles, Quong Tart's tearooms, Melvin's Ales, Dunlop and Perdriau tyres and acetylene lamps.[74]

A mug's game: gambling and corruption

Gambling was firmly established in Victorian Australia long before the advent of bicycles, the cycling craze and bicycle racing. Bicycle racing simply provided a new sport on which to gamble. The explosion in the number of bicycle racing events opened up the sport quickly to bookmakers (or 'pencillers') who had established their businesses at the horse and pony racing tracks and at pedestrian events.

Officially, betting was banned at most bicycle racing venues but these bans were blatantly flouted and generally ignored. Clubs placed prominent newspaper advertisements before meetings and abundant signage at the venues but bookmakers, the punting public, many competitors and numerous race officials, the latter of whom felt powerless to act, openly disregarded them. Warning notices about the prohibition of betting placed in the newspapers in the days leading up to race meetings simply reminded bookmakers about where they could field and reminded the punters to put aside a little cash from their pay packet for their wagers or 'flutters'. Everyone knew that the police on duty at the grounds would turn a blind eye, with some slipping a bet or two themselves.

Betting was usually on placegetters or the winner in match events involving just two competitors. In some races, bookmakers offered odds on who would beat whom out of pairs of riders they selected from a particular race card. So open was the gambling that newspapers occasionally published the odds. Predictably, prohibition failed.

Predictably, too, the scale and intensity of betting on bicycle racing led to a range of corrupt and fraudulent behaviour. Driven by the way they saw the handicap system working against the majority and by the big gaps paid as cash prizes between first place and the minor placegetters, numerous riders and their backers sought ways to game the system. One writer, who has argued that the resultant corruption did much to bring about a decline in bicycle racing by the turn of the century, summed up some of its forms this way:

> Some riders are alleged to have run dead for months so as to get a good handicap in a 'rich Wheelrace'. With the greater proportion of the prize money for first place – in other words, all for one rider – there was really no competition but for first place. There have been many riders who would not win a few pounds simply because they would show their hand and get penalised in their handicap. They would sooner get a cut from the winner of a big wheelrace and keep their handicap mark which had cost them many races and years to get. Some of the riders that got into the final realised that their only

chance of getting any of the money was by teaming with others, not to mutually aid one another with the best man to win, which would have been in the best interest of the sport but deliberately forego their chances, and help another to win for a cut of the prize money. They did not believe in it all going to one man – they practically cut up the money before the race started …

Many races were actually bought, the winners paying away the whole of the stake, compensating themselves by bets made on the results of the race … many racing officials who thoroughly understood the sport with an insight to the future, advocated a better system of allocating the prize money, but the various racing bodies apparently lacking the interest of the sport failed to see eye to eye with them. They did not trouble so much about the future as to how much profit they could make out of the meetings …

The rich wheelrace was an outstanding factor in the advertising columns and no doubt, mainly responsible for the crowded grandstands.[75]

Looking back over this worrying scene in 1901, one Melbourne bookmaker wrote in a cycling journal that, 'The racing cracks are by no means all punters' and went on to say, 'I can name quite a few that never had a wager in their lives'.[76] He did, however, confess to looking after his own interests by learning the codes of the signallers (or 'tintackers') who communicated by gestures their intentions before a race to confederates on the other side of the ground. With this method, that he described as 'more effective than Marconi wireless telegraphy in finding out all sorts of news', he fought back against the riding rorts to protect his business.

Another Melbourne bookmaker writing in 1901, again in a cycling journal, expressed the view that the touts with access to the dressing rooms were the ones doing the greatest damage to the sport. 'These touts, or information seekers', he argued, 'find out what is going and then go to well-known punters, who back a certain rider on the strength of the tout's advice. If their man wins, the punter gives the tout something out of his winnings. The tout is an evil'.[77]

The cycling news

The cycling craze and the success of bicycle racing as a sport spawned numerous journals and magazines. Some disappeared from newsstands almost as quickly as they arrived while others survived over many years. Most were specific to one city or one colony, although others attempted to serve wider markets across the continent. Among the first in the 1880s were *Bicycle*, *Bicycling News* and *Australian Cycling*. The *Australian Cyclist* began publication in 1893, was sold nationally and remained in print for over a decade. The *Austral Wheel*, published in Melbourne from 1896 through to 1900, was regarded as providing the broadest coverage.[78] After 1897, the *Sydney Wheelman*, official organ of the League of New South Wales Wheelmen, served well the interests of professional cyclists.

Other journals of note were the *Cycling Times*, the *New South Wales Cycling Gazette*, the *South Australian Cyclist*, the *West Australian Wheelman* and the *W. A. Cyclist*. The two Western Australian journals served both city readers and those on the goldfields, where cycling enjoyed widespread support for personal transport and where bicycle racing brought out close to the entire population of towns to race meetings.

Most journals were weekly publications. The *Sydney Wheelman* was published every Thursday morning, a popular time for journals to appear on the streets because it enabled them to provide late details of the weekend's events. The first issue of the *Sydney Wheelman*, on 15 August 1895, was cautiously priced at two pence but an immediate eager response saw the price reduced to only one penny after just five issues.[79]

Libraries, especially state libraries, hold complete or near complete sets of the contemporary cycling journals. Other sets survive in part or with fractured coverage. Review of a broad sample of what has survived reveals wide coverage of cycling matters. Club news including upcoming road races and track days is commonplace, as are reports of recent meetings, night racing, training tips, profiles of top riders and overseas news and trends. Features covered everything cycling from hill climbing to photography for cyclists. Maps often accompanied the touring notes and advice that summarised accommodation opportunities along cycling routes. Opinion pieces about controversial matters such as whether women should race, cycling on Sundays, new technology in the form, for example, of the development of tandem through to sextuplet pacing machines and motorised pacing machines, or changes in tyre technology as the cushion replaced the solid tyre and the pneumatic tyre replaced the cushion. Poems, some serious and some not so serious, were included, as were cartoons. Special pages and sections for ladies were a common feature although typically they occupied only a small portion of the publications in which they appeared.

Advertisements covered the full gamut of perceived needs of cyclists, including a bewildering offering of makes of new bicycles, cycling clothing and footwear, repair and maintenance kits, cycle parts and accessories such as tyres, wheels, saddles, pedals and tools. Tobacco and chewing gum brands were drawn to the attention of readers. The latest Chicago chewing gums were available. From Melbourne, MacRobertson's peppermint flavoured pepsin chewing gum was, they claimed, for cyclists and athletes. Chewing gum, said MacRobertson's advertising, 'tones up the system', 'makes, tissue, bone and muscle', 'gives increased power' and 'restores wasted energy'.[80] That and many other advertisements were illustrated with drawings or photographs.

Given the immense amount of public interest in cycling and bicycle racing it is unsurprising that newspapers devoted considerable space to the cycling interest. In the various colonies, almost every one of the city and country newspapers regularly addressed cycling issues with the advantage over journals of being able to publish updates on riders, entries and handicaps right up to, and including, race day. Where they published evening editions the city newspapers could very promptly publish results and commentary. Country papers reported their own local meetings and accounts of the larger city meetings, although a time lag of a week, sometimes longer, was not uncommon.

Sydney's *Daily Telegraph*, *Evening News*, *Sydney Morning Herald*, *Australian Star* and *Referee* were foremost in informing readers on cycling matters, with Newcastle and Maitland papers active in the Hunter Valley. In Melbourne the *Age*, *Argus*, *Australasian and Sportsman* were the leading city papers for cycling news with the *Geelong Advertiser* and the goldfields newspapers, the *Bendigo Advertiser*, the *Bendigo Independent* and the *Ballarat Star*, dominating provincial coverage. The *Brisbane Courier*, *Telegraph* and *Queenslander* were very active with cycling news, as were the *Morning Bulletin* in Rockhampton, the *Northern Miner* in Charters Towers, and the *Maryborough Chronicle*. South Australian readers were well served by the *South Australian Register*, the *Advertiser*, *Evening Journal* and the *Express and Telegraph* and Western Australian cycling enthusiasts looked to the *West Australian*, *Daily News* and *Coolgardie Miner*. Among the most vocal Tasmanian newspapers on matters to do with cycling were Hobart's *Mercury* and the *Launceston Examiner*.

Cycling columns were often titled for easy access. Predictable among the names chosen were Cycling, Cycling Notes, Cyclists and Cycling, Cycling Jottings, Cycling Chatter, Wheel Notes, On the Wheel and Hums of the Wheel. Some cycling columns ranged widely across cycling news, some were concerned exclusively or primarily with track and road racing.

Very rarely did cycling columnists write under their own names. They preferred pen names or nom de plumes. Some chose predictable names like Cyclist, Cyclo, Cyclos, Cyclophile, Wheeler, Wheelman, Freewheel, The Spokesman and Lapscorer. Others used a variety of catchy and sometimes eccentric names such as Toe-Clip, Scorcher, Back Pedal, Spindle, Puncture, Spokes, Pedal, Sprocket, Tyro-O, and, perhaps inevitably, A. Crank. Among the names more obscurely arrived at for the job-in-hand were Philabuster, Mercury and Velox (although the latter does mean swift and rapid).

THE SHAW FAMILY OF WOOLLOOMOOLOO

The family of William and Mary Anne Shaw

Five sons born to William and Mary Anne Shaw in Woolloomooloo, Sydney between 1864 and 1878 made their marks – at different but overlapping times – as upper-level competitive road and track racing cyclists from 1887 through until the early 1900s. William Nathaniel Shaw, who led his younger brothers into the new sport, was born in a rented family home in Palmer Street in 1864, soon after his parents and older sister, Janet (Jessie) Pitkethly Shaw, who had been born in 1862 in Glasgow, arrived in the colony. William's brother Samuel Robinson Shaw first saw the light of day in another rented Palmer Street house in 1870 and three other boys, Henry Tait Shaw, Frederick Ewart Shaw and Thomas John Shaw followed in 1872, 1876 and 1878. The three younger Shaw boys were born at various Riley Street addresses in Woolloomooloo as the Shaws frequently moved homes to accommodate a rapidly growing family.

The Shaw family included another son, James, born in 1866, but who was not involved in competitive cycling and two other daughters. Christina (Teenie) Shaw was born in Corfu Street, Woolloomooloo in 1868 and Mary Amelia Shaw was born in Riley Street in 1874. Christina went on to marry William Parrett a competitive sailor on Sydney Harbour and Mary went on to marry Brice Heber Thomas, a competitive cyclist and sailor and friend of the Shaw brothers. As well as his high-profile involvement in cycle racing, Frederick Shaw, as a youngster not yet able to compete on bicycles, involved himself in pedestrianism (foot racing) and then later, alongside his cycling career, made quite a name for himself skippering his sailboats on Sydney harbour and in the Brisbane River. The Shaws created themselves as a sporting family in unlikely and challenging circumstances.

The grocer and the grocer's wife

William Shaw earned his living in Woolloomooloo as a corner-store grocer and sometime clerk.[81] Born in 1832 in Saintfield, County Down, Ireland, the eighth of twelve children of a farmer turned linen warehouseman,[82] William, as a young man moved to Glasgow, Scotland for work. In the Glasgow house where he boarded while working in the linen trade he met Mary Anne Inch, who worked in the house. Mary Anne Inch had been born in the West Indies in 1841 but her birth was registered in Leith, Edinburgh, Scotland. Her father, Nathaniel Inch, managed the Zeelandia sugar plantation at Wakanaan Island, Demerara (Guyana). For reasons unknown, her mother, the former Jessie Pitkethly, returned to Scotland after Mary Anne's birth and went into service as a cook.[83]

By the time she was just twelve, Mary Anne Inch was working as an errand girl at the Blantyre Mill about twelve miles from Glasgow and living at Shuttle Row at the mill[84] where she received an elementary education in the evenings after working day shifts of up to twelve hours.

William Shaw married Mary Anne Inch on 16 June 1861 at Govan, Glasgow, Scotland.[85] Their first child, Janet (Jessie) Pitkethly Shaw was born in Govan in February 1862.[86]

William, Mary Anne and baby Janet (Jessie) emigrated on the Mackay and Company's Black Ball Line 1215-ton *Light Brigade* in 1863, arriving in Brisbane on 21 May after about 100 days at sea (reports vary between 98 and 102 days). On the passenger list William was shown as a farm labourer and he and Mary Anne as 'Scotch'. Their fellow passengers were largely farm labourers (or described themselves as such) and domestic servants but there was also a large contingent of displaced 'cotton operatives' from Manchester among the 411 passengers. Records of the voyage suggest that all on board had lived in extreme poverty prior to emigrating and that many charities helped support the emigrants before they departed from 'home'.[87]

If the Shaws had seen poverty before their departure on the *Light Brigade*, they certainly saw more of it when they were, in effect, dumped and abandoned in the fledgling Brisbane. As Thomas Keneally has written:

> On arrival in Queensland in the mid 1860s, the migrants [from Mackay and Co. ships] were put in the old military barracks in Brisbane. Many families found it so uncomfortable and unclean and the sewage so bad, they moved away and camped under trees. Their rations in the meantime were of very poor quality – flour, 'salt chunk of a consistency of the material comprised of a blucher boot', and tea. Tradesmen and professional men had to go on the road looking for agricultural work. Of one such family an immigrant wrote, 'That is what too many of our poor English come to ... he, and other deluded villagers, agree to rush out to Australia, only to scrape on as best they can ... little better all of them but walking skeletons, living in a mere log hut, and lamenting having left their English home.' Some accounts give the impression that Australia could never have been populated if the journey back home had been affordable.[88]

By mid-1863, after staying in Brisbane for only two months, the Shaw family was living in Sydney.

A move to Sydney may have been part of the Shaw's emigration plan all along. They may have had enough money in reserve to move on to Sydney, where they immediately had the welcome support of Tait Pitkethly, uncle of Mary Anne Inch/Shaw. Another possibility is that Tait funded the passages from Brisbane to Sydney. Tait Pitkethly, already well established as a stonemason and builder, lived in Woolloomooloo. And so the Shaws, less than six months after leaving Glasgow, found themselves residents of Woolloomooloo, or the 'Loo as it was affectionately known. Their world had changed. They had changed their world.

William reinvented himself as a grocer and storeman and ran his business from a sequence of small stores and shophouses in the bustling suburb. The family moved often, to chase better business opportunities or as bigger premises (they were still tiny, often described as 'snug cottages' and sometimes located in extremely narrow lanes), were needed to accommodate the growing family that grew from three to eleven between 1864 and 1878. Those needs were extended dramatically after the sudden and unexpected death of Tait Pitkethly on the last day of 1872. Tait, a widower, died intestate and the courts appointed William Shaw as the legal guardian of five Pitkethly children aged eight to seventeen.[89] William eventually gained permission to sell Tait's property to assist financially, but it seems some of the younger Pitkethly children moved in with the Shaws.

Two letters preserved in the National Library of Australia in Canberra, along with a diary, reveal something of the life in the Shaw household in Agnes Terrace, Bourke Street, Woolloomooloo. Both were written in March 1878 by Samuel John Shaw, a nephew of William Shaw, who arrived in Sydney in February aboard the *Tyburnia* and who was a guest, along with his shipboard travelling companion, in the Shaw home. At that time, Mary Anne was six months pregnant with her ninth child and the household was a cramped and busy one.

In a letter to two brothers the new immigrant mentioned that his uncle had secured a temporary job for him cleaning an engine but he had hopes of a new job within days in a 'green store' at £2/2/- a week, with the possibility of a rise.[90] In the other letter, to his mother and father, Samuel stated that his uncle and aunt lived very well, were very comfortable, that they were kind to him and that his uncle had found jobs for both him and his mate. He also mentioned that 'Uncle has a bit of ground and is going to build on it'. In that letter, he also commented on the children, 'I don't know if we will stay long here, as they have so many children, and they are a great pest, but if they keep us we will have to put up with them'.[91] This was the environment in which four of the young Shaw brothers, who were later to share cycle racing success, were being raised. The fifth was soon to be born.

William Shaw, his children and a portrait of their mother, c.1893.
Shaw family collection

THE 'LOO IN THE LATE 1800s

At first a 'pretty place', then docks, pubs, brothels and billiard rooms

Woolloomooloo, or the 'Loo as it was commonly known, now a harbourside inner city suburb of Sydney, was developed around the horseshoe-shaped valley immediately east of Sydney's first settlement at Sydney Cove, from which it was separated by Farm Cove. The settlement that surrounded the swampy shores at Woolloomooloo Bay was less than a mile from the centre of town, an easy ten-minute walk across the Domain and Hyde Park – and even much quicker on an ordinary or a safety. As Shirley Fitzgerald has written in her article for the online *Dictionary of Sydney*,[92] in 1845 Woolloomooloo was described as a 'pretty place'. She went on to note, however, that the development of the bay's cargo docks brought about a 'decline in amenity' and by the 1860s and 1870s the area became 'crowded with small houses, pubs, brothels and billiard rooms serving a maritime-focused population'.

While the *Picturesque Atlas of Australasia* had a little to say about Woolloomooloo and nearby Darlinghurst it did not offer any illustrations. This is simply because, by 1886 when it was prepared, Woolloomooloo was anything but picturesque. The 'poor quarter' of the 'Valley of Woolloomooloo' was indeed singled out for mention by the *Picturesque Atlas* as the least pleasing aspect of the outlook from the ridge at the top of Woolloomooloo Hill (now Darlinghurst, Potts Point and Kings Cross) because of its 'narrow streets and lanes in which rows of squalid tenements are huddled together'.[93]

Not surprisingly, the area suffered from public health issues. Outbreaks of typhoid fever plagued Sydney in the late 1880s and several of these outbreaks occurred in Woolloomooloo. One, in 1878, was attributed to contaminated milk. In August 1878, the *Sydney Morning Herald* reported a lecture on the topic of sewerage-induced 'house poison'. The speaker, the Secretary of the Health Society of New South Wales, talked of 'filth diseases', adding they were never absent from Woolloomooloo.[94] The 'Loo was no longer a pretty place but it was home to the Shaw family.

Sadly, Mary Anne Shaw died from the dreaded typhoid fever at her home, 5 Agnes Terrace, Woolloomooloo on 29 September 1879, aged 36.[95] Other members of her family and household were spared. Mary Anne was buried in the Presbyterian section of Sydney's Rookwood Cemetery. After being born in Georgetown in the British Guyana in the West Indies, growing up in Glasgow and working as an errand girl in the Blantyre Mill, marrying William Shaw and emigrating to Brisbane on the *Light Brigade* before voyaging on to Sydney and mothering nine children (eight of whom were born in Woolloomooloo), Mary Anne was never to know that five of her boys would embrace a bicycling craze, make names for themselves as competitive road and track cyclists, in some cases become champions or 'cracks' and then, again in some instances, enjoy success in other fields, including as businessmen. She would have been very proud of them, as she would have been of her other children.

Woolloomooloo Bay, c.1895. Powerhouse Museum, Sydney

Fishing boats and sailboats on Woolloomooloo Bay

Apart from the docks serving inter-colonial and international shipping, Woolloomooloo Bay hosted numerous small fishing vessels that gave rise to a daily wharf-side fishing market. Locals bought their fish there and the market attracted hawkers whose barrows of fresh fish were wheeled away for sale in nearby suburban streets.[96]

Young local lads, boys such as the sons of William and Mary Anne Shaw, were attracted to the waterside to watch the fishing boats, buy fish for the family, or fish for themselves, with no licences required. There they were exposed to the world of boats and boating and to the new high wheelers and safety bicycles on which men rode to work in the 'Loo or rode to the wharves to buy fish. They were also witness to leisure sailboats on the bay, to preparations for dinghy (small sailboats) racing on Sydney Harbour, and to the Woolloomooloo Regatta that had been established mid-century. This is likely to have been the early introduction to dinghy racing for several of the Shaw brothers, whose sporting interests and careers extended beyond highly successful competitive cycle racing to highly successful sailboat racing on Sydney Harbour and, in one case, also the Brisbane River.

CHAPTER 2

On Your Marks: William Nathaniel Shaw

William Nathaniel Shaw, the eldest son of William and Mary Anne Shaw, was born on 7 February 1864 at 18 Palmer Street, Sydney,[1] a street address that has long disappeared beneath the roadway of Sydney's Eastern Distributor, near where an overhead bridge carrying the Eastern Suburbs Railway now crosses high over that road.

Little is known of young William's early life and nothing about where he received his school education. As the eldest boy in the growing Shaw family, William is likely to have been called upon to assist his father in the family grocery stores, perhaps also making deliveries. As a young man he qualified through a five-year apprenticeship with McArthur and Company, tailors, of Sydney,[2] and worked as a tailor's cutter and, like other ambitious young men, is likely to have dreamed of one day owning his own tailoring business. Any achievement of this type, however, would require capital beyond that he could hope to quickly accumulate as a tailor's cutter and he may have been one of the many who saw the new sport of cycle racing as providing that opportunity.

Road racing in Sydney

Although William may earlier have owned ordinaries and safety bicycles, and ridden them as his personal transport and in touring events and participated in organised bicycle racing, it was not until 1887, when William was 23, that his name first appeared among widely available bicycle racing records. In that year he was a member of the newly formed Sydney Bicycle Club when he entered its members-only inaugural amateur road race to take place from the Waterloo tram terminus along Botany and Bunnerong roads, and finishing on Randwick Road between the toll bar and Sydney's first Zoological Gardens at Moore Park.[3] Gold, silver and bronze medals were offered and he was to race in the club colours of cardinal (vivid red) and black. William's allocated 8 minutes and 30 seconds handicap for a nine-mile race that was expected to be won in about 45 minutes suggest that the race officials saw him as a rank outsider, something to be expected of an unknown rider just entering this level of competition. Of the 30 riders listed to race in the days leading up to the event only 18 started. William was not among them.[4]

In 1888 William Shaw married Mary King.[5] In that year he again entered the Sydney Bicycle Club's members-only road race run over the same Waterloo to Randwick route of the previous year's race. William was allocated a handicap of 7 minutes and 30 seconds. The handicaps were decided not only on the merits of the riders but also to take account of the machines they had elected to ride, and this handicap suggests that William was mounted on a high wheeler. As the second front marker at the start, William was not thought, at least by the handicappers, to have much chance of success. Eighteen men started and this time William was among them. He was up with the leaders early in the race but 'fierce' southerly headwinds and dusty, rough roads made for hard riding and the stronger riders overtook the limit men, including William, before the competitors reached the half-way point at Botany.[6]

The race was not without incident. The *Australian Star* reported that 'A corps of red-coated military men were manoeuvring on the road behind the racecourse, but the commanding officer was good enough to wheel them off to meet some imaginary enemy, so as to give the bicycle men a clear course'.[7] Another problem arose when some competitors complained they were being blocked along the road by 'a few injudicious cyclists [including a former club member] racing them without being entered'[8] in what amounted to another form of scorching. Race reports tell that William Shaw was one of several riders who fell during the race, but not whether he recovered and resumed the race.

Strangely, after expressing this interest in the sport, William's name does not appear again in the racing records until mid-1892. He was a paid-up member of the Sydney Bicycle Club in 1891[9] but although two of his younger brothers, Henry and Samuel, began racing with the Sydney Bicycle Club that year William did not participate along with them.

William's re-entry to the sport got underway with his participation in the 1892 Sydney Bicycle Club's annual road race over what by now had become known simply as the Botany course. Again he was a front marker and again his handicap was 7 minutes and 30 seconds. Although the handicappers had not rated him among the strongest of the 27 riders who started, William Shaw, riding hard on a safety bicycle with cushion tyres, was placed fourth and was close to the leaders at the Botany half-way point. All riders were close at the finish.[10]

Two months later, William rode in the Suburban Bicycle Club's Open Road Race over the Botany course. Prizes offered were £5, £3 and £2 plus an expensive, donated Rudge bicycle to the winner. Racing on a handicap of 8 minutes and 30 seconds William was unplaced but his brother Samuel (Sam) Shaw, with a handicap of 3 minutes, was placed second in what was described as 'a great finish'.[11]

From road to track racing

Mid-1892 also saw the beginnings of a marked change of direction in William Nathaniel Shaw's racing interests when he switched from occasional entries in the now ten-mile Botany road race (supplemented perhaps with participation in club runs of which no records appear to have been kept) to path or track racing. In September, William entered in a two-mile open handicap race for the Sydney Club Trophy, a tea and coffee service and salver. On the Monday before the race many of those who would compete attended the Association Cricket Ground at Moore Park to train for the race. Heavy rain fell on race day and only 3,000 spectators braved the poor weather conditions. The track was heavy and sloppy and there were numerous spills among the 27 starters, four falling in the first lap. One rider had an expensive day out when he fell three times and on each occasion needed a new machine to continue the race. Only about a dozen finished and William Shaw, who was allotted a handicap of 260 yards, was again unplaced.[12] William's brother Sam and his future brother-in-law, Brice Heber Thomas, rode in other events at this meeting.

In the evening competitors enjoyed a smoke concert at 'Quong Tart's Rooms'.[13] Quong Tart was a highly respected Chinese merchant and philanthropist who made his expansive tea and grill rooms, 'of a scale and splendour never before seen in Australia',[14] available for many evening meetings, including those of cycling clubs. Quong Tart was a member of cricket, football, cycling, yachting, dinghy and swimming clubs as well as a member of the Highland Society, zoological society, agricultural and horticultural society and numerous charities. In cycling he was a member of the Burwood Cycling Club and, later, the League of New South Wales Wheelmen where he often officiated as a starter. His interest in cycling did much to interest and assist Sydney's Chinese community to become involved with the sport.[15]

The Austral Bicycle Club utilised the Botany course for its inaugural road race in September 1892. Prizes of £7, £3 and £2 attracted William and his friend Brice Thomas to enter and William was handicapped among the rear markers. He was unplaced, as was Brice. Cash prizes were unusual at this time in New South Wales (although not in Victoria) but were offered on this occasion 'to cater for riders who prefer cash to trophies'.[16] The hazards of road racing were again illustrated, in this race by the havoc a stray dog caused by running into the path of cyclists.

A common practice among city riders, particularly from Sydney and Melbourne, was to travel to provincial meetings where they knew there would be reduced competition and easier pickings. Provincial clubs often actively encouraged city riders in an effort to enhance their gate takings and expose locals to the culture of city cycle racing. Those clubs that welcomed city riders frequently reserved one or two races on their programmes exclusively for local competitors. Chasing glory away from the city, William Shaw's cycle racing career took a leap forward after he, and his brother Sam, headed out of Sydney by train with their bicycles to attend the Newcastle Bicycle Club's sports day at the Newcastle Cricket Ground on 1 October 1892. The Shaw boys had not wasted time. This was the Newcastle Club's very first meeting. Excitement was in the air, there was a strong contingent of mates from various Sydney clubs travelling with them and the meeting offered the opportunity of racing on the newly-laid gravel track that promised fast times.

The Newcastle meeting took place at a time when ordinaries had been all but superseded by safety machines but there remained some owners of ordinaries who still wished to race them, and the programme accommodated them. It was what was termed a 'mixed' programme that included both a One-mile Handicap for Ordinaries and a One-mile Handicap for Safeties. The other races, a One-Mile Maiden Scratch Race, a Three-Mile Mixed Bicycle Handicap and a Half-Mile Mixed Handicap were mixed in another sense, with all accepting entries both of ordinaries and safeties, a practice frowned upon in some quarters because of the extra danger involved. In the One-Mile Maiden Scratch Race W. N. Shaw won his heat and then went on to win the final. As this was a maiden race[17], for riders who had previously never won a first prize at any event, it is clear this was William's first cycle racing win.

William's win in the Maiden Scratch Race was added to later in the afternoon when he took out the Three-Mile Mixed Bicycle Handicap. As noted by the *Newcastle Morning Herald and Miners' Advocate*, William, riding with a handicap of 260 yards, overtook the early leaders over the last mile and led across the finishing line by 25 yards.

Had William Nathaniel Shaw arrived?

William's brother Sam, 'a splendid little rider', also had a worthwhile trip north, winning both his heat and the final of the Half-Mile Mixed

Handicap.[18] The strong sprints to the finish that were to become a feature of racing by all five Shaw brothers were in evidence by both men on the day.

As was the case with many provincial meetings, several metropolitan clubs were represented at the Newcastle Meeting with riders from the Sydney, Speedwell, Eclipse, Crusaders' and St Leonards bicycle clubs participating. As the *Australian Town and Country Journal* made known, 'The Sydney riders were very well treated by the Newcastle wheelmen, and were unanimous in their determination to visit the coal city again. There was a concert and supper in the evening after the races, and on the following day the Newcastle Club got up a run to Belmont, Lake Macquarie'.[19]

William's success at the Newcastle meeting did not immediately translate into success back in Sydney. He was unplaced in both the Half-Mile Open Handicap and the Five-Miles Open Handicap at the Championship Sports Meeting conducted by the Manchester Unity Independent Order of Oddfellows at Sydney's Association Cricket Ground in early November. That meeting had a programme of both cycling and foot racing. Advertising for it promised supporting attractions that included merry-go-rounds, swings and sideshows. William's entry in the five-mile race shows a continuing interest in longer forms of the sport, with that track distance being about half of that of the Botany road race route. A report of the meeting told that the five-mile race, the last on the programme, was run under very unfavourable conditions, with the track 'heavy and uncertain' owing to rain that fell during the afternoon. Racing was on a grass surface. Improvements to the cricket ground's track were something for the future.[20]

In December 1892 William raced for cash at Sydney's Association Cricket Ground. The occasion was the first day of an intercolonial cycling carnival and he put himself forward for the principal race of the first day, the Cyclists' Summer Cup run over two miles. Perhaps spurred on by his recent successes in Newcastle, William aimed high. The prize money of 50 sovereigns, 10 sovereigns and 3 sovereigns attracted riders from Melbourne, New Zealand, Singleton, Dubbo, Goulburn, Maitland, Newcastle and Bendigo. William was eliminated in his heat. A reminder about gamblers flouting the rules was provided in the report of the day's racing in the *Sydney Mail* that reported 'despite the notification that betting was strictly prohibited, the odds were called without let or hindrance in that portion of the ground outside the grand stand'.[21] The same report included a reminder about the dangers associated with bicycle racing with its mention that the competitors wore black-arm bands in memory of a New Zealand cyclist who had recently been killed in Melbourne when a dog caused him to fall from his machine. During the afternoon a trick cyclist from Ballarat was to attempt to lower the one-mile record on one wheel and 'Another attraction to the ladies on the lawn is that the City Band will discourse the choicest selections of music during the afternoon'.[22]

Events surrounding this meeting, and in particular the running of the Cyclist's Summer Cup, draw attention to how questionable decisions by carnival promoters could leave arrangements in disarray and damage the sport's image and attraction to the public. 'Cyclofile', writing in the sports newspaper the *Referee*, drew headline attention to the fact that the meeting's principal event, offering significant prize money to attract riders from near and far, was unresolved. The heats and final of that race had been set down for the first of two day's racing. However, the promoter shifted the final to the second day, a week later. When that was washed out the race was left in a 'glorious mess' and many of the competitors who had travelled long distances to the event were much out of pocket.[23] 'Cyclofile', in the same column, reported that the Sydney Bicycle Club, the club that William first joined, had expelled one of its members for breaching its rule that prohibited members from racing for cash prizes. Whether or not this was William Shaw is unknown but it is clear he would no longer have been welcome as a member of that amateur club.

Lillie Bridge

When William Shaw resolved his amateur/professional dilemma in favour of cash cycling he shifted his competitive focus, although not exclusively, to racing at the newly opened Lillie Bridge Grounds at Forest Lodge (Glebe), Sydney. Named after the Lillie Bridge Running Ground in West Brompton, London, the new grounds were developed privately by the Spencer brothers who converted five acres of low-lying wasteland by blasting cliffs and using the rock debris to level the site and create a pony-racing and foot-racing track.[24] Amid considerable fanfare and an advertising blitz, the Lillie Bridge Grounds were opened on New Year's night 1890. Inside the tiny quarter-mile circuit pony-racing track were four 150 yards sprint tracks. The grandstand could accommodate 4,000 spectators and the grounds were lit. The new electric light technology stood the ground apart from other venues and enabled night racing:

> The grounds are lit up by electricity, and the installation is on a most lavish scale. Altogether there are about 80 lights – 40 large Brockiepell [*sic*] arc lamps and 40 Swan incandescent lamps. The arc lamps are of 2000 – candle power each, and the globes are 20in. in diameter ... The electric plant is driven by a 14-h.p. engine.[25]

The same source noted that 'inducements will also be held out to the cyclists to make a venture upon [the grounds]', while another claimed, to have heard that 'the Lillie Bridge Grounds are the most perfectly arranged in the world'.[26] Perhaps the writer was also influenced by the elaborate fountains and lawns that were part of the landscaping.

It was not long before amateur cycling clubs recognised the attraction of the venue, close as it was to the city and adjacent to a tram terminal. Within eighteen months of the opening of the new grounds a bicycle race meeting was conducted there:

> The first Bicycle Race Meeting on the Lillie Bridge Grounds, Forest Lodge, takes place on Saturday afternoon next [30 May 1891], under the auspices of the Speedwell Bicycle Club. The pretty lawn and walks will be thrown open to the fair

sex, and plenty of seating accommodation is provided for the ladies comfort. The ground authorities have divided amongst the various clubs over 1000 ladies complementary tickets to be distributed among the members, so that a large and fashionable gathering is certain. Trams are to run at short intervals during the afternoon, and a special service of 'buses will also ply to and from the city. Every care will be taken to admit to the ladies' reserves only those whose presence is desirable, and an amusing and interesting afternoon will doubtless be spent. From a racing man's point only a fine day is required and a track second to none in the colony will be at the riders' disposal.[27]

Despite this fanfare, 'the ponies', with the addition of a bicycle and pedestrian race or two, were for the 'battlers and urgers' and catered for tradesmen and the working classes rather than the gentry. Their popularity, and that of venues like Lillie Bridge, was because of cheap admission, the presence of bookmakers willing to lay penny bets, and their sheer entertainment value. Pony and bicycle race meetings at the Lillie Bridge Grounds were well suited to the depressed times of the early 1890s.[28]

Presuming to take the initiative on the matter of gambling, the Secretary of the Lillie Bridge Grounds warned, 'Bookmakers are informed that (this being an amateur meeting) they will NOT be allowed to call the odds. Anyone infringing this rule will be immediately expelled from the ground'.[29] This rarely, if ever, happened.

William Shaw did not ride at the May 1891 meeting. His younger brother Henry did.

William began racing at Lillie Bridge in January 1893, by which time the proprietors of the grounds were heavily committed to conducting bicycle racing for cash prizes in association with pony racing. While the proprietors were prepared to allow amateur clubs to hire their facilities at weekends, their electric lighting enabled them to sponsor cash cycling on weeknights to add variety, and therefore crowd pulling power, to their pony racing programmes. Typically, programmes included just one bicycle race (these varied from meeting to meeting in terms of the length of the course covered) and two or (usually) three pony races.[30] These short programmes allowed working men, spectators and competitors alike, to fit nights at Lillie Bridge into their working week and family commitments. It was a smart business model for the proprietors, and it worked.

As if to herald in the New Year, William raced over one mile for £10 at Lillie Bridge on 5 January. While he won his heat he was unplaced in the final. Betting, so strongly previously banned at the grounds, was now part of the evening and recorded '5 to 2 v Shaw'. William Shaw enthusiastically embraced the night racing scene, so much so that a statement prepared for the proprietors in mid-August 1893 showing starts and payments of cash prize money to placegetters to that date revealed that he had raced on fifteen occasions. Unfortunately he had secured only one place in a final, a second paying £4, and in what amounted to a leader board of prize winners he was ranked 22 out of 25 in winnings. But even this amounted to the equivalent of about two weeks wages in his day job as a tailor and is likely to have contributed significantly towards his expenses in the sport from which he also took much personal enjoyment.

The second half of 1893 also saw William entered in numerous races under lights at Lillie Bridge. He raced over distances of half a mile, a mile, one and a half miles, two miles and three miles. Again, success was limited.[31] The fact, however, that William's entries for these races were accepted demonstrates that he was well regarded as a rider at this level when many would-be racers did not get a start. On the positive side, as well, there is abundant evidence that during this year he introduced his brother Sam and his friend and future brother-in-law, Brice Thomas, to weeknight cash racing under electric lights. No doubt, they enjoyed racing together. As the older and more experienced of the three men William exercised a leadership role.

Not all William's 1893 racing was at the Lillie Bridge Grounds and not all was path or track racing. Pacemakers were allowed, and attracted a good deal of excitement, when Sam and Henry Shaw and Brice Thomas raced together with William in the Speedwell Bicycle Club's annual road race over the Botany course in May 1893. The pacemakers took the men along at a good pace but the hope of pacemakers enabling fast times and records by their riders (pace followers) was dashed by very strong headwinds and a slippery road that caused several riders to fall. William rode a light 28 lb machine off a handicap of 3 minutes and 25 seconds. He was unplaced, as were his brothers and Brice.[32]

The Cyclists' Racing Board promoted a two-mile handicap race on 22 July 1893 to mark the opening of the track at the Agricultural Society's Ground, later known as the Sydney Showground, at Moore Park. The race was held in association with a football match. The unfinished track, predicted by the Agricultural Society to become the best in Australia when work was completed, was half a mile round and 30 feet wide. It was not intended exclusively for cycle racing. William and his younger brother Sam were among the 41 acceptances for the race. Four prizes were offered in an unusual arrangement: 'The race was for a sweepstake of 3s each, with £3 added, and trophies presented by Messrs. Bennett and Wood, Edge and Edge, I. Phizackerley, and H. A. Stanley and Co.'[33] All trophy donors were involved in the bicycle trade. Both William and Sam rode lightweight machines, William off 270 yards and Sam off 115 yards. Neither was a placegetter.

Another break from William's intensive 1893 Lillie Bridge racing programme occurred when he entered in a two-mile handicap race at the Sydney Bicycle Club's annual sports meeting at the Association Cricket Ground on 3 September. The race was for the Sydney Club Trophy, but neither that trophy nor any place prizes went to a Shaw.[34]

Following lengthy planning, the first meeting of the League of New South Wales Wheelmen took place at Punch's Hotel in Sydney on 21 September 1893. One of the first actions of the League (as it was immediately known) was for its handicapper to issue the marks for bicycle races on 2 October at a sports meeting at Rosehill Racecourse, near Parramatta. This meeting was not a League meeting but an Eight-Hour Day public holiday sports meeting that included a 125-yards Apprentices Handicap, a 100-yards Sack Race, a 75-yards Egg and Spoon Race, a one-mile and three-furlongs Bicycle Handicap, a 150-yard Novelty Race, a 150-yards Hurdle Race over six flights, an Old Buffers' Handicap (first prize four guineas and four pounds of tobacco), a two-miles and five-furlongs Bicycle Race, an Umbrella and Cigar Race on Horseback (in fancy costume, first prize £15), a one-mile flat race, a 100-yards Three Legged Race, a 150-yards Comic Costume Race and a Stilt Race. There were also Pick-a-Back and Barrel races but a scheduled balloon ascent did not come off due to strong winds.

William and Sam Shaw both caught the train or steamer from the city and raced in the one-mile and three-furlongs and the two-mile and five-furlongs bicycle races but without success. The distances covered, furlongs, adopted those covered by horses in the traditional use of the track for horse and pony racing. In the shorter of the two races William raced off 400 yards and Sam off 240 yards. Again in the longer race, they were the two front markers, William off 680 yards and Sam off 500 yards.[35] Had they taken their ordinaries with them for a fun day out?

The year 1894 was to be the last year in which William raced his bicycles. After two further races at Lillie Bridge, in February and March, William and his brother Sam, along with Brice Thomas, took their racing bicycles to Goulburn to race on the cinder track at Olympic Park.[36] That meeting was held under the auspices of the League of New South Wales Wheelmen, the colony's new peak body for professional or cash cycle racing. Before 800 spectators at this provincial meeting, William raced, without success, in the Two-Mile Cycling Handicap.

Life after bicycle racing

In mid-1894 William and Mary Shaw divorced, with each accusing the other of 'marital misconduct'.[37] It was alleged Mary 'drank very heavily' and in December 1893 'misconducted herself with … a lodger in the same house with her and her husband in Albion Street, Surry Hills'.[38] William promptly remarried, to Rachel Inglethorpe.[39] Five children were born to William and Rachel Shaw between 1895 and 1905.

William continued his work as a tailor's cutter for various employers and then, in January 1909, with capital of £80 borrowed from his wife, established his own wholesale tailoring business, the New South Wales Clothing Manufactory, at 150 Pitt Street, Sydney.[40] He employed three men and twelve girls in rented premises making garments that were sold to a variety of city retailers. William drew £4 a week from the business for his own use, paid rent and rented and bought sewing machines and cutting tables. He left much of the management to a trusted employee, who was also paid £4 a week, but who was not competent for the work of managing the small business and who neglected the accounts and the books. So did William.

The business owed money to a number of lenders, one of whom charged the increasingly desperate William Shaw exorbitant interest when he borrowed to meet weekly wages commitments. In a last, but ill-advised, effort to save the business William left it in the hands of his manager and took a job as a mantle (cloak) cutter with another tailoring company. By October 1911, William Shaw, who stated his address as Clifton Street, Little Coogee (now Clovelly) became bankrupt. In William's words in the Supreme Court 'my books are all upside down'. They had not been maintained for twelve months and it took some time for his debts of £161 to be identified and clarified and to establish his only assets, furniture in his home, described as 'a very poor and old lot', was worth £6 10s.[41] The family moved to North Sydney and William took work as a tailor's cutter for other employers. The New South Wales Clothing Manufactory was no more.

Fibbing about his age, William enlisted for war service with the Australian Commonwealth Military Forces on 2 June 1916. On his Attestation Paper completed at the Royal Agricultural Society Grounds, Sydney (where he had once raced bicycles), he stated his age as 44 years and four months although he was, in fact, 52 years and four months. The papers show he was 5'5" tall, weighed 149lbs, was of fair complexion with grey eyes and black hair (dyed to disguise age?). He had previously been rejected for service because of a double hernia but his medical examination now revealed that he had an operation for left- and right-side hernias two months previously. William Nathaniel Shaw was determined to enlist for war service.

William Nathaniel Shaw, c.1916.
Shaw family collection

Initially appointed to the Dubbo Depot, 53rd Battalion, 7th Reinforcements he was later transferred to Bathurst and then, as Private William Shaw (SN 2983aN34674) embarked Sydney for Plymouth on the troop ship *Ascanius* on 16 October, arriving 28 December. After service in France in 1917, William was transferred to the Command Depot at Perham Downs in June 1917 and returned to Australia on the troop ship *Galka*, arriving on 8 November 1918.

Following his return to Sydney, William resumed work as a tailor's cutter for various employers and maintained that work until his retirement. During that time he and Rachel lived at North Sydney, several addresses in nearby Milsons Point and at Cammeray, before moving to Sutherland in Sydney's south. William died in Newcastle in 1956.[42]

During his very long life, with all its ups and downs, William Nathaniel Shaw would have had many opportunities to reflect on the high wheelers and safety bicycles he first saw on the streets and in the lanes of Woolloomooloo, the bicycling craze that gripped the nation in his youth and the anticipation and excitement of racing. If he had dreamed of making his fortune from race winnings he would have been disappointed, but he clearly drew great pleasure from bicycling and cycle racing and the camaraderie of others enthusiastic about the sport. As well, he had every reason to be proud of the successes of his brothers and to have known that the leadership he provided sent them on their way. In that sense, William was the leader of the pack.

CHAPTER 3

'One of the Fastest Sprinters': Samuel Robinson Shaw

Samuel Robinson Shaw, the third son of William and Mary Anne Shaw, was born on 25 July 1870 at 199 Palmer Street, Woolloomooloo[1], where his father was the proprietor of a grocery store. The Shaw family lived above the store that was owned by Tait Pitkethly, Mary Ann Shaw's uncle.[2] As is also the case for his eldest brother, William Nathaniel Shaw, little is known of Sam's early life and nothing of his school education. Like William, and another brother, James, born in 1866 in Burrahpore Street, Wolloomooloo,[3] Sam completed an apprenticeship. While James, like William, became a tailor's cutter Sam's apprenticeship was in making and repairing shoes and boots, likely with John Hunter and Company.[4]

Sam Shaw later worked for John Hunter, who operated large boot factories in Sydney (Redfern), Brisbane and Adelaide, the City Boot Palace in Sydney, similar retail outlets in other cities and numerous provincial and suburban branches. Among the huge range of footwear sold by John Hunter was sporting footwear that included cyclists' shoes. The scale and success of Hunter's operations, comprising over 50 manufacturing and retail premises, apparently gave Sam a taste for business. One way forward towards that goal was to race bicycles for cash prizes, a sport to which his sporting talents were admirably suited.

Meanwhile Sam's brother James went very successfully into work as a tailor's cutter. His work became well known such that the city merchant-tailor who employed him (G. W. Lorking, 'Elegance and Durability') mentioned James by name as their cutter in numerous advertisements.[5] Over the period from 1912 until his death in 1835, Jas Shaw, as he wrote his name, was listed as a 'High-class tailor' in Castlereagh Street Sydney.[6] As far as is known, James took no interest in competitive cycling.

Off and away

Shortly after Sam's 21st birthday he raced in navy blue and white for the Crusaders' Cycle Club at the Sydney Bicycle Club's 10th Annual Amateur Championship Race Meeting on Saturday 22 August 1891, at the Association Cricket Ground, Moore Park. Twenty-one events were decided at the meeting, with the races run on a grass course and entries strictly restricted to amateurs. Sam Shaw rode in the second event, the One-Mile Maiden Scratch Race, with his entry in a maiden race establishing that he had never won a first prize in any prior event. He was placed third in his heat but was unplaced in the final.[7] Sam had paid one shilling at Quong Tart's chambers to enter. The race was a mixed one, open to ordinaries and safety bicycles. It is not known what type of machine Sam chose to ride.

In the following month Sam Shaw made the most of an opportunity to ride in another One-Mile Maiden Scratch Race, again at the Association Cricket Ground but on this occasion at a meeting of the Suburban Bicycle Club. Riding a roadster for the Crusaders' Cycle Club, Sam Shaw won his heat and the final. Reports of the race told that he led strongly away from the field in the final lap and won by about 20 yards.[8]

Following this success Sam did not compete again at this level until June 1892, when he entered to ride in a one-mile mixed race (for both ordinaries and safeties shod with different types of tyres) that was held under the auspices of the ten-day-old Austral Bicycle Club at the Drummoyne Park Fete and Garden Party. That get-together promised 'fun and frolic for old and young' with an events programme consisting of such varied activities as bicycle and foot racing, boat racing, kicking the football, lawn tennis, tug-of-war, and a quoit handicap supported by 'tableaux, living wax works and sideshows', all accessed from the city by steamers departing the King Street wharf.[9] Of the 22 safety bicycles entered, fifteen had cushion tyres, five had pneumatic tyres and two were still wearing the old solid tyres. Sam Shaw was one of the four competitors who chose to ride an ordinary. All four ordinaries were allocated big handicaps.[10] Sam was unplaced. Through this race the Austral Club signalled its intention to following the Victorian lead of racing for cash prizes.

Experimenting with road racing for the first time, Sam Shaw came close to what would have been far and away his biggest success to date. Riding in the Suburban Bicycle Club's Open Race over the ten-mile Botany course in August he rode well and won second prize of £3. In a very close race he lost by just five yards. The winner took away £5 and a quality Rudge bicycle.[11]

Riding in dark blue for the Crusaders' Club at a race meeting conducted by the Sydney Bicycle Club at the Association Cricket Ground on Saturday 3 September 1892, Sam started in the One-Mile Handicap Safety Bicycle Race and the Three-Miles Open Handicap Bicycle Race for the Ladies' Bracelets (twelve times around).[12] All races were run in rain on a heavy grass track, times were slow and spills were numerous. Sam was unplaced in both events.

The 'surprise packet'

Sam enjoyed better results at the St Leonards Bicycle Club's second annual race meeting in mid-September 1892, where, riding for the Crusaders', he comfortably won both the One-Mile Roadster Safety Bicycle Handicap and the Three-Mile Safety Bicycle Handicap. The *Referee* described Sam as the 'surprise packet'[13] at the meeting, which took place before a crowd numbering in the thousands as admission to the North Sydney Reserve was free. The narrow, quarter-mile, cinder track, 'fenced all round to keep out dogs',[14] proved dangerous: about a dozen spills occurred and several riders collided with the fence. Signs of the changing technology of the racing bicycle were that, at this race meeting, no wheelman rode an ordinary machine and air tyres (pneumatics) were in all but universal use.

Variations in reports about the spectator numbers at the North Sydney Reserve that put attendance at 3,000, 4,000 and 6,000 raise questions about reliability of the press. These widely varying numbers were no more than guesses because entry to the venue was without charge. Attendances at the Lillie Bridge Ground and the cricket and agricultural grounds at Moore Park were reliable and consistently reported because those entering the grounds passed through turnstiles. Indeed, the overall reporting of bicycle racing gives every appearance of having been reliable, with coverage of events by up to ten general and sporting newspapers being remarkably consistent. Cycling clubs issued their race schedules, prize listings and handicaps to the newspapers several days before meetings and made official results, including times, available immediately meetings concluded. Competitors and punters relied on this information and it was accurately reported. Some scope existed for independent reporting by cycling correspondents concerning descriptions of race highlights, and in opinion pieces, but this coverage was, in general, brief and free of hyperbole. Cycle racing competitors and the public were well served by the cycling scribes as are researchers today of the late colonial cycle racing scene. A wealth of information is preserved in newspaper accounts of the sport and those accounts are readily accessible online via the National Library of Australia's *Trove* database.

When the Newcastle Bicycle Club held its first meeting on 1 October 1892 at the Newcastle Cricket Ground, the meeting at which William Shaw won the One-Mile Maiden Scratch Race and the Three-Mile Mixed Mixed Bicycle Handicap, Sam followed up his success at the North Shore Reserve a fortnight earlier. In a 'splendid race until the last hundred yards, when Shaw drew out and won somewhat easily'[15], he won the Half-Mile Mixed Bicycle Handicap but, having won his heat, fell in the final of the One-Mile Safety Bicycle Handicap. Then, in November, Sam Shaw, racing from scratch at the Championship Sports Meeting conducted by the Manchester

Unity Independent Order of Oddfellows at Sydney's Association Cricket Ground, was placed third in the Half-Mile Amateur Handicap Bicycle Race. He ran second in the final and was second in the One-Mile Amateur Championship of New South Wales.[16] As the *Newcastle Morning Herald & Miners' Advocate* reported the close finish, 'P. E. Wootten won the one mile championship of New South Wales on November 9, getting home a yard in front of little Sammy Shaw'.[17]

'One of the three best amateur riders in the colony'

When, in January 1893, Sam Shaw 'went over to the cash' he was described by Sydney's leading sporting newspaper as 'one of the three best amateur riders in the colony'.[18] Riding for cash at the Lillie Bridge Grounds, Sam found his recent success counted against him in handicapping and he met with only limited success. Despite entering events on a number of nights it was not until mid-February that Sam won money, £2 for second place in the Half-Mile Handicap. In other events he ran second and third in finals of one-mile races, third in the final of a two-mile event and second in the final of a half-mile sprint.

In later years Sam Shaw was to give a considerable amount back to his sport through committee membership and by acting in various capacities as an official at race meetings. The first recorded mention of this work occurred in April 1893, when he was elected to the Committee of the Speedwell Bicycle Club, Sydney. Just prior to that he had visited Dubbo as a member of the Speedwell Club, to help promote their Easter Monday meeting.[19]

Shortly afterwards:

> Mr Sam Shaw … met with a severe accident … in Sydney, by falling from his 50-inch ordinary bicycle. His injuries consist of a broken arm and bruises on the head, and his many Newcastle friends will wish him a speedy recovery.

> Little Sammy made himself very popular during his short stay in Newcastle.[20]

Despite racing on safety machines, apparently Sam still rode his high wheeler in the city. As a 50-inch machine it had the smallest front wheel of the various sizes fitted to ordinaries and reflected its rider's small stature. The Shaw brothers were all quite short, something that was often referred to in newspaper reports.

Recovered from the fall from his high wheeler, Sam joined in the celebrations promoted by the Cyclists' Racing Board at half-time during a football match at the Agricultural Ground, Moore Park where a new cycling track was opened. With his brother William, both of whom were unplaced, he raced in a two-mile handicap event in which there were 41 starters. This track, an unusual half-mile around (those at cricket grounds were usually about half that), found many other uses in later years, including for trotting events, dirt-track motorcycle racing, stock car racing and of the Grand Parade at Sydney's Royal Easter Show.

Dogs running on to cycle racing tracks were a common menace. Spectators planning to attend the Grand Athletic Carnival to be held on 9 November at the Albion Cricket Ground at Maitland were cautioned 'not to being their little pets that they paid 2s 6d for a few weeks back, as all dogs found on the ground will be destroyed.'[21] They were also informed that a contingent of 25 riders from Sydney, under the management of the League of New South Wales Wheelmen, would arrive by boat to Newcastle and then transfer by train to Maitland. A procession along High Street, led by the Federal Band and with the cyclists wheeling their machines, was planned to precede the racing. Sam and Henry Shaw were entered in the Half-Mile Open Handicap and Sam was to race in the One-Mile Open Handicap and the Albion Stakes. In showery conditions that forced cancellation of the procession, Sam Shaw won the half-mile event and its £3 prize and was third over the two miles to pick up another £2.[22]

Scottish Highland Gatherings on New Year's Day each year were popular around the country and the Sydney Highland Society's sports at the Association Cricket Ground in 1894 was no exception. Over 13,000 crowded in for a day of mixed sports and activities, including bicycle racing under the rules of the just-formed League of New South Wales Wheelmen. Sam Shaw, riding in white with red sleeves, won his heats of the Half-Mile Bicycle Race and the One-Mile Bicycle Race but was unsuccessful in the Two-Mile and Three-Mile Bicycle Races. So many events were conducted at the meeting that up to seven were being contested at any one time. While Sam and his fellow cyclists were racing on the track, other events such as tossing the caber, putting the stone, a sack race, a wheelbarrow race, foot races, catching the greasy pig, pole vaulting, and highland dancing were under way in what was a colourful carnival atmosphere featuring bunting, kilts, bagpipes, dancing costumes and the City Band.[23] Sam Shaw was elected to the Committee of the League of New South Wales Wheelmen the following month.

On Easter Monday 1894 Sam and his younger brother Henry rode at the second cycling carnival to be held under the auspices of the League of New South Wales Wheelmen at the Albion Ground in Maitland. Among the contingent of riders visiting from Sydney was Joe Megson, the New South Wales champion. Megson won the final of the One-Mile Bicycle Race, was third in the final of the Half-Mile Bicycle Handicap and second in the Three-Mile Bicycle Race.[24] And Joe Megson beat Sam and Henry Shaw in the Slow Race[25] when both the Shaws slewed off the track. This meeting was just one of the many occasions when one or more of the Shaws raced against the Joe Megson and, no doubt, learned from the experience.

Sam and Henry Shaw, along with Brice Thomas, their future brother-in-law, were all entrants in one of the first road races to be run under the auspices of the League of New South Wales Wheelmen. Taking place on 5 May 1894, this race was over the full ten-mile Botany course. On top of cash prizes, a gold medal was on offer to any rider who broke the course record. Of the three, Brice Thomas, in tenth place, was best on the day.[26]

Goulburn calling

Racing at Goulburn was becoming attractive to Sydney riders and Sam, along with his brother William and mate Brice Thomas, were in town for the cycling carnival held at the Olympic Ground on 24 May 1894 to celebrate Queen Victoria's birthday. Sam's best race of the day saw him take out second place in the final of the Two-Mile Bicycle Handicap. The *Goulburn Herald* captured much of the flavour and excitement of the day:

> The most successful cycling event, and one of the most exciting and pleasant day's amusement ever held in Goulburn, took place on the Olympic Ground yesterday in the presence of about 800 spectators, amongst whom was noticed a large number of ladies, whose bright faces and neat costumes gave a very pleasing effect to the oval, and shows that the ladies are not going to be left out when there is a good day's sport to be enjoyed …
>
> Mr Magee of the Post-office hotel had a booth on the ground and appeared to be well patronised. A fruit-stall by Mrs Bigwood of Eastgrove was also liberally attended. A dressing-tent for the competitors had been erected under the shed at the western and of the ground, and the men were well sheltered from the wind. The track, which is laid down in cinders, was in splendid condition, and the riders expressed themselves as well satisfied with it, which speaks well for those who had the matter in hand. All the riders wore jockey costumes, which had a very pleasing effect. Most of the competitors rode racing machines specially brought from Sydney for the occasion.
>
> The principal event was the Two Mile Handicap of £35 divided into four prizes, viz., £25 first, £7 second, £2 third, and £1 fourth. This was won by the local champion (Reg. Everett), with S. R. Shaw (Sydney) second … The Novice Race fell to B. Thomas (Sydney) …

> The final contest for the Two-Mile Handicap caused a vast amount of excitement. Men cried themselves hoarse and threw their hats in the air; ladies clapped their hands, and without doubt the majority seemed to have only one thought and wish, and that was that the local favourite should win. The excitement reached the climax when Everett passed the post some ten or fifteen yards in front of Shaw. On dismounting, the winner was carried shoulder-high to the dressing tent.[27]

Back on the track in September Sam won his heat in a one-mile event run off in association with a football match at the Sydney Cricket Ground. Reports of the event, the League's first big handicap event, with 32 starters, stated that Sam Shaw rode 'right up to expectation' and that the League treated country visitors to the event to a theatre party at the Tivoli in the evening. This was early days for the League of New South Wales Wheelmen but the 'cash body is a long way ahead of the amateur union, and going ahead with rapid strides'.[28] In another League mile-race held a month later at Redfern Oval, at a sports meeting organised by locals in aid of the Redfern poor, Sam ran second in his heat.[29]

Another League-sponsored meeting at Goulburn called. Over-the-top display advertising for the two-day carnival set down for 9 and 10 November screamed that 'The Melbourne Cup will Only be a Circumstance to the Goulburn Wheel Race and the 10-Mile Championship at the Cycling Carnival. Olympic Ground, Friday and Saturday Next'. To attract the attendance 'a special reserve will be roped off for the ladies, and seats provided'.[30] More information about the meeting, its street procession and the 'Original Bone-Shaker'[31] on display in a van was available from A. H. Judd at the Music Academy in Goulburn. Newspaper reports told that 'a scoring board will be placed in the oval, so that visitors can ascertain the winners of heats, &c.' Among the tips offered was that 'S. R. Shaw will take a lot of beating if he rides up to last year's form'. However, before 3,000 spectators, Sam, off 200 yards, ran third in this £45 event that was won by A. H. Judd off 400 yards. Sam raced without success in the half-mile event and the Ten-Mile Championship of New South Wales. Prizes were paid over at the assembly room of the Music Academy on the Saturday evening.[32]

Beating Megson on New Year's Day

As was now usual, the cycle racing year commenced with events at the Highland Society's Gathering on New Year's Day. Again, a newspaper article captured the flavour and excitement of the day:

> The twenty-seventh annual gathering of the Highland Society of N.S.W. was held on Tuesday on the Association Cricket Ground, Moore Park, and was a decided success. Not only was liberal patronage bestowed upon the affair by the public, so that an attendance of upwards of 9000 was recorded, but the sports were numerous, and the competitions thoroughly representative of the cycling and athletic sections of the community …
>
> The appearance of the enclosure did not differ materially from that presented at previous gatherings of the kind. The grand stand was well peopled, it being estimated that there were nearly 4000 persons either seated thereon or watching the proceedings from the lawn in front. On the lawn was stationed the City Band, and it is almost needless to say that the music which it discoursed was almost exclusively Scottish. The grand stand was not the only structure which presented an animated and, having regard to the variety of the costumes, a somewhat gay appearance; but there was also a large contingent of visitors in the members' pavilion. The remainder of the circle formed by the spectators was broken at intervals by booths and sideshows, which helped to impart

> variety to the scene. The oval itself, wherein the sports and other competitions took place, was the rendezvous of many clans, some represented by pipers, and others by men, lads, and lassies, all clad in picturesque costume. There were representatives – and many of them worthy representatives, too – of the Rob Roy, the Royal Stewart, the Black Watch (the 42nd Highlanders, around whom so many memories of patriotism, and prowess, and dash cling), the Mackenzie, the Gordon, the MacLeod, the Macdonald, the Hamilton, the Argyle, the Campbell of Argyle, the Macduff, and the Macgregor clan … From time to time, and simultaneously with the dancing competitions, bicycle and other sports were carried out, and, the competitors being numerous and attired in the gayest of costumes, the effect of the scene altogether was quite kaleidoscopic. There was the inner ever-changing group of colours, and circling around this at times, in extended order (because of the handicapping), was a contingent of wheelmen, who, with the dancers, produced a chromotrope of remarkable brilliancy. Not only was the scene attractive viewed from the spectacular standpoint, but many of the exhibitions given were of a most exciting nature, and the vast audience freely bestowed its applause on the displays of skill, endurance, and judgment which were made. There were competitions which excited the enthusiasm and the stimulating plaudits of the spectators, and there were other competitions which gave scope for humorous situations. Especially was this the case with the obstacle races …[33]

Sam Shaw would have been pleased indeed when he won the Half-Mile Handicap from the scratch man, Joe Megson, a man widely regarded as the top rider of the day. Sam's 1895 was off to a great start. For a change of pace, Sam was chosen to play for the League of Wheelmen in a cricket match against the Redfern Bicycle Club at Redfern Oval on 12 January.

No record of individual performances has been located but the Wheelmen, chasing the Redfern Club's 6–151 were all out for 40.[34]

Always a 'club man', Sam was often involved in helping in the establishment of new branches of the League of New South Wales Wheelmen as the new cyclists' organisation underwent very rapid expansion. In January 1895, he entered for events at the first meeting of the Young branch to be held on Anniversary Day. No record of his participation has been found but if he did attend, like others visiting from Sydney, he would have been entertained by local riders in some gold-panning visits to the Lambing Flat diggings. In April 1895 he was elected to the Committee of the League and in July was elected the League's delegate for Armidale.[35] And for the new Parramatta Branch's Queen's Birthday meeting, Sam entered in the half-mile and one-mile races. From a visit of all of the officers of the League to Parramatta, an undated group photograph shows a dapper Sam Shaw with cravat and boater hat.[36]

Spills and wins

Accidents happen. In 1895, Sam Shaw had at least two, one on the track and the other on the road. In early April the *Australian Town and Country Journal* reported that Sam, in front of 10,000 people at the Sydney Cricket Ground, was among several riders who 'came a cropper'.[37] A week later Sydney's *Bird O'Freedom* reported the 'Merry little Sammy Shaw had a narrow escape … In Oxford-street he got run over by an un-handsome cab, and his machine was a perfect wreck. Luckily Sam got out of the way, he does not know how, and has only a few bruises to remember the incident by'.[38] This reporting of the dangers of cycling and cycle racing drew attention to only tips of the iceberg. Injuries were very common.

Cycling clubs commonly organised some special form of event to mark the beginning of a new season of sport and to rally members. The League of New South Wales Wheelmen inaugurated its second season, in May 1895, with an opening run (as distinct from a race) to Botany. Some 70 riders assembled at Martin Place and then watched by crowds along the way, rode via George and Regent streets to Botany. At Botany's Sir Joseph Banks Grounds a Half-Mile Roadster Race was run off among about 40 starters. Sam Shaw took third place. Then, in the evening, 'about 60 cyclists sat down to tea and afterward a very pleasant time was spent in harmony and amusement'.[39]

Once the season was underway the League ran its own programmes at the Sydney Cricket Ground and country centres and often sponsored racing at the half-time interval at major football games. Sam raced at several of these events at the Sydney Cricket Ground during the 1895 football season. He raced, but without luck, in the first week of June when the riders attired in coloured 'jockey caps and jackets ... presented a pretty sight as they spun around the track'[40] Sam won £7 when he took first place in the Three-Mile Open Cycling Handicap at interval in an inter-colonial football match between New South Wales and Queensland on 6 July. Twenty-eight started and 'little Sammy Shaw' raced home 'after a rattling spin' to win by a foot.[41] According to the *Newcastle Morning Herald & Miners' Advocate*, reporting Sam's win because he had a following in Newcastle, 'Everyone was pleased to see Sam's smiling face get home a winner'.[42]

Another spill and another win came Sam Shaw's way in late July at another of the races held at the football:

> The League riders have been congratulating themselves on the absence of accidents, but the two-mile race on Saturday was not free from a mishap which was nearly being serious. There was a fall just near the starting post, and Sammy Shaw came down on the fallen one. Middleton and others had to ride in or out to escape the obstacle. A little further on J. Williams, who would have bad a good chance on his recent form, also measured his length on the turf. ...
>
> Little Sammy Shaw came out of his shell in the second heat of the Mile Handicap last Saturday. He was on the 35yd mark. O'Brien and Middleton were on scratch, and at the

> back in the last lap O'Brien quickly settled the Victorian (whose saddle, it afterwards turned out, had gone wrong), and looked like winning easily; but Shaw went after the Parramatta man with a brilliant sprint, and, catching him in a short space, won by a dozen yards. The time (2min 22 3/4sec) is very swift ...'[43]

Samuel Robinson Shaw married Isabella (Bell) Wilson Hamilton at St Leonards in 1896.[44] Around the time of his marriage, Sam's cycle sport attention turned more towards administration of the sport and serving in several capacities as an official at race meetings. In October 1895, he was appointed as a member of the Racing Board of the League of New South Wales Wheelmen.[45] That board appointed him laptaker and lap-crier at League meetings in November and December and clerk of the course for the Cyclists' Union events held on New Year's Day 1896 at the Sydney Cricket Ground, where 20,000 spectators watched the sports. His laptaking work for the League continued throughout 1896 and he was reappointed to the Racing Board and made a member of the General Committee late that year and again in 1897 and 1898. League refereeing and timekeeping work came Sam's way in 1897.[46] Sam Shaw was clearly widely experienced and a highly respected member of the League's race administration team.

League of New South Wales Wheelmen

The League of New South Wales Wheelmen was also going from strength to strength as cash, or professional cycling, dominated the racing scene. A review of the League's history and activities published in July 1896 revealed the extent of its activities and how far it had progressed in less than three years since its formation:

> In 1892 several members of the Cyclists' Union, seeing that the sport so far as racing was concerned had no interest at all

from a public point of view, and encouraged by the success of cash cycling in Victoria, seceded, and formed the Austral B.C., the first cash organisation formed in New South Wales. Mr J. Williams, now official handicapper to the league; Mr E. C. Hughes, vice-president; and Mr J. Tracey, were the chief organisers. It was at first a struggle for existence, but presently the Speedwell B.C., one of the most popular of the Union, threw in its lot with the cash amateurs, and Mr F. G. C. Hanslow, then a prominent member of this club and late chairman of the interim council, united the Speedwell and Austral clubs and drafted a scheme upon which the League of New South Wales Wheelmen was formed, [on] September 3, 1893. To-day it has branches in every important town, in the colony, with a membership of about 4000. Its cosy George-street club rooms are the rendezvous of every cash amateur visiting Sydney, and the league is in front of such associations in Australasia.

At the first annual meeting in February, 1894, the credit balance was £30, and at the second, held in April, 1895, £330; at the last, held in February of this year, £1488; and this sum it is expected will be considerably augmented by the next report, as the income keeps steadily increasing. Last year it was £4314, against an expenditure of £2825, a very creditable showing for a body only in existence about two and a half years, and which practically started without funds.

The Racing Carnivals.

It is through its racing carnivals that the League is best known to the public. The first race meeting in Sydney for cash prizes was run before the formation of the league, in December, 1892, on the Sydney Cricket Ground. It was known as 'Lambton's summer meeting,' and could hardly be classed as a success, but it helped to pave the way for the meetings that have become so popular. The first racing under the rules of the League was at Lillie Bridge Ground, a series of weekly and fortnightly handicaps, but those who were able to see ahead succeeded after great opposition in getting the sanction to these races withdrawn, and thus the first real step forward was taken by the League.

On the 30th April and 6th March 1895, the first racing carnival run under the league rules took place on the Sydney Cricket Ground, and under the management of Mr Percy Hunter, the secretary, ably assisted by his brother officers, this initial effort was a pronounced success, both financially and from a spectator point of view. The prizes were about £350, and the racing men performed with a vim never before seen in the colony. The public flocked to the ground and the excitement was intense when Joe Megson, the League's champion, defeated the cracks from all the colonies in the half-mile championship of New South Wales and the five-mile championship of Australasia… The League's profit on that meeting was over £300, the largest sum up to that time ever gained by a cycle meeting in Sydney … November last filled the interval which completely overshadowed its predecessor. For weeks before 'Zimmerman' was the talk of the town, and 29,000 people passed through the turnstiles on the first day. On the second day Lord Hampden attended his first Sydney sports meeting. In spite of the rain, an attendance of 32,000 was registered, and hundreds who arrived late had to be turned away. Notwithstanding the enormous expense necessary in running such a gathering – the prize money alone was £500 – there was a credit of over £1800 after all charges had been paid.

The third carnival was held in March last. The Royal Agricultural Society having put down an asphalted banked track in their grounds, the race was held there instead of at the Cricket Ground, where the track was only grass and flat ...

The fifth carnival, the winter race meeting is set down for the 15th and 23rd August...

Each year the majority of country branches have held race meetings, and some of the more enterprising have now regular annual fixtures which are looked forward to with interest by the racing members of the league, and in addition to these the members of the league have competed at the Eight-hour Demonstration, Highland Gathering, and United Friendly Societies Demonstration ...

Many matters other than racing have not had the attention they deserve from the officers of the league, but the general wants of the members have been well looked after, and touring and social wants, two very important features, will soon be put upon a footing which will make the League in all departments second to none in Australia. It has club rooms in George-street with every convenience, such as telephone, billiards, piano, newspapers, games, and information re the progress of the league, its sporting fixtures, and touring. Smoke concerts are held every month, and the annual ball has gained much popularity. Dinners and picnics for the members are of frequent occurrence.

At the opening of the present season a picnic was given to the members with their families instead of the old style of united run, and its success probably ensured its becoming the annual opening fixture.[47]

During the time the League prospered and Sam Shaw accepted administrative and race official roles in the sport, he continued as a competitor, albeit with somewhat reduced and selective racing commitments. In June 1896, he raced without success as a placegetter in the League's One-Mile Handicap Race at the Agricultural Ground. In November, when he was officiating as lap-crier at the League's Summer Carnival he also raced, this time in the £130 Sydney Wheel Race.[48] In the Australia Fair sports at the Agricultural Grounds in February 1897, Sam raced in two League events, over a half-mile and two miles.[49] Later in the month he entered in several events at the League's carnival, including the Electric Handicap and Sydney Plate.

For Easter Monday 1897, Sam Shaw travelled to Bowral and the Moss Vale Grounds at Burrado in the southern highlands for the inaugural Grand Cycling Carnival of the newly formed Bowral Branch of the League. Heavily handicapped, he was placed second in his heat of the Open Handicap and second in his heat of the Bowral Wheel Race. His younger brother Fred also raced and gave an exhibition race at the Bowral meeting.[50]

At a cycling meeting held at the Sydney Cricket Ground on 5 June 1897, Sam Shaw beat Joe Megson to win his heat of the two-mile handicap. Then, 'In the final an accident occurred. Shaw touched Congden's wheel in the fifth lap. The former fell, and down over him came M'Innes, Meadham, and Megson'. As the *Referee* reported, the reason for the falls was that Sammy Shaw, riding very close behind Congden's wheel, touched it when that rider suddenly slackened pace, 'and Jill came tumbling after.' It went on to say, 'None of the riders who fell on Saturday were very seriously hurt. Sammy Shaw had his neck scraped by someone's pedal, Megson was bruised on the lower part of the body and leg, and Meadham described himself on Monday as sore all over'.[51]

The colony was awash in 1897 with 'record reign' events to celebrate Queen Victoria's record as reigning British monarch. The Queen's Diamond Jubilee on 20 June was the occasion of the sixtieth anniversary of her accession to the throne on 20 June 1837 and the League of New South Wales Wheelmen held a June carnival as their contribution to Sydney's celebrations. The *Australian Star* announced that the carnival

> will be run on up-to-date lines, with heavy purses, and lap and heat prizes, crowned by the £100 event – the Victoria Wheel Race. There will be two days' racing, Tuesday, June 22 (Commemoration Day), and Saturday, June 26. £350 will be distributed among winners. On the first day the programme includes: Queen's Cup, half-mile, first prize £15, second £5, third £3; Victoria Wheel Race, two miles, £50, £25, £10; Championship Sydney District, five miles, £10 (gold medal), £5, £3; One Mile Scratch, £15, £5, £3; Tandem Handicap, three miles, £20, £10. The second day's programme reads: Coronation Handicap, one mile, £25, £10, £5; First-class Handicap, one mile and a half, £15, £5, £3; Second and Third-class Handicap, £15, £5, £3; Ten Miles Scratch, £25, £10 and £5.

It went on to say, 'A race on the antiquated ordinary [penny farthing bicycle] will be included at the League's … carnival as a curiosity. How have the mighty fallen! Some old friends should mount the tall wheels, including, perhaps … [Sam] Shaw'.[52] As well, Sam Shaw rode in the Queen's Cup and the Victoria Wheel Race on the first day of this meeting and the Coronation Handicap and Second Class Handicap on the second day.

The Paddington Bicycle Club

The Shaw family moved from Woolloomooloo to the healthier and generally more desirable nearby suburb of Paddington, sometime after the death of Mary Anne Shaw in 1879. During the 1880s and into the 1890s they lived at several Paddington addresses, all close to the Association Cricket Ground and the Agricultural Ground. By 1898, Sam Shaw lived at 3 Point Piper Terrace, Point Piper Road (now Jersey Road), Woollahra (now part of Paddington)[53], a substantial terrace home that had been occupied by Sam's father and others of the Shaw family and which reflected their growing affluence.

Sam's interest in social runs was alive and well. In May 1899 he participated in, and completed, the Century Run, organised by the Cyclists' Union to mark the fast-approaching new century. The event was an all-day one:

> The Cyclists' Union century run on May 24 proved eminently successful. Punctually at 7a.m. 162 cyclists, including five ladies, started from Martin Place ... Parramatta was reached a little ahead of schedule time. Breakfast was provided at three hotels – the Park Gate, the White Horse, and the Commercial. The roads were fairly good, though dusty all the way to Windsor. But from thence to Penrith rough shingly roads were met, whilst a strong head wind made the riding heavy. The return journey was made according to time table, and the long line of cyclists passed through George-street, which was kept clear, and pulled up at the General Post Office at 6.30p.m ... 154 riders went right through, including the five ladies.[54]

Start of the Century Run, Martin Place, Sydney, 24 May 1899.
Town and Country Journal, 3 June 1899, p. 3

For some time, Sam Shaw, and numerous other prominent racing men who lived in Paddington had been giving consideration to the formation of a new local club that would be strong in numbers and pace. Their mid-

1899 proposal to form the Paddington Bicycle Club affiliated to the League of New South Wales Wheelmen was accepted and Sam was elected by the members (there were 130 within a month and that figure swiftly grew to over 250) to the position of Sub-Captain. The club originally met at Sinnott's Hotel on Oxford Street Paddington, later at the Paddington Town Hall. It adopted the colours of red and white and planned a host of activities including two five-mile road races over the Rose Bay course (one for amateurs, one for cash riders) a run to Bayview and a 'billy run'[55] to Narrabeen, both on Sydney's northern beaches. A winter dance and a ball were organised and the club held smoke concerts, undertook charity runs, established an ambulance class, proposed a military cycle corps from within its burgeoning membership and became a strong advocate of public cycle paths. Although it was first and foremost a cycling club, the Paddington Bicycle Club also experimented with holding cricket matches and swimming events, so becoming a precursor to latter day sports clubs.[56]

Sam Shaw's sterling efforts to help steer the new club to success were rewarded by his club mates at a smoke concert in September 1900. Described as the former secretary of the club, Sam, 'in view of the good services he had rendered to the club … was presented with a gold medal'.[57]

Political upheaval accompanied success. The Paddington Bicycle Club, within two years of its formation, became disaffected with the League. Then, when suspended from the League, it took matters into its own hands and seceded in August 1901 and sought affiliation with the New South Wales Cyclists' Union. Within two months it sought to change its name to the Eastern Suburbs Bicycle Club. After resolution of the underlying problems, the Paddington Bicycle Club and the newly formed Eastern Suburbs Bicycle Club co-existed. In December 1901, by which time he has moved to Winslow Street, North Sydney (now part of Kirribilli),[58] Sam was elected as Treasurer of the Paddington Bicycle Club. His varied club administrative experience would prove to stand him in good stead in his future sporting and business life.

Shaw Brothers, boot importers

In mid-1903 the firm of Shaw Brothers, boot importers, was established at 80 Miller Street, North Sydney, opposite the Marcus Clarke Emporium (department store).[59] The new footwear firm's registration papers[60] show that the persons carrying on the business were Samuel Robinson Shaw, Frederick Ewart Shaw (Sam's brother) and Donald Samuel Ewart Shaw, Sam's son who, at the time, was less than a year old.[61] Just what role Fred Shaw played in this business is not clear. He may have been a silent partner who in some way contributed to the establishment costs. A single man who had done very well racing bicycles and representing bicycle companies, he could well afford to have done so.

While the firm of Shaw Brothers was often listed as a boot importer it is clear from advertisements placed for salesmen and saleswomen, and the firm's product advertising, that, in addition to any wholesale business they may have been engaged in, they were also boot and shoe retailers and repairers. Separate men's and women's departments sold imported footwear from European, American and Australian manufacturers.

The Miller Street, North Sydney store remained the headquarters of the business for over 35 years[62] but prior to 1924 Sam opened several other stores in nearby suburbs and in the city. The first of these opened in 1908 and traded until 1922 at 10 Willoughby Road, Crows Nest/North Sydney. In 1915, 1916 and 1917 another store was located at 432 Pitt Street, Sydney, so that Shaw Brothers had three operating in those years. By 1918 Shaw Brothers were no longer in business in Pitt Street in the city but, in addition to the Miller Street and Willoughby Road stores at North Sydney, were now at Old South Head Road, Woollahra (Paddington). In 1918 they advertised at Bondi Junction.[63] It is possible another store was opened at Mosman. All stores were strategically located on busy tramlines, including at major junctions such as Crows Nest Junction and Bondi Junction.

Shaw Brothers boot and shoe store, 80 Miller Street, North Sydney, c.1921.
Sam Shaw is extreme right, his son Don Shaw extreme left.
Stanton Library, North Sydney

In association with his North Sydney business interests, Sam Shaw was elected to several sporting club positions, among them vice-president of the North Sydney Wednesday Football Club (1907) and secretary of the North Sydney Electorate Wednesday Cricket Club that entered first and second grade teams in the New South Wales Wednesday Cricket Association competition (1908).[64] Sam had been donating cricket trophies to the club and attending their smoke concerts since 1904.[65] In September 1908, at a meeting of its 130 members, Sam Shaw was elected to the council of the Willoughby Bicycle Club. He kept up his riding and riding fitness and in June 1910, a month prior to his fortieth birthday, rode *from scratch* in a ten-mile road race over the Chatswood course in an event organised by the Crows Nest Bicycle Club, of which he was a member and official.[66]

Later in life, Sam was elected to civic positions. He was secretary of the North Sydney Chamber of Commerce (1924) and treasurer of the North Sydney Ratepayers and Citizens' Association (1934). In 1925 he was unsuccessful in his bid to win the right to represent Victoria Ward on the North Sydney Council.[67] As well, he served on the sports and other committees of the United Grand Lodge, Wollstonecraft and was a member of the Loyal Orange Lodge.

Between 1902 and 1907 Sam, Bell and young Don lived at 20 Winslow Street, North Sydney. Afterwards, and until his death, he lived in a substantial home built across two building blocks, at 10 Sinclair Street, Wollstonecraft (near North Sydney).[68] As a weekend and holiday retreat Sam enjoyed a large block of bushland at Newport Beach, in the area local estate agents now know as the 'golden triangle', and there he built a small weekend and vacation home. Relatives and friends visited the property, and these included his cycling mates: for example, in November 1908, 'At the invitation of Mr S. R. Shaw, [members of] the Crow's Nest [Bicycle] Club held a stump picnic at his grounds at Newport' that involved a programme of sports for which prizes were awarded.[69]

Sam Shaw at the wheel of his 1907 Argyll car, NSW 484, at his Newport Beach weekender, c.1912. Shaw family collection

Motorcycles and motorcycle sport

His prospering stores enabled Sam to move on from his early cycling interests to motorcycles and cars and in the first decades of the twentieth century he became one of Sydney's motoring pioneers. He owned a c1907 Argyll touring car registered NSW 484 followed, perhaps among others, by a 1917 Buick tourer, a 1920s 'bullnose' Morris, a Buick and a Hudson. The number plate NSW 484 moved from car to car because he was proud of his early association with motoring in New South Wales. That plate was later used by his son and remains in the Shaw family.

Sam's interest in motoring led him to compete in motorcycle and car club events, the latter sometimes in competition with his son. In late 1919 he was elected president of the Northern Suburbs Motorcycle Club, a role in which he was immediately active and popular:

> A huge success describes the opening run to Long Reef on Sunday. At 10.15 a.m. one heard low hums rising, then a metallic click as low gear engaged second, then top, then silence and 21 different outfits were on their way.
>
> The fairly bumpy ride to the Spit was compensated for by the glorious views from the heights. From here on the road improved, but another bumpy stretch awaited the party near Long Reef. Packed hampers, smiling faces and good fellowship was the order of the day.
>
> Upon arriving at Long Reef hampers were unpacked, billies boiled, events mapped and flagged out, and a sojourn made for lunch. What can beat a good lunch out in the open. Lunch over, hampers were packed and chats over the programme commenced …
>
> The prizes were presented by President S. Shaw, who was very much in attendance. President S. Shaw was elected to his position this year and has proved the wisdom of the club's selection. He is popular among the boys.
>
> The attendance at the run was 17 side car outfits, two solos and two cars, carrying altogether 48 adults and the children. Messrs. Perce Boyce, Les Vandenbergh and S. Shaw were very active in the running of the events.[70]

In early December 1919, four hundred spectators watched the start of a two-day motorcycle reliability trial at Lee's Garage, Parramatta. Among the machines competing on a ride that would take them to Katoomba, Lithgow and Mudgee and return were two Indian motorcycle-sidecar outfits. Sam Shaw rode as passenger/navigator in one while his son, Don, aged sixteen, rode the other that also carried a passenger/navigator. Sam was introducing his son to motorcycle sport at an early age, and enjoying the experience himself.[71]

Under Sam's leadership (1919–25), the Northern Suburbs Motorcycle Club also conducted one-day and half-day reliability rallies of this type over shorter distances. Other competitive events included quarter-mile acceleration tests and hillclimb contests and the club's social events included billy runs. Events were not always centred on motorcycles. 'By President Sam Shaw's invitation', fifteen members of the club joined a snapper fishing expedition.[72] As president of the club, Sam presented prizes at club meetings and smoke concerts. He was also a generous donor of prizes, including some valued up to £10/10/-. In 1925, he became the first president of the Motor Cyclists' Association of New South Wales.

Newspaper reports of Sam's 1920s motorcycling achievements often referred to his earlier success in bicycle racing. Among the comments made were that Sam Shaw was a 'once great cyclist', that he was 'one of the fastest [bicycle] sprinters in Australia 20 years ago', 'the great cyclist of the Megson days', 'a crack cyclist of other days' and 'a great cyclist in the boom days of 25 years ago [when] he won many races from short marks'.[73]

Bicycles led to motorcycles. Motorcycles led to cars. While Sam did not race cars, he enjoyed using the cars he proudly owned to compete in acceleration events, hillclimbs and motoring gymkhanas. Most of the events in which he entered were sponsored by the Northern Suburbs Motor Club, of which he was a member.

Sam Shaw had come a long way from his native Woolloomooloo.

Samuel Robinson Shaw continued to operate his very successful boot and shoe business and maintained his interest in bicycles, motorcycles and cars until his sudden death in a private North Sydney hospital on 15 October 1939.[74]

Donald (Don) Samuel Ewart Shaw

Sam Shaw influenced many people but none more so than his son Donald (Don), with whom he shared his business and sporting interests for nearly four decades.

With his family, Don, as a five-year-old, moved from North Sydney to 20 Sinclair Street, Wollstonecraft about 1907. Little is known of his early education but records establish that he attended The Sydney Church of England Grammar School in his senior years at school, enrolling early in 1917[75] and leaving early in 1919.[76]

In 1919 Don Shaw went to work full-time with his father in the North Sydney footwear business, now effectively Shaw and Son (although the business name was never changed). At the same time Don followed in his father's footsteps and became active in sport, particularly motor sport with the Northern Suburbs Motor Cycle Club.

In September 1919, just after his seventeenth birthday, Don Shaw, before 'a good muster of motor cycling enthusiasts' won the club's flexibility hillclimb, an event for riders of solo and sidecar machines that involved executing both slow and fast hill trials. The winner was the rider with the greatest difference between those times, after allowing for handicap.[77] Later that month, Don was one of four riders, from 22 starters, in a 100-mile reliability trial that lost no points and tied. Don Shaw who, 'still in his teens, joined up as a novice two months ago, and straightway bagged the first two events he entered for', was eliminated in a subsequent trial to decide among the four who had tied when he damaged his machine and it suffered mechanical problems.[78] Don's remarkable early success in motorcycle sport suggests that his father allowed or encouraged him to ride motorcycles, perhaps on the Newport property, well before he was able to join the club and compete.

In July 1920 Don took first place in a standing quarter mile event, effectively a short drag race. He repeated that win in a similar event in November, the winner's trophy having survived in the possession of his daughter.[79] Later that year he took second place in a youths' single skulls handicap at the Pittwater Regatta.

In February 1922 Don, riding his Excelsior motorcycle with sidecar, was an entrant in the fourth annual 24-hour reliability trial of the Northern Suburbs Motor Cycle Club. Leaving from the club's rooms in Crows Nest, the route included Katoomba, Bathurst, Crookwell, and Goulburn and then returned to Crows Nest via Tom Uglys Point in Sydney's southern suburbs.[80] In October that year he took second place in a club event for solo machines held at Willoughby; also that month, he won a 75-yard foot race run at a meeting of his motor cycle club at Lane Cove. At the club's annual general meeting in October, when his father was again elected president, Don was elected club captain.[81]

Don Shaw (left) on his Excelsior motorcycle sidecar outfit, c.1921.
Shaw family collection

In 1923 Don Shaw was again an entrant in the club's 24-hour reliability trials. In November 1923, riding his Excelsior motorcycle, Don took second place in a hillclimb event. The following month he was competing on an AJS machine. Then, riding the AJS, he was an entrant in the club's 1924 24-hour reliability trial.[82]

When, in 1925, the Northern Suburbs Motor Cycle Club became the Northern Suburbs Motor Club Don was elected press correspondent; his father was elected president.[83] This father-son sporting association was evident again in 1926 when they competed against one another in their club's car 'speed-judging' event, Don driving a small French Amilcar two-seater sports car and his father, Sam, driving a large Buick tourer.[84]

Throughout the 1920s and 1930s Don worked in the family footwear business at 80 Miller Street, North Sydney. The prosperity of the business provided Don with the resources to spread his sporting interests to speedboats. In October 1936 he successfully raced his *Dee Shaw* to second place in competition conducted by the Australian Motor Yacht Squadron on Middle Harbour. The following year his *Wee Dash* won the second heat of a speedboat handicap conducted by the Australian Motor Yacht Squadron.[85] To build and maintain these boats, his cars and motorcycles, and to build a caravan, Don kept a very comprehensively equipped workshop at his Northbridge home. Neighbours and friends often borrowed tools from this workshop but, after he had trouble securing the return of lent tools, he erected a sign in his workshop that read, 'The man who lends his tools has gone to Alaska'. Among his other interests in the 1930s and 1940s, Don was a regular spectator at the wrestling held at the old Sydney Stadium at Rushcutters Bay and an active ice skater at the Glacerium near Central Railway Station. Don's interest in boating and motoring continued into the 1940s. In 1941 he owned a boat built of huon pine and equipped with an outboard motor. In 1947 he still owned a Royal Enfield motorcycle.[86]

Shaw Brothers was sold in late 1948 or early 1949 to Mr G. H. Lane of Mosman (the Shaw Brothers name remained with the business until 1954). After the sale of Shaw Brothers, Don Shaw briefly ran a small boot stitching business at 105 Pacific Highway, North Sydney.

Donald (Don) Samuel Ewart Shaw, aged 46, died suddenly at his home, 34 Woonoona Avenue, Northbridge, on 23 April 1949. His probate papers described him as a shoe shop proprietor. Don's estate included property at Wollstonecraft, Northbridge, Mona Vale, Castlecrag and Tambourie Lake, Shoalhaven along with a 1936 Ford V8 sedan, previously his father's, and a caravan.[87]

CHAPTER 4

Soldiering On: Henry Tait Shaw

Henry Tait Shaw was born to William and Mary Anne Shaw on 7 August 1872 at Riley Street, Woolloomooloo. His birth certificate shows the name of Tait Ewart Shaw but apparently William and Mary Anne changed their minds and when their son was baptised on 15 September the name was recorded as Henry Tait Shaw.[1] On occasions Henry was known as Harry (written as Hy). On many more occasions his name Tait, a family name, was misspelled, most commonly as Tate. In the bicycle racing community he was usually known as H. T. Shaw.

Having learned his trade with R. D. Brauch, a large clothing manufacturer of Castlereagh Street, Sydney, Henry followed in the footsteps of his brothers William and James and worked as a tailor's cutter. William and Henry Shaw became respected tailors employed by Sydney tailoring firms. Both were nominated to give evidence in an industrial dispute in the clothing trade before the Court of Arbitration in 1904.[2]

Joining the wheelers for one-mile racing

With older brothers swept up by the cycling craze and engaged in the sport of bicycle racing, it is not surprising that Henry joined with them and began cycling, first as his personal transport and recreation, and then in racing. But, as was common for cyclists new to the major track and road events, Henry's years in the sport began slowly. His entries for events had to translate into acceptances. Decisions had to be made about what race distances might suit his abilities and which meetings were appropriate for his introduction to the sport. He was fortunate, however, in having the support and guidance of his brothers and in benefitting from their experience.

Henry raced under lights, on 30 May 1891, at the first bicycle race meeting conducted at the Lillie Bridge Grounds at Forest Lodge, Sydney. The occasion was the Grand Amateur Autumn Race Meeting of the Speedwell Bicycle Club, when seven bicycle races were decided. Riding for the Crusaders' Bicycle Club in blue and white, Henry was unplaced in the One-Mile Open Bicycle Handicap for Roadsters.[3] The fourteen starters included the champion Joseph Megson.

One-mile events were Henry's first competitive interest. Shortly after his Lillie Bridge debut, and again in the Crusaders' blue and white, he contested the Mile Mixed Roadster Handicap in the Grand Amateur Championship Race Meeting run by the St Leonards Bicycle Club at St Leonards Park Oval on 18 July.[4] A month later, riding for the Crusaders', he rode in the One-Mile Maiden Scratch Race at the Association Cricket Ground, Moore Park, at the Tenth Annual Amateur Championship Race Meeting of the Sydney Bicycle Club.[5] His brother, Sam, also contested this event and ran fourth.

Other one-mile events beckoned. Still eligible to ride in a maiden event, Henry Shaw raced, again in the Crusaders' blue and white, in the One-Mile Maiden Scratch Race at the Suburban Bicycle Club's Sixth Grand Amateur Championship Race Meeting at the Association Cricket Ground on 26 September. The race was ridden on roadsters with a minimum weight of 35lbs and pneumatic tyres were barred.[6] Henry was unplaced in his heat but his brother Sam won the final. As well as entering these various bicycle club events, Henry was listed to compete in the One-Mile Safety Handicap at the Highland Society's Sports meeting at Moore Park on New Year's Day 1892.[7] Henry was unsuccessful in taking places in any of these events but he was a newcomer to this level of the sport. He was rubbing shoulders with some of the greats of the day and developing track sense and competition strategy.

Changing tack?

While the Shaw brothers were most focussed on cycle racing, they often tried their hand at other sports, with these including sailing. For the Australian Anniversary Regatta on Anniversary Day 1893 (26 January), Henry and brothers William and Sam, along with their future brother-in-law Brice Thomas, were members of the 20-man crew of the 24-foot *Regina* competing against 20 other boats in the Australian Anniversary Handicap. The Sydney Harbour course for the race was from the flagship, the steamship *Cintra,* around Fort Dennison, around the lightship and the Sow and Pigs reef, around Shark Island, back to the flagship and finishing between the flagship and Clark Island. Prizes for this race were £25, £15, £5 and a championship medal to the captain of the winning boat.[8]

Captaining the *Regina* for this race was George Parrett, whose son William (Will) Parrett later married Christina (Teenie) Shaw.[9] Sports-minded members of the Shaw, Thomas and Parrett families had similar sporting interests and were close. It seems likely that Henry Shaw, along with his brothers and Brice Thomas again crewed on the *Regina* in 1892 on the numerous other occasions it competed on the harbour, often very successfully, under Captain George Parrett. However, that is not confirmed as it was rare for crew lists to be published and no other lists for this boat have so far come to light. It also seems likely that Henry's flirtation with sailing took him away from cycling at this time. Records of Henry participating in upper level cycling events in 1892 are sparse indeed.

Back on the saddle

By May 1893, Henry was back on the saddle, when he joined William, Sam and Brice Thomas to ride in the Speedwell Bicycle Club's annual road race over the ten-mile Botany course. Henry's handicap for the road race, a race that allowed pacemakers, was six minutes, a time that was based on the weight of the 33 lb machine he rode. None of the four men was placed. In November of that year, he was a member of the 25-strong contingent that travelled from Sydney to Maitland by steamer and train under the management of the president of the League of New South Wales Wheelmen to compete in the Maitland Club's Grand Athletic Carnival at the Albion Ground. Henry was set down to ride in the half-mile event. At this time, photographers were beginning to ply their trade at bicycle club race meetings. While capturing images of quickly moving machines was still proving difficult, prospective spectators for this meeting were informed that 'the committee have secured the services of an expert photographer, who will photograph people who look over the fence'.[10]

Very late in 1893 Henry returned to racing at the Lillie Bridge Grounds. While he was unsuccessful in the One-Mile Bicycle Handicap on 13 December, he won the Two-Mile Bicycle Handicap on 20 December from 270 yards. That race attracted 25 starters, among them Joseph (Joe) Megson, at that time the foremost rider in the colony, who rode from scratch. While Henry's 270-yard start undoubtedly contributed to his win, he had the satisfaction of beating the famous champion and taking home the prize money.[11]

Racing in pink silk and riding a 27 lb machine, Henry was eliminated in heats of the Half-Mile Bicycle Race and the One-Mile Bicycle Race at the Highland Gathering Sports held at the Association Cricket Ground on New Year's Day 1894.[12] Sam Shaw and Brice Thomas were also eliminated in the heats of these two events.

Henry's wins in 1893 had their downside. Handicappers, now recognizing Henry's racing talent, considerably shortened his handicap. While Henry raced often in 1894 it was not until September that he enjoyed another win when, at races conducted by the Suburban Bicycle Club, 'H. Shaw annexed the Half-Mile Open Handicap in 1min 10sec'.[13] In the nine months leading up to that win Henry raced in numerous half-mile, one mile, one-and-half-mile and two-mile handicap events at race meetings held at Lillie Bridge, The Association Cricket Ground, Redfern, Maitland and Goulburn and he also competed in another ten-mile road race over the Botany course.[14] Much of this racing was done in the company of his brothers Sam and, from July, Fred and Brice Thomas and also many of the racing greats.

The pattern now apparent in Henry's cycle racing was repeated in 1895. He raced in the top league, often over varying distances with brothers and mates, and often in the company of the 'cracks'. While he almost certainly enjoyed the racing, the company and the camaraderie he rarely won a place in competition.

The first major cycling carnival of the League of New South Wales Wheelmen for the year took place at the Sydney Cricket Ground over two days on 30 March and 6 April. When a Newcastle rider fell in the first heat of the £130 Sydney Wheel Race and fractured his collarbone and a Goulburn rider fell over him, Henry gained some notoriety when he 'cleverly rode over one of the prostrate men without losing his balance' and was placed fourth in his heat. On the second day, the 'form' said that Henry, off 140 yards in the Metropolitan Handicap for £100, £15 and £5, was 'well spoken of' as a chance. He was unplaced. Also on the second day, a day that attracted 12,000 spectators, Henry won his heat of the Second Class Handicap over one mile off a short 65 yards in 'a pretty race' in which he 'rode with dash' and 'ran away in the last lap to win easily'. He raced in the final, but like Joe Megson, was an 'unplaced wheeler'.[15]

This carnival was the largest cycling meeting ever held in Australia up until that time. Over 400 accepted riders were competing in 38 events, many with multiple heats, for £400 in prize money. The meeting was the first inter-colonial event sponsored by the League under an inter-colonial agreement that each colony with a League of Wheelmen (Victoria, South Australia, Tasmania, New Zealand, Queensland and New South Wales) must send its champions. It was also the first time pacing tandems, brought from Melbourne for the meeting, made a track appearance in New South Wales.

The racing men were given every opportunity to practice. The Sydney Cricket ground was open to them every afternoon without charge and was extensively used for practice by local riders in the weeks leading up to the meeting and by the visitors from other colonies when they arrived in Sydney a week before the races. Much of that training involved the men travelling on the track at pace for six to ten miles (four times around to the mile) and then sprinting for the last half lap. Two weeks before the meeting the *Sydney Morning Herald* reported that, 'The track at the cricket ground represents a very busy appearance every afternoon, fully 50 cyclists being at work there' and went on to say, 'a large number of spectators assemble each afternoon on the track for the purpose of watching the men at work'.[16] Three days before the meeting the *Australian Star* commented:

> Megson was out, but only did slow work. R. W. [Bob] Lewis [second only to Joe Megson as a local star], still with sweaters on, appeared on his new machine, which looks a beauty, but took it steady at first. He did a couple of good laps with H. Shaw and Fred Shaw hanging on. One of these latter two should make things sultry in the half-mile.[17]

Very little information is available about other training regimes followed by racing cyclists but, unsurprisingly perhaps, there was no shortage of advice about exercise. As one British cycling book of the time vaguely suggested, the would-be racing man should be 'temperate in all things'. It is easy to doubt that many Australian racing men took this sometimes vague but sometimes alarmingly precise advice on board:

> Plenty of exercise, good, sound food, and early retiring, are essential. In summer rise about seven, in winter a little later. On getting out of bed a cold bath should be indulged in, followed by a brisk rub up rather than down. A few minutes exercise with dumb-bells or India clubs might follow … a little outdoor exercise before breakfast will also prove beneficial, and for this purpose a gentle walk will be found best.[18]

The same authors also had something to say about tobacco. The racing cyclist, they said, should give up smoking, or 'considerably restrict himself in the use of the weed', although latter-day trainers, they went on, 'incline to approve of a confirmed smoker enjoying a pipe in the evening'.[19]

Buoyed by the success of its two-day March/April carnival the League planned a Monster Racing Carnival, as they called it, for 16 and 23 November 1895. The earlier carnival had netted £400 profit, enough to elaborately set up the League's 420 George Street clubrooms, and the League hoped to repeat that financial success. Again, the venue was the Sydney Cricket Ground. Henry was among the acceptances for the carnival that attracted entries from Sydney, Italy, Queensland, Victoria, Tasmania, South Australia, Western Australia, and from League branches in New South Wales at Parramatta, Broken Hill, Newcastle, Maitland, Bega, Nowra, Goulburn, Mudgee and Picton.[20] Also listed to race was Arthur Zimmerman, the American champion. Local fans were intrigued by the prospect of Zimmerman's clash with Joe Megson, now the half-mile, one-mile, five-mile and ten-mile champion of Australasia. Dubbed 'the greatest of all pedallers',[21] Zimmerman was the talk of the town and added many thousands to the spectator tally that topped a record 65,000 over the two days of racing.

Prize money for the carnival, advertised in the League's journal in September as £375,[22] had climbed to £500 by race day, by which time 428 riders were listed to compete.[23] Among them was Henry Tait Shaw, who raced in 'all pink' off a handicap of 290 yards, for £100, £15 and £5, (and £1/10s first in heat, 10s second in heat), in the first heat of the Sydney Wheel Race at the Sydney Cricket Ground on 16 November.[24] In his heat, Henry, the limit man, held his lead until the third lap but was then outpaced.[25] On the same day, the first of the carnival, he rode, again in 'all pink' off a handicap of 95 yards, for £10, £2 and £1, in the Second Class Handicap of 'about one mile, four times round'.[26]

In the interval between the two big League carnivals in 1895, Henry Shaw raced in handicap events run over half-a mile, one mile and two miles in association with football matches played at the Sydney Cricket Ground in May, June, July and August.[27] In those races, and others over two miles at Parramatta and Rosehill in October, he apparently continued to enjoy the competitive cycling even when he raced without gaining places.

Still excited by the rush of the League's two-day events, Henry, along with his brother Fred, entered for the half-mile Federal Stakes and the two-mile Australian Cup at the March 1896 Autumn Racing Carnival at the Agricultural Ground. The Federal Stakes, for which the entry fee was just one shilling, offered prizes of £15, £3 and £2. The Australian Cup had entry and acceptance fees of two shillings and six pence and prizes of £40, £7 and £3, plus £1 for heat winners.[28] Henry Shaw was assigned a handicap of 90 yards for both races.[29] When the completed list of entries was published, Henry was shown to race also in the Third Class Scratch Race (with brother Fred) and the One-Mile Second Class Handicap (with his youngest brother Tom).[30]

The League's advertising for the event called it an International Carnival and made much of the fact that riders from America, England, Italy and New Zealand were among 'the most celebrated string of riders ever seen on an Australian path' and entered in what the League promised would be 'two days of the most sensational racing ever seen in Australia'. In something of a rebuff for the management of the Sydney Cricket Ground that had hosted previous two-day carnivals of the League of New South Wales Wheelmen, the advertising for this meeting on the adjacent Agricultural Ground highlighted that, rather than racing on an unbanked track, competitors would enjoy 'a racing path, with high banks on the corners, similar to the English, American and French tracks' that would allow riders 'to display their true form'. Much was made, too, of the 'many improvements in the enclosure [grassed areas and an improved grandstand], that it now rivals in point of public accommodation any ground in the colony'.[31]

A detailed reminder, told with a touch of humour, about the dangers of racing that were magnified on this fast, new asphalt track, came from reports of mishaps during the first day's racing:

> There was sensational racing, and exciting finishes were seen, and there were several falls. As a British community we naturally do not countenance anything so inhuman

as a bullfight, but we are conscious that the sight of an ambulance corps taking off the slain from a cycle track or a steeplechase course adds considerably to the zest of the day's outing. To those so minded there was plenty of zest. In the third heat of the Federal Stakes, Boyd, the New Zealander, came down and hurt a leg, which affected him for the rest of the day, but the fifth heat of the same race and the second heat of the Australian Cup provided the greatest thrill. It was just opposite the dressing room that Pearson came down, just as the big field was going at top speed. In an instant Moore and Rathgen were over him, and M'Innes and Boyd over them, other riders going one side or the other to avoid the prostrate wheelmen. The slender racing cycles were twisted and buckled in all directions, and one cut right through the water stand pipe beside the fence. Pearson was insensible, having sustained concussion of the brain, and he was taken off the field by the Civil Ambulance and Transport Brigade, two representatives of which dressed his wounds and took him home, Dr Muskett attending to his injuries. Beyond the loss of flesh gouged out on the asphalt, the others were not badly hurt. The element of tragedy having been removed, comedy soon took its place. The high pressure water began immediately to spurt in a great fountain through the cut pipe, drenching the crowd around, and pouring volumes of water across the new track. Gentlemen wearing official badges gave orders intended to meet the emergency, and misguided individuals endeavored to stop up the pipe with clay and wood plugs, and so forth, the only result being that they had to retire dripping and discomfited amidst the cheers of the crowd. Then, as the track rapidly flooded, emissaries were hurried hither and thither to procure a spade with which to cut a channel. Finally, a bystander was seized with an inspiration, which

> resulted in one of the boundary flagpoles being successfully driven into the pipe, and a drain having been cut, the track was cleared and racing resumed.
>
> The final sensation was in the second heat of the Australian Cup. Here again there was a large field, and the finish was being contested at clinking pace. Just as riders with set teeth entered the straight, Fisher and Payne bumped, and the Victorian came down heavily, while M'Innes, who was finishing at a great pace, ran clean over him and fell face downwards on the track. Both men were evidently badly injured, and lay insensible on the asphalt bleeding from ugly-looking wounds. The Ambulance Brigade was in attendance without delay, and bound up the wounds, being engaged for almost 20 minutes in affording temporary aid to the still unconscious riders. Stretchers were brought into requisition, and the wounded men carried off the field to a building, where they were attended to by several doctors.[32]

Henry Shaw did not figure in any of this mayhem but in the final of the Third Class Scratch Race, having taken third place in his heat, his 'tyre burst when half the journey had been accomplished'.[33]

The Megson–Lewis benefit and the motocycle

The League of New South Wales Wheelmen conducted a benefit meeting at the Agricultural Ground before 13,000 spectators on 25 April 1896 for Joe Megson and Bob Lewis, who proposed to visit the 'old country', America and Europe from May to try their luck on the fast tracks on the other side of the world. An amount of £350 was raised to assist them with that ambitious cycling excursion.

The 'motocycle' featured in an exhibition ride at the Megson–Lewis benefit meeting. *Sydney Mail*, 2 May 1896, p. 913

Henry Shaw was appointed a League referee for this meeting, his brother Sam a laptaker. Younger brother Fred was a competitor. All three thus had the opportunity to see and experience close up the 'motocycle' featured as a drawcard to the meeting. The machine in question, the first in the colony, had arrived in Sydney to the Austral bicycle agency a month before, when 'fully 5,000' people turned out to watch it run down George Street from the agency to Circular Quay and back. Bob Lewis and another rider followed on a tandem bicycle but were unable to keep up with it. It was then announced that the motocycle would give an exhibition at the Megson–Lewis benefit meeting by pacing Megson or Lewis for a mile and then running five miles at its top speed.[34] Advertising for the meeting by the League highlighted the 'marvellous motocycle' and prominently displayed a drawing of it.[35]

On the day, the exhibition did not go according to plan. Sydney newspapers reported vaguely that the motocycle's 'full capabilities could not be shown' and that 'a fair speed was attained'. At a distance, the *Armidale Chronicle* was more forthcoming but also light on detail when it reported that 'owing to something or other being wrong 18 miles an hour was the highest speed obtained'.[36]

While the formally dressed Henry and Sam carried out their official duties at the meeting, young Fred raced in the two-mile Lewis Handicap for £15, £3 and £2. Having easily won his heat by four lengths, Fred took fourth place in the final that almost resulted in a dead heat between those who were placed second, third and fourth.[37]

Start of the second heat of the One-Mile Scratch Race at the Megson–Lewis benefit meeting, Agricultural Ground, Sydney. Joe Megson is on the second machine from the right. *Sydney Mail*, 2 May 1896, p. 913

Marriage, a hawker's licence, a ball, a business and bankruptcy

The bicycle racing days of Henry Tait Shaw were over. He continued his work as a tailor's cutter and, on 24 February 1897, married Emily Agnes Breakwell at St John's Church of England, Darlinghurst.[38] Shortly after his marriage the Water Licencing Court granted Henry a hawker's licence for a packhorse.[39]

Henry continued his association with cycling and bicycle clubs. In September 1899, he was a referee for the Paddington Bicycle Club's road races over the Rose Bay course.[40] As well, he supported social activities of the League of New South Wales Wheelmen and, now a proud father, involved his wife:

> SOCIAL ITEMS ...
>
> The League of the N.S.W. Wheelmen held their sixth annual ball last Friday evening in the Paddington Town Hall, and judging by the manner in which everything passed off, must rank as one of the most successful functions ever held by that body. There were some 360 persons present, including representatives from kindred clubs, and the floor being first-class, a programme of twenty-one dances was vigorously gone through ... Some very pretty gowns were worn by the ladies, the following being the most conspicuous ... Mrs S. R. Shaw, pale green satin, cherry velvet and roses ... Mrs H. Shaw, white satin, chiffon and poppies.[41]

About the same time, Henry began his own tailoring business in Hunter Street, Sydney.[42] By 1901, while residing at Brougham Street, Darlinghurst, Henry was secretary of the Cutters and Trimmers Association that met fortnightly at the Trades Hall.[43] However, Henry was unable to make a success of his tailoring business and disposed of it.

With no prior experience in grocery retailing, other than assisting in his father's grocery stores first at Woolloomooloo and then Paddington, with £10 Henry Tait Shaw opened a grocery store in early 1903 at 54 Denison Avenue, Rozelle, near Balmain in Sydney. At that time a friend, Hamilton Nicholls, acted as guarantor. On 28 July 1903 Henry entered into a Deed of Partnership with Hamilton Nicholls to operate as Shaw and Co., grocers at 54 Denison Street, Rozelle. Nicholls, a watchmaker who worked in the city, was a silent partner and took no part in the day to day running of the business, which was immediately in financial trouble.[44]

On the 28 September 1903 a sequestration order was made in the Supreme Court of New South Wales in Bankruptcy against Henry Tait Shaw and Hamilton James Nicholls, trading as Shaw and Co., grocers, at Denison Street Balmain (Rozelle). The Statement of Bankrupt's Affairs on that date showed liabilities to unsecured creditors as £129/4/6 and assets of £38/9/4. There was no cash at the bank and none in hand. In a Statement of Bankrupt's Separate Affairs submitted on the same day, Nicholls declared liabilities of £5/5/- and no assets.

Accounts presented to the court on 30 December showed the affairs of the business to be in an even poorer state than had been set out earlier. Liabilities totalled £164/11/6 and the expectations about the amounts that could be raised by the sale of stock had proven overly optimistic. Henry was living at 92 Goodhope Street, Paddington and Nicholls was living at the shop and dwelling property at Rozelle.[45] Henry was made bankrupt.

By 1904, Henry was again employed as a tailor's cutter in the city.[46] From 1905 to 1912 he and his growing family lived at Granville, near Parramatta. In 1913 and 1914, Henry Tait Shaw, tailor, was at Chestnut Street, Wynnum, South Brisbane.[47] His wife, Emily, did not appear on those rolls but in 1913 Henry Taite (*sic*) Shaw, tailor, and Emily Agnes Shaw were at Argyle Street, Parramatta.[48]

Private Henry Tait Shaw, ANZAC veteran

Henry Tait Shaw enlisted in the Australian Commonwealth Military Forces on 1 September 1914 at Liverpool, New South Wales. Aged 38 years and one month on enlistment he was recorded as having been born in Woolloomooloo, Sydney, and as being 5'3", 8 stone 4 lbs of fresh complexion with blue eyes, dark brown hair and with a scar on the bend of his left forearm. His occupation was shown as a tailor and he, with his wife, lived at 36 Suffolk Street, Paddington. As a private in the 4th Battalion, he embarked from Sydney on board the transport ship *Euripides* on 20 October 1914.

As a member of the 4th Battalion, Henry was part of the second wave of landings at Gallipoli on 25 April 1915. On or before 20 November of that year Henry's sight was affected, with this caused by the exploding cone of a shell during the Gallipoli campaign. In 1915 Henry was hospitalised on at least five occasions. He spent time at Camp Mudros and the Sanpi Rest Camp on the Greek Island of Lemnos, at the Red Cross Convalescent Hospital at Montazah Palace, Alexandria and the Agricultural Hall in Cairo, sometimes with relatively minor ailments and later with his continuing eyesight problem. From January to early March 1916, he was a patient in the Australian Hospital, Heliopolis and was invalided to Australia on 3 March 1916. Henry returned to Australia on the *Argyllshire*, via the Suez, arriving 11 July 1916 for discharge as medically unfit because of chorditis of the right eye.

From 12 July 1916 Henry Tait Shaw was granted a war pension of £3 per fortnight. Fortnightly pensions were also granted to his wife Emily Agnes, £1/10/-; his children Desdemona, William Charles, Meta Jean, each 10/-; his son Percy Inch, £1; and his son Sydney George, 15/-. All were living at 14 Wortley Street, Balmain. These pensions were lowered on 30 August 1917.[49]

Henry enlisted a second time, again at Liverpool, on 16 November 1917 and now aged 44. He served in the staff cook's unit. Papers show Private Shaw as a tailor's cutter, and as 5'4½", 9 stone, with medium complexion, blue eyes, and brown hair. He was discharged from this position in November 1918 at the termination of his enlistment.[50]

Henry, apparently intensely patriotic and enjoying the stability of army pensions and pay, enlisted for a third time. On 24 June 1919, aged 46 years and 10 months he enlisted for Home Service. He was recorded as being a tailor, was 5'4", 126 lbs, of medium complexion, blue eyed with brown hair and had defective eyesight. He lived at 23 Regent Street, Paddington and served as a cook in the Australian Army Medical Service at Randwick, Sydney.[51]

Henry Tait Shaw died, aged 49, on 3 September 1921 at Granville, Sydney. A death notice recorded that he was late of the 4th Battalion, AIF (Anzac).[52]

A fitting recognition and tribute to Henry's war service and abilities was made by his former cycling colleagues and the Newcastle cycling community in 1916, after his return from active service:

> RETURNED SOLDIERS' ASSOCIATION
>
> PROPOSED ATHLETIC CARNIVAL
>
> The members of the Returned Soldiers' Association in Newcastle are promoting a sports carnival, which it is intended shall be held on January 26 (Anniversary Day). The object of the carnival is to supplement the funds of the association, so that it can be made a useful body in assisting disabled returned soldiers to the fullest extent. Mr Harry Shaw, who bas been appointed official organiser, saw service on the Gallipoli Peninsula, and returned wounded. In the boom days of cycling he was a noted performer on the racing path, and was well known in Newcastle along with his racing brothers, Sam and Fred Shaw, the latter winning the Newcastle wheel race in 1898. The officials of the R.S.A., together with a committee of the association, will work in conjunction with Mr Shaw. The programme will comprise foot racing, cycling, and other athletic events. The ladies of the Red Cross Society and other patriotic organisations have promised their assistance in the movement, support from various athletic bodies, and individuals In Sydney, has been promised. Donations will be welcomed by the association for the prize fund.[53]

A subsequent report on the Returned Soldiers' Association Sports highlighted Henry Shaw as the organiser of the 'clean, interesting cycling and foot events' that had been run on the day at a meeting that boasted a world record set for womens' hurdles, music by the Lone Pine and Stockton bands and four events run by the Newcastle Motorcycle Club.[54]

CHAPTER 5

'A Man of Great Determination': Frederick Ewart Shaw

Frederick Ewart Shaw was born on 20 July 1876 at 81 Hill Terrace, Riley Street, Woolloomooloo, Sydney, the eighth of nine children, and fifth son, of William Shaw, grocer/clerk, and Mary Anne Shaw (née Inch).[1] The Shaw family of Woolloomooloo had moved again.

Frederick was commonly known as Fred or Freddy/Freddie. More formally, in cycling, sailing and business he was almost always referred to as F. E. Shaw. For reasons that will become clear, he was sometimes referred to as Mr 'Etna' Shaw.

Pedestrianism

A series of over 20 listings of an F. Shaw in Sydney's *Evening News*[2] suggest that Fred Shaw engaged in competitive running and walking, then called pedestrianism, that preceded and then briefly overlapped his competitive cycling career. The first of these listings was published on 29 October 1890 and the last on 11 May 1895.

None show a fuller name than F. Shaw so it cannot be concluded with absolute certainty that this was Frederick Ewart Shaw. It is telling, however, that the first listing occurred when Fred would have been fourteen and that listing was for a nursery event. Many that followed were for nursery, novice and youth's events. About half of the listings were for events held at the Lillie Bridge Grounds (later Harold Park) where Fred, along with his brothers, competed in bicycle races conducted at meetings that included athletics and cycling events in addition to pony races. Other venues where F. Shaw ran and walked competitively were the Marrickville Running Grounds and the Carrington Ground, a part of Centennial Park.

At these venues, running and walking races attracted large fields of entrants that often numbered over 100. Events involved numerous heats leading to a final. F. Shaw won his heat on several occasions. He was fourth in the final of a 200-yard walking race at the Carrington Ground on 9 May 1891. That race carried a first prize £15, as was common for races at that ground, but paid nothing to other placegetters.

It is also telling that Fred Shaw occasionally competed in informal running races at mixed sports events he attended, primarily to race bicycles, in later years.[3] There is no evidence that he earned much prize money from 'ped' racing, as it was commonly known.

Following his brothers into bicycle racing

Fred Shaw was admitted as a member of the Crusaders' Bicycle Club[4], his brothers' club, when he turned eighteen in July 1894.[5] Sporting his club's blue and white, Fred rode later that month in a two-mile amateur handicap event at the University Athletic Club, in a half-mile handicap at a meeting co-hosted by the Suburban Bicycle Club and the Darlinghurst Harriers in August and another half-mile handicap at a further joint meeting of those clubs at the Sydney Cricket Ground in September.[6] In the latter, he 'led all the way and won [the final] handsomely by eight yards' in a time of one minute and ten seconds. His prize was a trophy presented by the two club presidents.[7] In September, he was placed third in his heat in a half-mile race and was unplaced in a three-mile race at Redfern Oval at the Redfern Poor Relief Sports. With the support of his elder brothers Sam and Henry, young Fred was being cautiously introduced to the intricacies of the sport, and its ups and downs, at this highly competitive level.

That was also the story for 1895. In March, Fred raced, with Sam and Henry, in the two-day carnival organised by the League of New South Wales Wheelmen at the Sydney Cricket Ground. On the first day he raced in the League Cup over half a mile and in the £300 Sydney Wheel Race. On the second day his rides were in the Metropolitan Handicap over one mile and the Second Class Handicap. When the League conducted another two-day carnival in November, Fred Shaw, in red and white sash, and before a crowd of 27,000, raced in the Second Class Handicap of 'about one mile, four times round' for £10, £2 and £1.[8] Although Fred, in the language of the day, 'failed in annexing' any of these races, or others he rode in 1895 at the half-time intervals in football matches in Sydney or at a sports meeting in Maitland, he continued to enjoy the sport at this top level, to learn more about it and to practise regularly and build a reputation as a determined stayer.

Race experience, and the extensive on-track training that accompanied racing, began to pay off for Fred Shaw in the following year.

For the two-day, March 1896 carnival of the League of New South Wales Wheelmen at the Agricultural Society's Ground, Fred Shaw raced in the Federal Stakes over half a mile and the Australian Cup over two miles on the first day. On the second day he tackled the Sydney Cup over one mile, the Second Class handicap and the Third Class Scratch Race, in which he was placed third in his heat.[9] At this meeting, the eighteen-year-old Fred Shaw met and raced against international and intercolonial competitors, rode on the ground's new, banked asphalt track that enabled higher speeds and witnessed several serious mishaps on the track resulting from the faster racing.

Fred's next challenge was to contest the Lewis Handicap over two miles for £15, £3 and £2 at the Megson–Lewis benefit meeting at the Agricultural Ground, the object of which was to assist local champions Joe Megson and Bob Lewis gain northern hemisphere racing experience. In front of his older brothers Henry Shaw, who was a referee at the meeting and Sam Shaw, who served as a laptaker, and a crowd of 13,000, young Fred won his heat and was placed fourth in the final in what was judged to have been almost a dead heat between him and the second and third placegetters.[10]

As will be seen, Fred Shaw went on to a lifetime career as a bicycle, motorcycle and motor vehicle mechanic. It is likely that the presence of the 'motocycle' demonstrated in Sydney before and at the Megson–Lewis benefit meeting made a strong impression on the mechanically minded Fred Shaw. Maybe that machine was the catalyst that led Fred to a lifetime interest in motors and machines.

Gambling and its underbelly among the meeting's punters was also clearly evident despite 'ostentatious' advertisements bellowing that betting would be strictly prohibited. As one Sydney newspaper told the story of the shenanigans on the day:

> Betting? No, there was no betting. The Authorities had laid themselves out to put a stop to such a thing, but they had not put a stop to absolute robbery and welshing. Between the door of the dressing-room and the entrance to the course, where stewards were observant – as they should be – every hour of the afternoon, a gang of the greatest spellers and ne'er-do wells were taking in the silly gulls who were fools enough to trust money in their hands.[11]

Racing at League carnivals and under League rules at football matches at the Agricultural Ground (otherwise now known as the Hampden track[12]) during the winter of 1896 added to Fred's experience and growing reputation. Among Fred's successes was winning, by ten yards, in one minute and four seconds, the final of the Half-Mile Handicap on 27 June. Newspaper accounts of the race praised the ride, for example: describing 'little Shaw [as] staying well, and winning by ten yards'; and highlighting that this 'is Fred Shaw's first win under League rules and he rode like a veteran. In the final he finished exceptionally well, and justified the good opinion which many had formed who had been watching him doing his work [training] during the week'. Others took notice and called him 'a promising young rider' and said that he 'rode remarkably well in the final and fully deserved the prize of £7'.[13]

Goulburn to Sydney road race, 1896

While road racing over relatively short courses such as Sydney's ten-mile Botany course had become commonplace, long-distance road racing was in its infancy in the colony. Fred Shaw was one of the very few Sydney riders to jump at the chance of competing in the first 130-mile (209 km) Goulburn to Sydney event in 1896. One of only nineteen starters, Fred was handed a handicap of 42 minutes and left Goulburn at 7.18am on the frosty morning of 25 July. It was unlikely that he was attracted by the meagre prize money of £5, £3 and £2 on offer, although the winner was also promised a new Humber road racer bicycle from Goulburn's Austral Agency, and a pair of Morgan and Wright tyres were to be awarded to the rider with the fastest time. After debate with the Railway Commissioners, the League won a concession fare of eleven shillings and two pence for the one-way trip to Goulburn for Sydney riders, with this fare including their bicycles.

The route chosen for the race by the League of New South Wales Wheelmen was that of the main southern road, via Berrima. Because of the poor condition of the road, and because several riders had been injured in falls while practising on it for the race, arrangements were made to have members of the St John Ambulance Association follow the race on a tandem. Much of the press coverage, indeed several dozen reports, of the race focussed on the disruption caused by a large number of metal tacks, their 'business side uppermost', that were strewn across the track causing numerous punctures and delays for repairs and the £25 reward offered by the League for apprehension of the 'tack strewer'. Fred Shaw was not among the first eight riders to finish the course. It is not clear from any of the race reports whether Fred Shaw finished, was a victim of the tack attack or whether he withdrew for some other reason.[14]

The Goulburn to Sydney road race became an annual event from 1902, when the Dunlop Rubber Company assumed responsibility for organising the event.

A smoke concert and back to the path

An unusually detailed report of a smoke concert organised by the League of New South Wales Wheelmen between the first and second day's racing at their Grand Winter International Racing Carnival, held on the Agricultural Ground, provides rich insight into the format of these social evenings, their appeal to members and their role in entertaining visiting carnival participants:

> The League, held a monster complimentary smoke concert last evening at Aaron's Exchange Hotel, Gresham-street. About 500 members of the League and their friends, including all the intercolonial and country visitors to the carnival, were present ... Mr Percy Hunter occupied the chair, and in a very humorous speech opened the ball. The full strength of the Balmain Premier Coldstream Band, rendered a charming overture, 'In the Limelight,' and Mr G. Weatherall opened the vocal proceedings with a pretty rendering of 'Moonlight at Killarney,' and later on sung 'I'll Await My Love.' Among the most brilliant successes of the evening were Messrs. Bobby Watson and George Hellings. The former was in his best vein, and sang several songs during the evening, among others, 'Things Were Lively,' 'She Was in My Class,' 'Can't Stop,' and a parody on 'The Song That Reached My Heart.' Mr Hollings was also very happy in his selections, and his song 'Hoopoziti' was received with enthusiastic applause. Among the other gentlemen who kindly contributed to the immense success of the evening were Messrs. J. Harper, 'Paradise Alley'; W. Stent, assisted by the members of the American Banjo Club 'Washington Post March'; Master Allan Jeffkins, cornet solo; Mr A. Cantor, 'I'm Blowed if He Can Call Hisself His Own'; Mr Peterson, 'Pilgrim of Love'; A. Glynn, 'She

> Wanted Something to Play With,' and 'Four and Twenty of Us'; and Mr Frank Leston, who rendered several of his very best elocutionary efforts in his own inimitable, style. Mr L. de Groen acted as accompanist all through the evening, and assisted in no small degree to the success of the entertainment. The thanks of the League are also due to Mr W. Aitken, manager of the Exchange, for his untiring efforts on their behalf, and also to Messrs. Nicholson and Co., who kindly lent a 'Grand' piano for the occasion. After the entertainment Mr B. Barnard, who conducted the 'smoker' on behalf of the League, entertained a few of the principal guests at supper. Several very complimentary speeches were made ... The evening was unanimously decided on all hands to be the most enjoyable ever experienced by the League, and the fun was kept going fast and furious to a late hour.[15]

Fred Shaw, along with one or more of his brothers, is likely to have attended this social. He certainly was a participant in racing at the Winter Carnival of which it was a part. On the first day he ran second in his heat of the two-mile Hampden Wheel Race but was unplaced in the final. On the second day, riding a Beeston Humber before 18,000 spectators, he won his heat ('Shaw dashing home won comfortably') and second place and £5 in the final of the Second and Third Class Handicap of 'about one mile', when 'Shaw went away for all he was worth, but the pace was too much for him, and Leech caught him and beat him home by a wheel'.[16]

When the League's Spring Carnival was contested in September, Fred Shaw raced again. Continuing his strong riding, he won his heat in the Spring Handicap and then was placed second, by just half a length, in the final and took home £10.[17] Further, at the November carnival conducted by the Goulburn Branch of the League on their newly asphalted track to mark the Prince of Wales' Birthday, Fred was placed second in his heat of the Goulburn Wheel Race. He won his heat of the Half-Mile Open Handicap. 'Many ladies' were among the 4,000 spectators, 'Mr Clancy of the Imperial

Hotel had the publican's booth, and did a good business' and there were refreshment stalls and sideshows available to feed and entertain patrons.[18]

Fred Shaw returned to Goulburn for the Highland Gathering Sports on 26 January, Anniversary Day, 1897 with high hopes for a half-mile open race and the two-mile Burns Wheel Race. Cycle racing formed only part of the day's activities:

> Yesterday, as is the custom on each Anniversary Day, every local Scotchman either donned kilt and sporran, or if not possessed of these articles, gave evidence of his patriotism by wearing some national emblem, or sporting a rosette of some particular tartan. The general public, too, or a great many of the public, recognised the occasion by a liberal display of tartan, worn either as hatbands, neckties, or rosettes. So far as Goulburn is concerned, yesterday was really what one gentleman on the ground described as 'Scotchman's Day'...
>
> The weather was fine, though exceedingly hot, the thermometer being 96 in the shade …
>
> The Gathering as a gathering may safely be said to commence on the day before the 26th, as visitors generally begin to arrive a day before, and from the time of their arrival the interest and enthusiasm become manifest, The pipers and drummers arrived in Goulburn on Monday night at 9.15, and as usual marched to the strain of the pipes to their hotels. A great number of people assembled at the station to witness their arrival and escorted them down the street. The demonstration was commenced by a procession which was of a very interesting nature. A contingent of the local volunteers assembled at the corner of Auburn and Clinton streets at 9.30, and headed by the District Band … marched down Auburn-street. At the same time the members of the Sydney Scottish Rifles team assembled at Campbell's corner, and headed by the Pipe and Drum Band, marched up the street.

> The two processions met near the post office, where they were merged into one, and proceeded to the show ground… on the programme was an event known as a bayonet competition, in which the competing teams were the Scottish Rifles and the Goulburn Volunteers …
>
> The privileges of the ground were held by the following local business people … No. 1 publican's booth, Mr D. Campbell, Exchange Hotel; No. 2 publican's booth, Mr Chas. Magoo, Post-Office Hotel; No. 1 refreshment-stall and luncheon-booth, Mr Thos. Byrne; No. 2 refreshment-stall, Mrs McDonald.
>
> There were the usual accessories of sports – such as gaming tables, and other forms of 'speculation,' where 'yer pays yer shillin' and yer takes yer chance.' There were also bookmakers and sweep-promoters in galore. A good deal of speculation was indulged in, especially in the bicycle and foot races …[19]

Fred was unplaced in his heat of the half-mile open race and was scratched from the Burns Wheel Race.

Following its successful 1895 and 1896 carnivals, the League of New South Wales Wheelmen, always an innovative body, aimed even higher for its 1897 March Carnival held on the newly asphalted and banked track at the Sydney Cricket Ground.[20] The carnival jumped from having been a two-day meeting to a four-day one, with some of the racing at night, in a first for the venue, under electric light which promised to 'brilliantly illuminate' the track and the ground. Other attractions were Lesna, 'the Illustrious Frenchman, the most celebrated pace follower in the world' in a race over 20-miles with local riders 'paced by an Army of Multicycles' that, with their riders, had been brought from Melbourne for the occasion, and British champions.[21] Some idea of the advances, and expense, pacing was bringing to cycle racing was illustrated by Lesna, who had 'a quint, three quads, four triplets, and two tandems, to man which thirty-three picked riders will be required'.[22]

The first of the four meetings was run on 4 March, Federation Polling Day, and patrons were advised by advertisements to vote early and go to the cricket ground by special trams in the afternoon to watch racing from 2.30pm.

At this first meeting Fred Shaw raced in the Federation Handicap for £20, £7 and £3. Off 275 yards, he won the first of five heats and then went on to take out second place in the final[23] but was beaten by a wheel in his heat of the Sydney Wheel Race (first prize £100). Apart from the £7 he won, Fred was able to take away from this carnival his experience of the new, electric-lit track at the cricket ground, the experience of seeing several of the world's top cycling champions and first hand sighting of the complexities of multicycle pacing over the 20-mile race. He must also have benefitted from the experience of numerous practice sessions with many experienced riders on both the Sydney Cricket Ground track and the Hampden track at the adjoining Agricultural Ground over the month leading up to the carnival when both tracks were 'alive with racing men'.

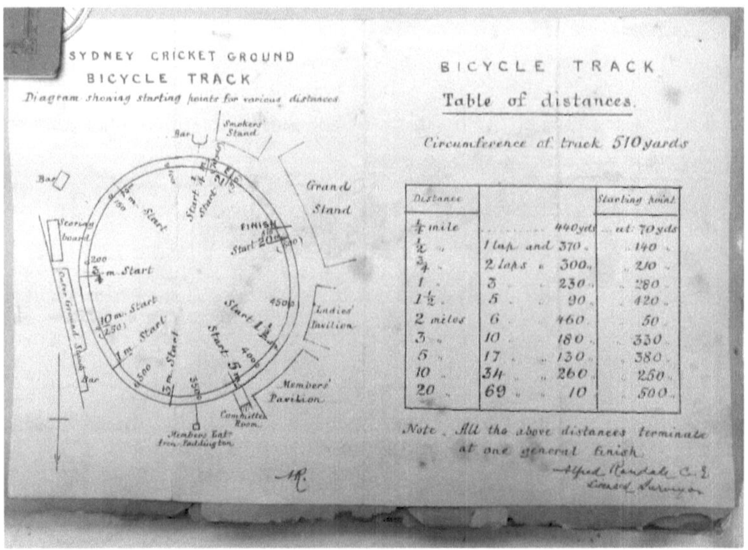

SYDNEY CRICKET GROUND
BICYCLE TRACK

BICYCLE TRACK

Table of distances.

Circumference of track 510 yards

Distance		Starting point
¼ mile	440yds	at 70yds
½ "	1 lap and 370 "	140 "
¾ "	2 laps " 300 "	210 "
1 "	3 " 230 "	280 "
1½ "	5 " 90 "	420 "
2 miles	6 " 460 "	50 "
3 "	10 " 180 "	330 "
5 "	17 " 130 "	380 "
10 "	34 " 260 "	250 "
20 "	69 " 10 "	500 "

Note. All the above distances terminate at one general finish

Plan of Sydney Cricket Ground bicycle racing track showing the one finish line and start positions for various race distances, undated. W. H. Kavanagh, *Album Collection of News Cuttings, Tickets, Invitations, Business Cards and Other Memorabilia Related to Australian Cycling 1886–1912*, State Library of New South Wales

Winning the 1897 Newcastle Wheel Race

Newcastle was the largest of the League's branches and the Newcastle Wheel Race, over two miles, was the premier event on its calendar. Fred Shaw made his name in bicycle racing by winning that race on 27 March 1897 in 4 minutes and 34 seconds. With the win came a prize of £35, a substantial amount and by far Fred's most lucrative prize to that time. The *Newcastle Morning Herald & Miners' Advocate* reported that Fred, 'one of the youngest riders at the meeting' 'rode with the coolness and judgement of a veteran, and with a well-timed sprint of 50 yards from the finish snatched the prize … by inches only'.[24] A Sydney paper recognised that 'he rode a brilliant race, and his win was a highly popular one'.[25] Fred's win was on a Cleveland brand bicycle and it is likely its agents, the Sydney Cycle Company, added handsomely to his earnings from the race when it immediately initiated a series of advertisements for the Cleveland and its bicycle riding school highlighting that 'Little Freddy Shaw On His Cleveland Racer Won The Wheel Race'.[26]

There was more for Fred than winning the prestigious Wheel Race when he became the toast of the after-parties:

> The visiting wheelmen were loud in their praises of the manner they were treated by the local branch. A first class smoke social on the Thursday night was followed by a splendidly arranged picnic on Sunday. The branch … took the visitors by train to Cockle Creek, where the steamer Maggie Johnson steamed round the shores of the Lake, landing the party at Swansea. A splendid dinner … was laid on the grassy sward under the cooling shade of the gum trees, and to say that the feed was heartily partaken of is totally adequate [*sic*]. A half-hour's stay at Toronto was made and Cockle Creek reached on the return journey in nice time for the Sydney and Newcastle men to catch their respective trains. The picnic was a huge success, and visitors were highly pleased at the treatment by the Newcastle branch.[27]

A fortnight later the newly crowned champion racer gave an invited exhibition mile race at the Bowral and Moss Vale Grounds at Burradoo in the southern highlands. He was 'paced by a tandem and covered the distance in two minutes and eighteen seconds, passing the tandem near the winning post'.[28] At the same carnival, as a competitor in the Bowral Wheel Race with older brother Sam, Fred was riding well when he lost a tyre from his machine.

Bicycle racing in the 1890s certainly had its high and low points. More of each followed.

Fred continued to stamp his mark on bicycle racing. Among other competitive rides, on 22 May 1897, he ran second in the final of the Half-Mile Handicap at the League's Winter Handicaps meeting and took home £7. A week later he ran twelfth, despite a mishap, from 40 starters in the 22-mile, wet and muddy Manly to Bayview Road Race in which pacing bicycles were employed. In June he was placed fourth by just a foot in the final of the Coronation Handicap, for £25, £10 and £5, over one mile at the League of New South Wales Wheelmen's Jubilee Carnival, just missing out on the money. He competed in the 53-mile Penrith Road Race in July and won third place in a half-mile handicap on a new track at the Junee Racecourse in August. Later that month, ahead of Megson and De Lissa, Fred took home the £7 prize for second place in the Open Handicap of 'about two miles', missing out on the £20 first prize by 'only a few inches'. On 28 August, Fred was placed third in the Naumann Handicap over two miles at the Jubilee Charity Carnival, a Chinese carnival. Again he rode impressively but just missed out on the big prizes, a new bicycle valued at £25 for first place and a pair of Dunlop tyres and Westwood rims for second place. Also at that meeting, out of a field of 33, he ran third in the Town Hall Handicap over three miles to win £3.[29]

Bicycle racing was only a part of the programme of this Chinese charity fair. Something of the colour of the day and of the many varying circumstances under which colonial cyclists sometimes raced is revealed in the following account:

The great attractions were the Chinese procession and Chinese football match. The costumes worn by the Celestials who took part in the procession were valued at £3000, and the blaze of colour was a perfect shock to European eyes. There were costumes of the most weird and gorgeous description, and many of the wearers walked about the ground before the procession started with conscious pride. The excitement amongst the Chinese was intense. As early as 8 o'clock, though the carnival was not timed to start before 11.15, the Chinese arrived from all parts of the city and suburbs …

'The balloon ascent' took the form of sending up a few small paper affairs, which occasioned not the least excitement. Then the rumour became current that the football match would not be held, as the Mongolians did not understand the game, this creating great disappointment.

The Chinese bicycle race was about the funniest thing seen on the ground. There were three starters. One came out in most picturesque attire and jockey cap. In front of his jacket he wore a large bouquet. Neither of the other two deigned to wear extravagant dress, racing in their singlets and braces. The distance was two laps, and the Chinaman in costume at once went to the front. His name was Hock Sing. Bing Hing made a fairly good race with him but tired at the finish, Hock Sing winning easily. He was not sure when he passed the post that he had won, and went round another lap, gazing anxiously behind him to see that his rivals stole no march on him. When he was informed that he had won his joy was unbounded. He insisted on riding round with his hands off the handle bar, whereat the crowd cheered in a good humoured sort of way. The Chinese Zimmerman then rode round half a lap, waving his jockey cap in the air. His next manoeuvre was to get his feet on the rests and go round in that way. He would have ridden round till the evening probably had not Mr Quong Tart, the starter, peremptorily called him off. It transpired that Hock Sing had won a race somewhere in the country. He was persuaded to endeavour to lower the mile record and started out full of confidence. The record was not damaged.

The scene on the ground was peculiar. There were Chinese here, there, and everywhere, in the most glaring toggery. In the middle were a group of aboriginals throwing the boomerang. The cadets were lined out on one side, and in another part of the ground a military display was given of jumping, rescue work, and cleaving the Turk's head.

A second Chinese bicycle race brought out four starters. One could not get going till the others had covered half a lap, and complained that the shover-off had sent the wheel round the wrong way. The people shrieked at his efforts to get under way. Bing Hing, who was second in the first race, was again second …

By 3 o'clock there were nearly 20,000 present. The clashing of Chinese cymbals and tom-toms just before 3 o'clock announced that the processionists were getting ready for the march past …

The procession was so extraordinary and outlandish as almost to defy description. All those who took part were arrayed with full Celestial splendour. There were banners innumerable, and great clashing of kettledrums and squeaking of trumpets. Several Chinese females with painted cheeks were carried round. There was a small regiment of soldiers, who wore hats of the shape of inverted bowls. The higher class Chinese, or rather their representatives, were on horseback, one Chinese lady also being mounted. At the head of each fiery steed was a man, whose duty it was to see that the animal did not become recalcitrant. A huge dragon brought up the rear of the procession. It had a huge head, the man underneath, which kept it moving continually up and down. The dragon was about 80 yards long, and was made of red, yellow and green material. At intervals of about two yards the representation of the reptile was supported by men underneath, who endeavoured to impart to it an undulating motion. The turnout was the first of its kind ever seen in Sydney, and the novelty was greatly appreciated.[30]

Rumours of a visit to England

By late 1897 pacing was well established on the Australian bicycle-racing scene. It made for faster racing and more spectacular spills. Spectator numbers had been falling at race meetings and it was hoped that paced racing might bring back the paying public. Tandems were widely used in paced races, and machines carrying three, four, five and even six riders appeared at major events. The 'moto-cycle' pacer[31] had been demonstrated the previous year in Sydney.

In Australia, pacing had been pioneered in Melbourne and interest there was high. In March 1897 a Melbourne newspaper published the following summary statement about mechanised and electric pacing:

> A British syndicate has recently been engaged building electric pacing machines for pacing bicycles in racing. The motors are fixed to tandem machines, and are situated quite close to the ground, the weight of the whole machine is not much more than that of a quad, with four men up. At the present time there are scores of riders in England who practically earn their living by riding pacing machines. Naturally these men are very much opposed to the introduction of artificial pacers, which will take away their bread and butter. All sorts of dismal pictures are painted of the dire accidents

> which may befall cyclists following the wake of a motor if it should break down suddenly. There is really less danger from motor pacing than from the present multi-cycle system, for, whereas with the motor cycle only one or two men would be employed, on the other hand, with quads, triplets, and tandems, quite an army of cyclists would be required to fill the seats on the pacing machines. One of the great drawbacks to motor pacing is the smell, which almost suffocates the rider who tries to hang on. The electric motor will, however, overcome this difficulty, and at the same time cheapen the cost of pacing very considerably, as the number of riders will be reduced to about one tandem team.[32]

There were even proposals for steam-powered pacing bicycles. While some neat designs emerged, this idea kept cartoonists busy imagining and illustrating exploding steam-powered bicycles causing mayhem, destruction and serious injuries to riders.[33]

Australian riders lacked the experience of their English, French and American counterparts with paced racing and some who had shown promise were rumoured to be likely to be sent to England to improve their pacing skills in racing. One report singled out Fred for mention saying that 'Freddy Shaw, the youthful rider, who won the Newcastle Wheel Race of £50 in March last, has shown marvellous improvement. Behind the pacing machines he sticks like glue, and there is some talk of the little fellow going to England shortly to train behind the Dunlop pacing machines'.[34] Another source said it was rumoured that Fred Shaw, 'a somewhat diminutive youth, who had previously distinguished himself on the Newcastle track … will be taken to England, where he will be set to learn to ride properly behind pace.'[35] While Fred never visited England, it is clear that he was a determined and very capable young man regarded as having a notably promising future.

Getting about

Because four of the front men in the Junee Wheel Race, for £20, £5 and £2, held on 2 August were disqualified the Junee Branch of the League of New South Wales Wheelmen was required to re-run the race. When that occurred in September, Fred Shaw took out third place and spoke in the evening at a dinner at the town's Loftus Hotel, where the 'settling took place', to thank the local branch on behalf of the visitors for their hospitality.[36]

In late 1897, Fred, now aged 21, began taking an interest in racing in Queensland with it being reported that 'Little Freddie Shaw, of Sydney, has been winning in North Queensland on his Red Bird Special'.[37] It is possible that interest commenced earlier that year when, in April, the *Northern Miner*, published in Charters Towers in north Queensland, wrote that, 'A young rider named Shaw won four out of five events at Rockhampton. He had ridden previously, but was not credited with such form'.[38] Then 'the speedy Shaw' won his heat, the final, and £8, in the One-Mile Open Handicap in front of 3,000 spectators at a meeting of the Newcastle Branch of the League of New South Wales Wheelmen in late October.[39] He passed through Sydney to race in the richest event in the history of the colony, the £300 Sydney Wheel Race over two miles, but was in Goulburn within a week to be 'greatly applauded' when he won his heat of the two-mile Goulburn Wheel Race.[40]

Melbourne was Fred's next port of call. At the meeting of the Melbourne Bicycle Club, the club that sponsored the high-profile Austral Wheel Race, Fred raced on the Melbourne Cricket Ground's unbanked, grass track in December. The rich Austral Wheel Race, for £200, £100, £35 over two miles, attracted 214 entries including men from Italy, England, Ireland, New Zealand and all the Australian colonies. Fred was one of eighteen starters before a crowd of 25,000, in the eighth heat (of ten) but, racing off 120 yards, failed to win the first or second place required to go forward to the final. At the same meeting, although he rode well and was described as a 'class rider' and 'a man of determination', he was also eliminated from contention in the MBC (Melbourne Bicycle Club) Plate for £50, £20 and £5 over a mile and a half and the Victoria Mile for £15, £7 and £3.[41]

Fred Shaw was at Melbourne's Exhibition Building and grounds on 26 January 1898 for the ANA (Australian Natives' Association) Fete Cycle Races, at which he raced in the £400 ANA Wheel Race over two miles and the One-Mile First Class Handicap for £25, £10 and £5. The Wheel Race attracted 190 entries 'from nearly all the riders in Australia with a track reputation'[42] and was decided after heats and semi-finals. Fred was again eliminated in his heats of both races. In association with its fete, the ANA sold shilling tickets in an Art Union. First prize was a vase of 250 ounces of polished gold valued at £1,000.[43] It seems likely that Fred also chased that prize with a ticket or three.

Australian Natives' Association (ANA) Great Fete Cycle Races, Melbourne Exhibition Grounds, 26 January 1898. State Library of Victoria

North to Brisbane, and beyond

When the Australasian United Steam Navigation Company's 2114-ton steamship *Arawatta* arrived in Brisbane on 9 June 1898, it brought with it 'the most famous contingent of cyclists that has ever yet visited Queensland'. The group consisted of five cyclists from Melbourne and Sydney, of whom Fred Shaw was one (Joe Megson and another cyclist were to arrive two days later), a quint pacing team and two quad teams. The visitors were met at the wharf and conveyed by 'two drags and cabs to the League [League of Queensland Wheelmen] … a procession being formed behind the vehicles by numbers of wheelmen who had been in attendance at the wharf'.[44]

The southern riders had been brought to Brisbane to compete in the inaugural winter carnival of the League of Queensland Wheelmen on the Brisbane Cricket Ground, Woolloongabba (the 'Gabba') to commence on 18 June. Their participation was lavishly highlighted by the press:

> Last Saturday will doubtless long remain a red letter day in the cycling annals of Brisbane, inaugurating as it did the great winter carnival of the League of Queensland Wheelmen, a carnival which stands out from anything that has preceded it by virtue of the quality of the men engaged. Never before has Brisbane entertained such a galaxy of cycling talent as is at present within her borders, and, apart from the naturally existing desire to see the famous visitors in action, there was also great curiosity as to the manner in which our own local men would compare with them. These and many other reasons caused the attention of all and sundry to turn in the direction of the Brisbane Cricket Ground, Woolloongabba. The roadway opposite the ground was thronged by 1.30, at which hour the gates were thrown open, and from then until late in the afternoon the people poured in, until the total must have approximated over 8000. The weather had borne a threatening aspect throughout the day, but the clouds were considerate enough to contain themselves. The competitors included representatives of England, and of N. S. Wales, Victoria, and Tasmania, while Gympie, Ipswich, Rockhampton, Barcaldine, and Bundaberg had each sent

> their men along to assist the Brisbane riders in upholding the Queensland reputation.[45]

Fred Shaw won his heat of the Half-Mile Open Handicap but was unplaced in the final, and was second in his heat of the Brisbane Wheel Race, for £50, £10 and £5, over two miles or six laps of the cricket ground. During the afternoon an exhibition was given of a 'motor tricycle' and a multicycle race involving a tandem, a triplet, a quad and a quint was run off. On the following Monday evening the southern riders were entertained at a smoke concert in their honour. On the second day of the carnival Fred was placed fourth from the sixteen starters in the final of the Brisbane Wheel Race.[46]

Within a week on the conclusion of the League's winter carnival, the following announcement and comment appeared in the *Brisbane Courier*:

> Fred E. Shaw, the Sydneyite, who rode so pluckily at the late sports, has obtained a situation in Brisbane. He should be an acquisition to the League, and it is more than likely that the brilliant sprinting powers he possesses will land him past the post first before he has competed long with the local riders. His chance for the Brisbane Wheel Race was much fancied by his Southern friends.[47]

Just as Fred had travelled to race at regional League meetings in New South Wales, so he did in Queensland. In late September 1898 he raced successfully at Maryborough at its branch of the League's first cycling meeting. That event was held at the town's Newtown Park, whose unbanked improvised cycle track had corners described as nearly square. In the lead-up to the meeting, the local paper, noting Fred's entries, wrote, 'F. E. Shaw is a Sydney crack, and is described as a little wonder'. Fred's handicaps were '10 yards in the Lap Dash, 60 yards in the three-mile race, and 25 yards in the race for ladies' bracelets'. Horse-drawn buses, for a fare of three pence, transferred patrons from the town to the distant park gates every half hour and an estimated 500 to 600 attended the meeting. Prominent cyclists from Adelaide, Melbourne, Sydney, Brisbane, and the Queensland towns of Rockhampton, Charters Towers, Gympie and Bundaberg, as well as local riders, contested the events. Fred, with a strong sprint home on his Red Bird Special, won the Three-Mile Handicap over nine laps to earn £3 and was second in the final of the Ladies' Bracelet race to win a bracelet. To complete a successful day on the track, Fred led a Brisbane team of four to beat a Maryborough four in the team race for a share of £10. A smoke concert and 'settling up' was held at the town's Customs House Hotel on the Saturday night, after which the majority of visiting cyclists boarded a late train for Brisbane.[48] Picking up on this news, Sydney's *Referee*, noted 'Fred Shaw ... who for his size is a rare bit of metal, is racing with success in North Queensland'.[49]

Fred Shaw was among the 30 competitors who started in the 37-mile Swift Road Race run under the auspices of the League of Queensland Wheelmen in mid-October for a No.1 Swift road racing machine, £10 and £5 from Kangaroo Point to Cleveland and back. He was unplaced.[50] Outcomes were much better for Fred at a Prince of Wales' Birthday sports carnival at Roma, 470 km west of Brisbane. At that meeting, again riding his Red Bird Special, he won £4 for first place (by a yard) in the Two-Mile Bicycle Race, £7 for first place (by a foot) in the Three-Miles Bicycle Handicap and 10 shillings for third place in the one-and-a-half-mile Special Scratch Bicycle Race. He also rode in the Mile Bicycle Race Handicap and the Half-Mile Bicycle Handicap. It was reported that attendance at the sports was good 'despite picnics held by the Wesleyans and the Salvation Army' and that, 'In the evening a very successful and well-attended dance was held at the Oddfellows' Hall' as a send-off to the visitors.[51]

In December, Fred Shaw was back in Maryborough for its third meeting held under the auspices of the League of Queensland Wheelmen. Over 1,500 spectators turned out to watch the racing and the 'ladies were well represented, which is not to be wondered at considering that they are such ardent cyclists themselves off the track'. In one event, Fred and one other rider tangled with a dog that ran into their path and 'how both riders did not come to grief was simply nothing short of a miracle'. The publican of the Globe Hotel catered for the 'thirsty souls' in the trying heat, while nearby 'a bevy of 'Y' Union girls ran a temperance stall'. Even the local newspaper admitted the handicappers favoured the locals. Fred rode well in his heat of the Maryborough Wheel Race over two-miles for £40, £7 and £3 but not well enough to make the final. However, he won the final of the Open Five-Mile Championship of Maryborough and took away a £6 prize. A description of the race provided more detail, including of Fred's meeting with the dog:

> … some smart sprinting was witnessed at the end of the different laps through a small additional prize being offered to the competitor who scored the greatest number of laps to his credit. A good racing pace was maintained throughout the distance, and the event wound up with a real genuine lap sprint which witnessed the closest finish of the day, Shaw just pipping Morrison on the post. Time 15 mins. 15 secs. During the progress of this race a small dog got on the track, and Morrison and Shaw rode over it. Both men were going at full speed at the time, but fortunately they were not upset, and the dog, who was the intruder, got all the worst of the interview …[52]

Fred also won £2/10/- as one of the four riders in the group that won the Team Race over three miles at Maryborough. Fred raced his Red Bird Special at the meeting. Other bicycle brands involved in the day's racing included Stearn, Massey Harris, James Racer, Beeston Humber, Swift, Ariel and Advance. All were familiar to the bicycle racing Shaw brothers.

Again, Sydney's *Referee* took notice, saying that 'Little Freddie Shaw, of Sydney, who is a loss to the local racing brigade, continues to do well in North Queensland'.[53] Sydney's *Sunday Times* wrote: 'Freddie Shaw, the midget Sydney rider, is now a scratch man in Queensland League ranks, having captured many races in that colony, including the recent important championship scratch races. Shaw is one of the smallest racing cyclists on the path'[54] and the *Newcastle Morning Herald & Miners' Advocate* told its readers that 'the crimson flash' is … doing well in Queensland.[55] 'The crimson flash' was a nickname Fred had acquired in Queensland and was derived from the crimson colour of his Red Bird racing machine. Advertisements sung Fred's praises and that of the Red Bird. One highlighted 'Freddie Shaw, the midget, wins all Queensland Championships and other events, All on Red Birds …For your '99 mount ride a Red Bird'.[56]

As an employee of the Goold Bicycle Company in Brisbane, agents for Canadian Red Bird bicycles, Fred almost certainly earned more from the Maryborough and Roma race meetings than his £25/10/- and bracelet race winnings. Cycle racing was lucrative for the 'cracks', although they were often responsible for the expenses of pace making. In addition to prize money, successful riders received gifts from firms that supplied their machines and their tyres. As well, betting took place on all principal racing events and there were various ways riders could exploit this.[57]

Fred was of small stature, being just a little over 152cm (five foot) in height and weighing around 52 kg. Newspapers variously referred to him as 'little Shaw', 'the little fellow', 'a somewhat diminutive youth', 'Little Freddie Shaw', 'the midget Sydney rider', 'the NSW midget' 'the game little fellow', the 'little southern crack' and 'one of the smallest riders'. Those remarks, made fondly rather than as put-downs, were often combined with generous positive comment as, for example, 'the popular little rider', 'that sterling little rider', 'the little wonder' and 'the game little Red Bird rider'. Others, a little more imaginatively, referred to 'Fred Shaw, of Sydney, who for his size is a rare bit of metal' to 'a good one for his weight' and characterised him as 'a rare bit of stuff for his inches'. Fred achieved much as 'the plugger', 'the crimson flash' and 'a man of great determination'.

Dinghy sailboating, a new interest

Apparently flush with cash from his Queensland winning streak, in November 1898 Fred Shaw commissioned Fred Yarrow of Brisbane to build for him a 14-foot dinghy sailboat. It was one of five such competitive

14-footers being built in and around Brisbane at the time. The sailboat, named *Etna*, owned and to be sailed by Fred Shaw, was entered in test races conducted by the Brisbane Dinghey[58] Club on the Hamilton and Lytton Reaches of the Brisbane River in preparation for a coming intercolonial sailing championship to be contested in Sydney. The build was not completed in time and it did not sail in these tests.[59]

The small dinghies of the time, that were steered with the aid of a centreboard and carried enormous sails for their size, were different from much larger yachts.[60] Unlike yachts, they were open boats with no deck and thus highly susceptible to taking water and capsizing. Dinghy racing was not a part of the established and inherited yachting establishment but, rather, was a uniquely Australian sport that originated with the battlers of the working class waterfront suburbs of (initially) Sydney and Brisbane, whose small boats were derived from the working boats carried on all large ships, watermen's skiffs and small fishing boats operating in protected waters.[61] According to one historian of Australian sailing, there was nothing like these 'skiffies' anywhere else in the world.[62]

A considerable amount of detail about Fred Shaw's *Etna* was available by mid-January 1899. No expense had been spared:

> A batten carvel 14-footer is now nearing completion at the shed of Mr F. Yarrow, South Brisbane. It is expected to have her afloat in a day or two, and during next week she will be shipped by steamer for Sydney to take part in the coming carnival. She is a big-bodied dingey with a fine entrance and very bluff and short bows. She has a very sharp rise of floor, and a deep and heavy looking tuck. Her beam is extended well fore and aft, and at the widest part is 6 feet 9 inches outside the planking, while across the tuck she measures 5 feet 7 inches. Amidships her depth is 23 inches, and forward and aft 27 inches. There is a spring in the keel of 4½ inches forward und 3½ inches aft. She is to be entirely open, and will carry a large square board. Her plunking, thwarts, battens, case,

> and tuck are of cedar, and her timbers, keel, and sternpost are of yellow wood. The stem is of crow's ash, mouldings beech, stringers Oregon pine, and knees honeysuckle. The boat is neatly planked and well put together. Her sails of Japara are locally made, and the mainsail when stretched will measure 24 foot on the foot, 13¾ feet on the luff, 14 feet on the gaff, and about 28 feet on the leech. Her jib will be about 21 feet on the luff, 13 feet on the foot, and 15 feet on the leech. Her bumpkin will he 11 feet outboard, and she is to be christened Etna for her owner, Mr F. Shaw.[63]

Again in mid-January, the *Brisbane Courier* reported that Fred was about to depart by steamer for Sydney to compete at the electric-light [bicycle races] and that he 'will take with him also his new 14-footer boat, and with that and his bike he expects to show his old friends in his native town that he is some pumpkins[64] since he came to Queensland. He will endeavour to fill his craft with prize money and bring it all back to Brisbane'.[65] In Sydney, Fred, who had joined the Johnstone's Bay Sailing Club, sailed *Etna* in intercolonial challenge races in Sydney Harbour at the Anniversary Regatta on 26 January. Fred sailed his new boat from scratch, for £4 and a trophy, £2 and £1, over a course from a line between the starter's boat and the Orient buoy, round the P & O buoy, round the flagmark moored off the flagship, thence round Shark Island and outside the Pile-Light and buoy, back around the flagmark moored off the flagship, round the P & O buoy, and finishing between the gunboat and the flagship. The flagship on the day was the lavishly decorated 10,566-ton North German Lloyd's *Koenigin Luise*. *Etna* took 4 hours 6 minutes and 52 seconds to complete the course but was unplaced.[66] In July 1899, Fred Shaw was elected to the committee of the Brisbane Dinghey Club for the 1899–1900 sailing season.[67]

It is not known how Fred's interest in sailing began, although it must certainly have begun before he commissioned the building of *Etna* when he was 22 because he would have needed considerable experience on sailboats before he was ready to skipper his new boat in competition. His interest in sailing may well have originated in his boyhood years around Woolloomooloo Bay, where he had ample opportunity to watch fishermen and watermen on a daily basis as well as weekend and holiday racing.[68] Many of the small sailing boats on the harbour were crewed by working-class men from waterside suburbs like Woolloomooloo.[69]

The *Marjorie*, a 14-footer dinghy sailboat (almost identical to Fred Shaw's *Etna*) on Sydney Harbour, 16 January 1899. William Hall Collection, Australian National Maritime Museum, Object #00002616

Races among sailboats gave the impression of being leisurely affairs, although it took a lot of raw strength and courage to sail the open boats successfully.[70] Commonly races occupied many afternoon hours, often between three and seven. Sailing competitions generally appeared quiet and orderly. They were carried out well away from the betting they invariably attracted and at a considerable distance from the crowds that gathered on the foreshores and headlands to watch or that travelled in the hired harbour and river ferries that followed the races. About the most dramatic event that could befall the sailors, usually after a sharp change in weather conditions, was 'taking a bath' when a boat capsized or a man fell overboard. Competitive sailing was notably different from competitive cycling, where the pace was often frantic, the yelling touts were never out of earshot, the crowds were noisy and demanding, danger was always present and races, with the exception of road races, were often completed in a matter of minutes.

Both, however, combined a man (or men) and a simple machine pitted against similar combinations, and subject to the vagaries of local conditions. For Fred, the two sports were complementary in that sailing was a summer-month pursuit while most, but not all, bicycle racing was conducted in autumn, winter and spring. Sailing and cycling helped Fred, always the lively sportsman, to be competitive across the whole of each year and each sport helped him keep fit for the other.

Cycling and sailing

Bicycle racing paid more handsomely than sailboat racing and, as Fred Shaw was employed in the flourishing Queensland bicycle trade, cycling continued to dominate his sporting activities. In its notes about training for the March 1899 St Patrick's Day events, the *Queenslander* wrote that 'judging by his riding [Fred Shaw] is in splendid fettle'.[71] From 33 starters in the Three-Miles Bicycle Handicap at that meeting, for £9, £3 and £1, Fred finished third, having run 'half through the field in style'.[72] In April's Ambulance Sports, in aid of the City Ambulance Brigade, at the Brisbane Cricket Ground, he 'raced beautifully to the finish', described elsewhere as a 'slashing finish', in the Three-Mile Handicap and took away £6, and was second in the final of the One-Mile Handicap that added £2 to his winnings for the day.[73] In both Ambulance Sports events he raced from scratch. Fred again raced from scratch in the May Day Sports at the Exhibition Ground the following month (reflecting his recent successes, he was now often a 'scratch man') but in his heat, finding the distance between himself and the field too great, he 'sat up' to signal his withdrawal.[74] Fred was now becoming a victim rather than a beneficiary of handicapping, perhaps never more so than when, with no prior warning, he was forced to race from 200 yards *behind* scratch at a meeting in country Toowoomba, where he represented the 'Red Bird stable', in late May. The *Brisbane Courier* said, 'Shaw reports that the track was a terrible one, over grassy hummocks and holes, notwithstanding the assistance of three tandems [as pacers], his time for the mile was – well, something to make the little fellow blush.'[75]

Another month later Fred was road racing once more, this time over a four and a half-mile track at Rocklea nine kilometres south of the city. Three amateur and one professional club raced over the same route: The South Brisbane Bicycle Club, the Brisbane Safety Bicycle Club, the Brisbane Bicycle Club and the League of Queensland Wheelmen. Fred rode in the League Electoral Race, as it was named, organised by the League. Five teams represented electoral districts within Brisbane (Enoggera, Bulimba, Brisbane South, Woolloongabba and Brisbane North). Fred's Brisbane South team was second in a dead heat. Fred was awarded an acetylene bicycle lamp donated by the Goold Bicycle Company for being the first rider to finish.[76]

1899 illustration from the AC cycling poster/race bill, printed in five colours, and with accompanying space for meeting details, available to clubs to promote race meetings. *Australian Cyclist*, numerous issues, 1899

Other large cycling meetings at which Fred competed in 1899 included the Queensland League's August Carnival, where he 'cleverly won' the James Challenge Cup over five miles on his Red Bird from sixteen starters. Riding a tandem, he and Mick Healy, the two 'cash champions of Queensland' were placed second in a multicycle race[77] and the two champions then fought out a match race, about which more will follow. He also raced at the Hospital Sports Meeting at the Exhibition Ground in October, taking third place in the Two-Mile Cycle Handicap. Later that month he was unplaced in one-mile and three-mile events at the Gympie Sports when he 'had to give away starts' when he raced from scratch in both events.[78] He was not likely to try Gympie again.

In September, October and November of that year, Fred sailed his 14-footer in handicap events on the Brisbane River. In the November race, *Etna* 'gave her crew a bath, and was assisted ashore by a passing boat and righted'. In November, too, Fred skippered the 10-footer *Our Own* in races on the Milton Reach of the river, taking a second place that carried a prize of just ten shillings for five and a half hours' sailing. Fred Shaw did not sail for monetary reward. *Etna* capsized in a race conducted by the City of Brisbane Sailing Club in the Hamilton and Lytton reaches in December, the crew of four taking another 'bath'.[79]

Sailing, Hamilton Reach, Brisbane River, Brisbane, Queensland, c.1895. Australian National Maritime Museum, Object #00009338

Fred Shaw celebrated New Year's Day 1900 by skippering *Etna* to second place in a handicap race in more open water at the Sandgate Regatta on Bramble Bay, an embayment of Moreton Bay, Brisbane. He sailed *Our Own* in the Ten-Footers' Championship at the City of Brisbane Sailing Club's Dinghy Championships at Milton Reach on 20 January but capsized and did not finish. He also sailed his *Etna* in the 14-Footers' Championship but was late to the start and was unplaced. In similar races in early February he took out places with both boats (with each race taking the best part of five hours) and racing again in early March, won the 10-footers' event. And, racing for a first prize of a case of wine, *Etna* was entered in a twelve-mile 'cruising race' held by the Brisbane Sailing Club on 7 April to mark the end of the sailing season. The race commenced at the Dry Dock and finished at the Indooroopilly Bridge. There was no race luck for Fred Shaw and his crew, who, like other crews, 'camped at Indooroopilly on Saturday night, and returned down the river' on the Sunday.[80]

In a quite different type of race, in late March Fred and his *Etna* engaged in a privately arranged match race with *Skip*, another 14-footer, on the Hamilton and Lytton reaches of the Brisbane River. The event, for which each side put up a £10 stake, was watched by spectators from the riverbank and from the chartered steam launch *Urdine*, which also carried the race referee and other officials. *Skip* won the race in 5 hours 18 minutes and 49 seconds, with *Etna* only about five minutes behind in 5 hours 22 minutes and 18 seconds.[81] Like cycle racing, dinghy sailboat racing, that began as weekend outings for enthusiasts, was commercialised as a spectator sport[82] and was often accompanied by flotillas of spectator craft aboard which gambling on race outcomes was commonplace.

In January 1900, Fred competed in only one major cycling event, a nine-mile League road race. Prizes for this event were a silver claret cup, valued at five guineas and a silver-mounted meerschaum cigar and cigarette-holder, valued at one guinea, with a third prize consisting of 50 per cent of the entrance money, the remainder of which was divided in the proportion of 25 per cent each between the second and third men. While he rode the fastest time for the race (23 minutes and 2 seconds), Fred saw none of these prizes because he was placed fifth on handicap. He may have enjoyed the evening more when members of the League and friends were entertained at a smoke concert at Roberts's Sovereign Hotel.[83]

After a trip to Newcastle in June, where he ran second in a one-mile handicap, Fred entered in several events at the two-day Winter Carnival of the League of Queensland Wheelmen at the Brisbane Cricket Ground (the 'Gabba') in July. He ran third in the Five-Mile Invitation Scratch Race and won a place in the final of the Brisbane Wheel Race. But at that meeting a highlight and principal attraction was a Motor Paced Tournament over three miles, the pacing machines being Dunlop motor pacing tandems. When he won his heat on the first day, *Table Talk* ventured the opinion that the final, to be run the following week, 'should be a good thing for Freddy Shaw, who proved himself adept at pace following whilst residing in the southern colonies'. They were not wrong. Riding 'prettily' Fred went on to 'dash splendidly' and win the final, set a three-mile record from the 'fast and furious' pace, attract 'great applause' as he finished, and take away £15 and a gold medal.[84]

One cycling historian wrote about motor pace racing that it was 'was glamorous but dangerous. Falls were common, largely because bicycle tires tended to burst at speed. The riders wore neither helmets nor gloves. They depended on fast reflexes, the rude health of youth, and luck'.[85] Early motor pacers, such as the Dunlop machines featured at this Brisbane carnival, were under the control of two men and were known as motor pace tandems. The man at the front controlled the engine and thus speed while the man behind him steered. Later, they evolved to be one-man machines. The rider now sat, but often was near standing, well back on the machine to maximise the slipstreaming effect for the 'stayer', as the bicycle rider behind was called. This configuration of the motorbike meant that the handlebars were up to a metre long. This type of racing was sometimes referred to as stayer racing and the machines as stayer bicycles. With smaller front wheels and handlebars known as drop bars that curved downwards and towards the rider, these stayer bicycles were designed to take maximum advantage of the slipstream created by their pacer motorcycles. Pacing motorbikes, in addition to their use in both track and long distance races, were used in training where they helped improve 'leg speed' and helped riders become used to the higher track and road speeds the pacers made possible. Motor pacers tended to blow tyres at speed. When this happened carnage often followed, with multiple cycle and motorcycle riders injured in single accidents. On occasions men died.[86] This was a brave new world for Fred Shaw, the boy from Woolloomooloo.

Interest in cycle racing had been waning in the late 1890s and the Dunlop motor pacers were brought to Australia in 1899 in an attempt to generate publicity and spectator crowds. The French-built De-Dion powered Jaluu motor pacing tandems did just that.[87]

The Brisbane Butchers Employees' Union held their annual picnic and sports at the Brisbane Cricket Ground in late July. Fred won the Two-Mile Professional Bicycle Race, run under the auspices of the League of Queensland Wheelmen, in Queensland record time of 4 minutes and 17 seconds. For his efforts he took home £5. Some idea of the overall character of the picnic day can be gleaned from the nature of other events that included a Cash Carters' Race, Shopmen's Race, Slaughtermen and Beef Carters' Race, Butchers Employees' Handicap, Ladies Race, Boys Race, Girls Race (all foot races), Maiden Trot for bona fide butchers' working horses, All Comers' Trot and a Tug of War, butchers v. grocers. The two-mile Professional Bicycle Race was the only cycling event on the programme.[88]

Since soon after he arrived in Brisbane Fred worked for the Goold Bicycle Company, riding their Red Bird racing machines and rising to the position of foreman in their workshops. This changed in May 1900 when he went into the employ of Jas. Smith and Sons, agents for the famous Stearns path racers manufactured in Syracuse, New York. His first task for them was to visit Cunnamulla and the western districts of Queensland demonstrating Stearns Yellow Fellow machines and assisting the establishment of agencies for them. Fred had swapped red bicycles for yellow ones, but not for long. By August he had quit, quite possibly when he learnt that, in April, the Rockhampton manager for Jas. Smith and Sons had ridden a Stearns Yellow Fellow more than 800 miles over a circuit west of the town in search of new business. It was soon reported that Fred Shaw, 'the popular little rider, who has shown up so brilliantly on the cycle track, has now thrown in his lot with the Cleveland Cycle Company where he is employed as salesman' and that, 'his brother, Mr Tom Shaw, is now sub-agent for the above high-class wheel [manufactured in Cleveland, Ohio] at South Brisbane'.[89]

Challenge racing

Challenge racing between two top 'cracks' at cycling carnivals became popular in attempts to reignite interest in the sport after notable drops in spectator attendances at race meetings became widespread in the late 1890s. These two-man contests usually came about when one rider challenged another to a race over a stated distance or distances for a stake, often a substantial sum, put up by both on a winner-takes-all basis. In effect, the riders were betting, backing themselves to win. However, there was scope for the promoters of race meetings, and bicycle agencies, to make further substantial behind-the-scenes incentives available to riders who would compete at their carnivals or ride their brand of bicycle. At a time when falling spectator numbers were being blamed, at least in part, on the handicap system that often made it difficult to tell who was winning[90], the paying public was attracted by the prospect of seeing the best of the champions racing one another without handicaps.

Fred Shaw first became interested in challenge racing in early 1899 when he placed a notice in the *Brisbane Courier* issuing a challenge for a match race over one, three and five miles, paced or unpaced, for a 'purse not to exceed £50 (preferred), or for the Bicycles we ride, or for fun'. Fred stated his address as 'Care L.Q.W. [League of Queensland Wheelmen] Rooms'. Two weeks later the same newspaper reported that 'The challenge issued by Freddy Shaw, the game little Red Bird rider, to race the self lauding and boastful Swann has not received any response ... Shaw is waiting hopefully, however, and expresses himself as willing to race for money or marbles, wherever and whenever the "downy" one is ready'. In the public posing that tended to take place before this type of event, the challenge was accepted a week later and it was claimed that 'Freddy Shaw [was] jubilant' and 'has spared no effort to bring the match to a finality'. Then, as the posing continued, Swann headed off to north Queensland and requested that the challenge race take place at Charters Towers or Bundaberg but then said he did not know where he would be on the date of the proposed match.[91] No evidence has been sighted to suggest the Shaw v Swann challenge race ever took place. After the announcement of a handsome stake and much publicity there appears to have been no action.

There was, however, plenty of match-racing action for Fred at the League of Queensland Wheelmen's August Carnival, one of the most prominent meetings of the Queensland racing calendar. Much interest had been generated in a match race between 'the cash champions of Queensland' Mick Healy and Fred Shaw, good mates but fierce competitors. Display advertising for the carnival in the Queensland press promised 'A Grand Challenge Match between M. Healy and F. Shaw, over a distance of five miles, for a stake of £25 a side, paced by the crack riders'. The race, under the auspices and sanction of the Queensland League of Wheelmen, was paced by single riders with the men being limited to six pacers each over the course of the race. A race report explained further the process of pacing, the alternating fortunes of the competitors and the exciting finish:

> This match has been the subject of much controversy during the last two seasons, and great interest was taken in the issue. Both men had many supporters on the ground, who heartily cheered them as they rode. Martin, Mutton, and Harvison paced Shaw; and Carpenter, M'Donald, and Eaton did the same duty for Healy. These names are a sufficient guarantee of a warm pace, and the event proved it so. Healy was the first to take the lead, but in the second lap Shaw, under Martin's guidance, displaced him. At the beginning of the fourth lap Healy and Eaton went to the front. Martin again took

> Shaw past Healy in the next lap. In the sixth lap Eaton paced Healy to the lead, and in the eighth Martin again aided Shaw to displace his opponent. Positions frequently changed, and at the last lap Shaw was leading. At the dressing-room Healy seemed fatigued, but he soon recovered, and, spurting brilliantly, passed Shaw and won by half a wheel. The excitement throughout the race was intense, and the scene at the finish was one of great enthusiasm.[92]

Another race report captured more of the excitement of that race:

> A fine start was effected, Carpenter and Harvison taking the men out for the first lap, M'Donald and Martin next, and Eaton and Mutton following. Healy and his pace went to the front at the start. Martin seemed to do the lion's share of the work for Shaw, and each time he went on he escorted the little fellow to the front. The excitement was most keen as the race progressed, and at the fourteenth lap Harvison took Healy to the front. At the bell the pacers came off, and Shaw led round to the back of the track, with Healy a machine's length behind, and lying in a nice position on the inside. Mick now shot to the front as the sheds were approached amidst loud cries of 'Healy! Healy wins!' 'No, no!' 'Yes, it's Shaw!' 'No, Healy!' Freddy spurted beautifully when the sheds were passed, and the machine's length which had separated the men was slowly closed up, until as the tape was crossed it had been closed up to about a quarter of a wheel, by which distance Healy won one of the most interesting match events that could be witnessed anywhere.[93]

Within weeks, the *Brisbane Courier* noted, 'Freddy Shaw is endeavouring to secure another match with Mick Healy. If these two cracks could be brought together again for the Hospital Sports it would prove almost as big an attraction as all the rest of the programme together. It is said that Shaw has another £25 to wager on his chances'.[94] The proposed rematch did not take place.

In early 1901 Fred Shaw was looking for another challenge and demonstrating that he was again prepared to heavily back himself. In Sydney, the *Referee* carried this note:

> 'Sammy' Shaw, one of the original Leaguers, tells me that his brother, Fred, wants to make a match with any cyclist in Australia. The little fellow will be remembered as a rare bit of stuff for his inches when he used to ride In Sydney. He has been in Brisbane for a while but will be down at Anniversary time for the sailing races on the Harbor. His Idea is to meet any rider in Australia at his weight, 8st 2lb, in three events, say, one, three, and five miles, paced or unpaced, for £50 or £100 a side, the race to take place in Sydney. Now, is there anyone willing?[95]

There is no sign that there were any takers. However, by late September a match race for £25 a side between Freddy Shaw and Freddy Rickards, both of whom had previously worked together in the Red Bird workshops in Brisbane, was arranged for the Woolloongabba track over one, two and five miles and to be 'paced by all the multi-cycles which can be got together between Brisbane and Toowoomba'. On the day, the pacer riders included Fred's younger brother, Tom Shaw. Fred Rickards won the first race over one mile. Fred Shaw won the two-mile race. In the third race, the five-mile event, 'an unhappy calamity' occurred with Fred Shaw 'coming a heavy cropper' that saw him taken away by ambulance after sustaining heavy bruising and an injury to the hip. Barrackers for both riders protested loudly, each blaming the rider other than their own but the race and the challenge was decided, after a protest, in favour of Fred Rickards. Fred Shaw was up and about again ten days later when he sailed for Sydney, cabin class, on the steamer *Peregrine* with his sailboat *Etna* 'to look for victories on the water'.[96]

Texas Jack v. Fred Shaw, Horseman v. Cyclist

BRISBANE CRICKET GROUND.

SATURDAY NEXT, 10th FEBRUARY,

AT 3 P.M.

Texas Jack

VERSUS

FRED. SHAW.

HORSE VERSUS CYCLE.

LAST SATURDAY'S EVENTS WERE UNANIMOUSLY PROCLAIMED BY THE PUBLIC TO BE THE MOST NOVEL AND EXCITING RACES YET SEEN.

TEXAS JACK will Race Horses (changing his mount every half-mile) against the Well-known Cyclist FRED. SHAW, in THREE RACES of 1, 2, and 5 Miles.

CYCLIST IS TO USE TRIPLET AND QUADRUPLET PACING IN ALL EVENTS.

DON'T FORGET TO SEE THE NEW PROGRAMME

WILD WEST SPORTS AND BUCKJUMP RIDING CONTEST.

ADMISSION, 1s.; Grandstand, 1s. Extra.

Advertising for Texas Jack v Fred Shaw challenge.
Brisbane Courier, 8 February 1900, p. 2

Following a similar show a week earlier involving Mick Healy, who lost the clash, a contest was arranged between Texas Jack, a visiting American horseman, cowboy and showman and Fred Shaw, 'the crack cyclist pace follower'. To take place at the Brisbane Cricket Ground, the challenge pitched Texas Jack on horseback against Fred Shaw on his Stearns bicycle in three races. Texas Jack could change horses (remount) once in a one-mile race, three times in a two-mile race and every two laps in a five-mile race. Fred was to use triplet and quadruplet pacing. Apart from these three races, this 'wild west' show offered three other attractions, an 'exhibition of sharpshooting with rifle and revolver on the back of a galloping steed', 'feats with the lasso' and a buckjumping contest.

Fred had a good afternoon on the triangular track laid out for the racing. He won the one-mile race by about 30 yards. In the two-mile race Fred was overtaken late in the race but appealed on the grounds the horseman cut the last corner. The appeal was upheld and Fred was awarded the win, and he then went on to win the five-mile race by about 60 yards. Thus, Fred won his challenge match with Texas Jack and went home well rewarded, although financial details of the arrangements were not made public.[97]

Spruiking Ayer's Sarsaparilla

Ayer's Sarsaparilla advertisement featuring Fred Shaw. *Evening News*, 16 June 1900, p. 7

Fred Shaw was a product ambassador for Ayer's Sarsaparilla, a nerve tonic billed as 'The World's Greatest Family Medicine' that claimed to remove 'all feeling of exhaustion, braces you up, makes your work easier, gives strength to the muscles, refreshes and invigorates and, best of all, takes out every impurity from the blood'. In a display advertisement for the tonic, Fred was quoted as saying it 'makes you have a good appetite, tones up the stomach, steadies the nerves and puts the go into you', all especially important for training and racing in the extreme heat of a Queensland summer. That advertisement featured a drawing of Fred cycling on the track, along with his testimonial that, 'I tell you, I am a great friend to Ayer's Sarsaparilla'.

Whether or not Ayer's Sarsaparilla contributed to his bicycle racing ascendancy, and medical views are that it likely did not, Fred Shaw's bank account must have been considerably enhanced by his support for the product. The advertisement appeared in a total of 56 newspapers in New South Wales, Queensland, Victoria, South Australia and New Zealand on over 260 occasions between June 1900 and July 1904.

Fred was not alone among champion cyclists in supplementing his track income by endorsing commercial products. As the *Sydney Sportsman* reported in 1902:

> Crack cyclists are being sought after by business people as a means of advertising their wares just now, judging by the pictorial advts. in Sydney dailies, in which Joe Megson appears as an advocate for a certain brand of electric belt, and Freddy Shaw, who now resides in Queensland, figures, as a cyclist whose success is solely [?] attributable to the use of a certain invigorating tonic. 'Jack' Parsons, erstwhile champion of Australia, has his name associated with cycling shoes, clips, valises, and other accessories.[98]

More cycling, more sailing

In Sydney in late January and early February 1901, Fred Shaw sailed *Etna* in several inter-state[99] races on Sydney Harbour as a representative of Queensland and then returned north.[100] Back in Brisbane cycling, Fred won the final of the One-Mile Handicap, and was placed third in the Two-Mile Handicap at the St Patrick's Day Sports in March.[101] At the Eight-Hour Day Sports at the Brisbane Cricket Ground in May, racing under the auspices of the League of Queensland Wheelmen, he ran third in the Two-Mile Handicap 'by a nice bit of riding' but in the final of the One-Mile Handicap, 'Freddy Shaw had something go wrong with his machine at the start, and he had not got properly going when he had to ride off'.[102] This was a mixed sports meeting that featured the usual complement of sideshows, boxing-booths and refreshment stalls, and, as well as cycling events, the meeting's competitions included foot races (for Amalgamated Carpenters, Typos, Shop Assistants, Shipwrights and Boilermakers and an 'Old Man's Race over 75 yards'), a novelty race, running high jump, a potato race, throwing the hammer, a newsboys' race and a young ladies' race. It seems there was something for everybody.

In the cycling carnival conducted at Brisbane's Exhibition Grounds by the League of Queensland Wheelmen in July 1901 Fred was beaten for first place in the James Challenge Cup by Fred Rickard and was also placed second in the Challenge Cup, a five-mile scratch event.[103] He raced at the Grand Cycling and Pedestrian Carnival in Toowoomba that month and, from time to time, was entered in events at Charters Towers. Back in Sydney in October after the challenge match race with Fred Rickard, Fred sailed in races sponsored by the Sydney Dinghy Club and the Johnstone's Bay club. Appropriately the dinghy club began its sailing season with a 'miniature regatta' that involved its entire fleet of dinghies ranging from six to fourteen feet. While Fred didn't succeed with *Etna* at that October meeting, he took second place in the 14-footers' handicap in a race conducted by the Johnstones's Bay Sailing Club in November. By the end of December he was back in Brisbane at the tiller of the New South Wales'-owned 14-footer *Irex,* entered by A. Welch, in a three-day series of inter-state races on the Brisbane River.[104]

Irex was a boat very familiar to Fred because he had raced against it on numerous occasions on Sydney Harbour. *The Yachtsman's Guide to Sydney Harbour*, published in 1898, chose *Irex* to illustrate the challenges of open-boat skiff racing:

> This is a mighty fine sport but a wee thing damp. See *Irex* smashing to windward against a black nor'easter, there is nothing more beautiful in this world; but see her mainsheet hand five seconds too late in the jibe around Bradley's and you will get a fine view of that boat's famous bottom which is beautiful, but better where it belongs.[105]

At the United Ground in Townsville Fred raced in the League of Queensland Wheelmen's New Year Carnival on 5 January 1902. In the New Year's Handicap, for £7, £2 and £1, he won his heat and was placed third in the final.[106] During the remainder of 1902 Fred raced without success at two meetings at Charters Towers, an Eight-Hour Day sports meeting in Sydney in October and a League carnival In Sydney in November.[107] At the November meeting, from a large field that saw six heats run off for the two-mile Australian Handicap, Fred Shaw gained third place in the final. The year saw Fred's commitment to bicycle racing dramatically reduced in favour of sailing.

Fred campaigned *Etna* in numerous races in 1902 and 1903 under the auspices of the Sydney and Waterview Bay Dinghy clubs, the Johnstone's Bay, Neutral Bay and St George sailing clubs, at Anniversary Day regattas at the Drummoyne and Hunter's Hill Regatta, and the Middle Harbour, Balmain and Gosford regattas. In these races, most of which occupied over five hours, Fred gained considerable respect as a skipper and more than his fair share of success, with several wins each yielding £3/10/- and a trophy. In September 1903 he sold *Etna* to a Western Australian syndicate and the boat immediately left Sydney for Perth. Earlier, from January 1903, he had begun racing tiny 8-footers, particularly *Zephyr*, that sometimes sailed with just a one-man crew. In 1904, with Fred at the tiller, *Zephyr* won the Waterview Bay Dingy Club championship. That year he turned again to 14-footers' events, successfully skippering the new *Wandeen*, such that its owner, Mosman indent merchant George Hauer, presented him with an inscribed sovereign as a token of his appreciation. For another owner, Fred occasionally sailed the 14-footer *Geisha*[108] and in February 1904 he took second place and £3/3/- in the 14-footer *Wanderer* in a race on Botany Bay, a race that was followed by a smoke concert at Linck's Hotel, Sandringham.[109] In early 1905, he sailed the 10-footer *Charmant* on Sydney Harbour with some success[110] and continued his association with sailing in Sydney in 1907 as a member of the committee organising the Balmain Regatta.[111]

Building bicycles at Newtown, Sydney

By April 1902, Fred Shaw had moved from Brisbane back to Sydney and was proprietor of a small bicycle shop at 117 King Street, Newtown on the main road leading south out of the city and about four kilometres from the city centre. Several times in May and June 1902 Fred placed a display advertisement in the *New South Wales Cyclist and Motor Review* saying that he was a bicycle builder and that he kept a large stock of second-hand bicycles, sundries and all accessories.[112]

An advertisement in the *Australian Cyclist* placed by a dealer at The Strand, Sydney makes clear that the term accessories included such after-market and replacement items as bells, pumps, lamp brackets, graphite, locks, saddles, valves, oil lamps and bike stands.[113] Other advertisements of the day suggest additions to this list: tyres, tubes, cycle handlebars, cyclometers, oil, polish, puncture kits, bicycle valaises, tool bags and even chewing gum and rifle and fishing rod mounts for those riders contemplating a hunting or fishing trip.

Shaw Brothers, boot and shoe importers and retailers

As revealed in Chapter 3, the firm of Shaw Brothers, boot importers was established at 80 Miller Street, North Sydney in mid-1903. While Fred's brother Sam, who had extensive experience in the footwear trade, was the driving force behind this firm, registration papers show that the business was carried on in the names of Samuel Robinson Shaw, Frederick Ewart Shaw and Sam's infant son, Donald Samuel Ewart Shaw.[114] It is not clear what role Fred Shaw played in this business, with the possibilities existing that involvement was at first active through to the perhaps more likely circumstance that he was a silent partner who contributed capital to get the firm up and running.

Whatever the circumstances of his role with his brother Sam in the North Sydney firm of Shaw Brothers, it is clear that Fred's involvement continued until at least late February 1904 when Messrs. Shaw Brothers offered a trophy as a prize in a sailboat race on Sydney Harbour for the Sydney Dingy Club's open-boat 14-footers, an event in which 'such veterans as … Fred Shaw … will steer the boats'.[115]

The Bicycle Depot, Camden and Fred Shaw's Etna brand bicycles

In May 1904 Fred Shaw moved to Camden, then a small 'Edwardian market town',[116] about 65 kilometres southwest of the central business district of Sydney (and now a boom spot that is transforming the town, and surrounding farmland, into one of the outer suburban growth areas of Sydney). Shortly after his arrival in Camden, Fred established the Camden Bicycle Depot in Argyle Street to cater for the needs of cyclists.[117] He was soon in the business of using his experience as foreman of the Goold Cycle Works in Brisbane to manufacture his own brand of bicycle, named, like the 14-footer sailboat he had sailed in the Brisbane River and Sydney Harbour, the Etna.

While bicycles were relatively simple machines they had complex cast and machined parts that were beyond the production capacity of a small cycle works. Weekly cycling publications such as the *Australian Cyclist* (1898–1901) that became the *Australian Cyclist and Motor Car World* (1901–1904) carried numerous advertisements from suppliers of locally made and imported bicycle components such as wheels, rims, spokes, tyres, valves, hubs, brackets, pedals, chains, cranks, gear wheels, ball heads, fork crowns, saddles, lamps, brakes, pumps, tool bags, gear cases, and handles of felt, cork, celluloid or leather. While there were several large city-based cycle manufacturers, Fred Shaw was one of a very large number of small-scale manufacturers who traded on their personal competition successes and addressed local markets. Many of his cycles were made to order. As essentially a bespoke manufacturer, Fred Shaw could advise customers, whether they wanted a bicycle for racing or for general use, on the available component options and then make the bicycle to meet their needs. Fred's only cycle making competitor in Camden was Fred Duck, who manufactured Duck and Victory brand bicycles cycles.

There must have been many who asked Fred Shaw why he chose the name Etna both for the 14-footer sailboat he had built in Brisbane and for the bicycles he built in Camden (and likely those he built at Newtown in Sydney from 1902). In a 1907 advertisement for his bicycles in the *Camden News* Fred explained:

> Everyone is familiar with the mountain of that name, which is likely to burst forth into activity at any time. In the case of the Bike, it has already done so. Then again it has this peculiarity: – if you read it backwards it makes the word *ante*, which as every schoolboy knows is the Latin prefix *before*. Now we intend this machine to be before every other.[118]

The advertisement, that headlined Fred Shaw's Etna bicycles were built to order to satisfy personal requirements, stressed that they were 'designed and built by F. E. Shaw, who, having won distinction in different parts of Australia as a track rider, is qualified in no small degree for building a scientifically perfect wheel', and went on to say, 'Experience has taught the expert, that, to obtain the best possible results, certain means are resorted to, to secure an even distribution of weight, and correct angle, to get the greatest possible effort with the least exertion'. The advertisement also highlighted that Fred was a skilled mechanic who could repair all types of machinery including steam and petrol driven motorcars, guns, rifles, revolvers, separators, sewing machines, farm machinery, gas generators and gas engines and that his workshop was 'fitted for the most difficult class of Mechanical Work'. Two weeks later, a coachbuilder, general blacksmith and horse shoer in the nearby town of Campbelltown advertised that he was an agent for 'F. E, Shaw, General Mechanic, Etna Cycle Works, Camden. Bicycles Built. Guns and Machinery of all Descriptions Repaired'.[119]

By June 1906, the *Camden News* was singing the praises of Fred's 'mechanic's shop' and his ability to service and repair motor cars, few of which, it must be said, had found a home in Camden at that time. Great fanfare was attached to Fred's acquisition of a lathe, the only one in town save for a specialist one at a woollen mill. An American Barnes machine, Fred's lathe could make parts 'to an ace of accuracy' to repair cars, bicycles, cream separators and guns that previously had to be sent to Sydney for attention.[120]

At the 1907 Camden Show Fred Shaw exhibited his Etna bicycles at a stand in the main hall. In what was described as a very creditable display, the exhibit showed 'different machines that were built to order for local gentlemen, and also the numerous accessories, conveying an idea of what is in stock at his business premises'.[121]

An Etna bicycle built by Fred Shaw at the Bicycle Depot, Camden.
Undated but believed c.1907. Shaw family archives

Designs adopted by Fred for the bicycles he made were sometimes innovative. In an account of a fastest time in a Bathurst to Sydney road race won by a Fred Walcott it was reported that, 'Riding an Etna cycle, built by Fred Shaw of Camden, his mount was of unorthodox design, with a sloping top bar and low head, and the back wheel close built to the centre bracket'.[122]

Fred was quick to make known the successes of the Etna bicycles he built for track and road racing. For example, in a January 1907 advertisement he listed 32 wins, places and fastest times taken out by Etna cycles over the previous six months at track meetings at Camden, Goulburn, Westbrook and Sydney and in the Camden to Sydney, Goulburn to Sydney and Picton road races and reminded readers he was 'Late foreman to the Goold Bicycle Co.'s Works, Brisbane'.[123] And having seen prize donors gain publicity, and won many prizes himself in competition, he was at the forefront of offering prizes at Camden and district cycling meetings. Prizes he donated varied from cash prizes for individual events to contributions towards the prize pools for meetings, and they also included trophies, a set of racing tyres, a tea service and a flash Etna racing bicycle, the latter valued at £30.[124]

Fred Shaw's skills as a mechanic were not restricted to bicycles as he showed willingness to find engineering solutions to a variety of problems. For example, as the *Camden News* reported in February 1907:

> As a matter of record the removal of the whole of the CAMDEN NEWS plant from the premises of the estate of the late T. C. Whiteman to the permanent printing office adjacent to the Camden Post-office, Argyle-street, was entrusted solely and absolutely to Mr F. Shaw, a practical engineer of Camden. The big Wharfedale machine on which the CAMDEN NEWS is now being printed was permanently laid down by Mr Shaw. The conveyance of the machine weighing nearly three tons, was intrusted to Mr F. Dowle, North Cawdor, with his team of four horses.[125]

Fred had not yet abandoned bicycle racing. In mid-1904, and now living at Camden, at his request he was re-instated by the Cyclists' Union as an amateur[126] and was set down to race in a meeting conducted by the Union in a Half-Mile Handicap (in red with white bands), a Two-Mile Handicap (in blue) and in the One-Mile Championship of New South Wales (for the Northern Suburbs Bicycle Club). These events, conducted at the Sydney Cricket Ground were part of a three-day Diavolo Cycling Carnival,[127] among the main features of which were performances by Diavolo, 'The Looper' (W. H. Barber), a trick cyclist who attracted crowds to bicycle race meetings as an entertainer and lent his name to the entire programme. Diavolo's main act, the one that brought in crowds across the world, and which he performed each day of this Sydney carnival, involved him riding a bicycle down a narrow staging 100 foot in length, entering a loop of 50 feet diameter at an estimated 90 miles an hour, spinning round the inside of the circle, and emerging on the opposite side. The whole journey occupied about five seconds, with the momentum carrying the bicycle and its rider nearly halfway across the grassed area of the cricket ground after the exit from the loop.[128] While Fred Shaw was not moved to emulate Diavolo, he could not fail to have been impressed that the Diavolo meeting at the Sydney Cricket Ground on 3 December included a £100 challenge race between two privately owned 14.6-horsepower Knowles–Darracq motorcars. It seems likely indeed that Fred Shaw, who went on to become a car owner, motor mechanic and new and used car dealer, would have been excited to witness this event. There were no cars in Camden at this time and Fred was about to contribute to changing that situation.

Perhaps in an attempt to help reintroduce his Etna bicycles to a crowded Sydney bicycle market, Fred Shaw entered a half-mile League of New South Wales Wheelmen's race at a football match at the Agricultural Ground, Moore Park in mid-1906. Beating Meadham, the champion, he won that race by a machine's length.[129]

'Camden to Queensland by Motor'

Late in 1907 Fred Shaw, as engineer/mechanic, accompanied Dr Francis West and his wife when they left Camden in their new 'motor' (car) on a holiday road trip to the doctor's parents' sheep property, Pilton Station, Clifton, near Warwick in south-east Queensland, on roads not made for motoring. On the third day of their outward journey, when the car was started at Scone, it emitted 'a fearful noise' caused, as Fred discovered, by a loose flywheel. Over that day and the next Fred repaired the car but soon after the party left Scone it developed gearbox problems. After Fred dismantled the gearbox and attended to its problems, Mrs West returned to Scone and then continued her journey north by train. After leaving Tamworth, Dr West and Fred, who travelled in daylight and camped out at night, were delayed again in a blacksmith's shop straightening an axle bent during a creek crossing. On the return trip to Camden, via Toowoomba, Kempsey, Port Macquarie, Taree, Gloucester, Maitland and Parramatta, the car experienced further flywheel problems, there were breakdowns in the car's electrical system and the carburettor caused trouble. Fred Shaw made the 1,754 miles (2,822 km) trip possible by solving the car's mechanical and electrical problems as they arose.[130] He earned his keep and at the same time enhanced his reputation as an able mechanic. Fred remained good friends with the doctor, a cyclist, all-round sportsman and community leader, for over 20 years.

Within two weeks of Fred's return to Camden he was asked to act as an agent for Mr C. Statham, a Camden's solicitor, for the purchase of a new eight-horsepower De Dion car in Sydney and to drive it back to Camden. The *Camden News* reported that after 'some very severe trials, viz, driving to Picton and back, over Razorback,[131] with three passengers, and over the steepest hills between here and Sydney carrying five passengers. Mr Statham informs us that he is more than satisfied with the car, and with a little more of Mr Shaw's able tuition he feels sure that he will have every confidence in taking any of the trips both for business and pleasure, for which his new purchase was intended'.[132]

Marriage, and Etna motorcycles

On 21 October 1908 Frederick Ewart Shaw married Rosa (Rose) Mabel Smith of Camden at St John's Church of England, Camden.[133] In the context of the major pioneering contribution made by Fred Shaw in introducing the motorcar to Camden, it is worthy of note that Rose Shaw was the first bride to be conveyed to St John's Church, Camden by motor vehicle.[134] Following the reception at Wandeen[135], the Hill Street home of Rosa's parents, the newlyweds left Camden 'for a motor tour through the South Coast'.[136]

By January 1908, F. E. Shaw, in an advertisement highlighting the success of his Etna bicycles (1st, 2nd and 3rd in the Thirlmere ten-mile road race in December 1907, 1st, 2nd and 3rd on Boxing Day 1907 in the One and a Half-Mile Road Race and the Youths' One-Mile Road Race at Mt Hunter and with successes in the Camden Wheel Race and Camden District Championship), billed himself as a 'Motor & Cycle Builder',[137] with the 'motor' meaning motorcycles.

On the June holiday to mark the birthday of the Prince of Wales, the first motorcycle race to be held locally was contested at the Camden Cycling Club's Sports meeting. Four machines competed over three miles. The three riders who finished all rode 1.5-horsepower Etna motorcycles made by Fred Shaw. The back marker, Fred Shaw, quickly overtook his three opponents after the start but finished second. The winner's time was 5 minutes and 53 and three-fifths of a second.[138]

Just how many motorcycles Fred made is not known, nor is it known when he made his first. As early as 1896 mechanics attached small combustion engines to safety bicycles and the motorcycle was born. Some of these early motorcycles were employed as 'motor pacers' at cycling events and Fred had been closely associated with Dunlop motor pacers in Brisbane and Sydney from 1900. No doubt he took a keen interest in their design and construction as well as their function and performance. It seems likely that Fred had experimented with building motorcycles well before the 1908 race at Camden in which he and three of his machines competed.

Fred Shaw's bicycle shop (Camden Bicycle Depot), Argyle Street, Camden, October 1908. Accompanying a letter from Neville Shaw, Fred's son, to a representative of the Camden Historical Society, 20 September 1989

No details of any Etna motorcycles, nor any image of one, have been located. It is certain, however, that Fred's motorcycles, like the tens of thousands then being made around the world by myriad entrepreneurs,[139] took the form of a standard safety bicycle to which an engine and improved braking system had been fitted. The earliest designs used 'clip on' engines, many of which were manufactured by Minerva in Belgium and imported into Australia via a London agent.

'Minerva kits' comprised an engine, petrol tank (that could be painted and brand-named locally), carburettor, electrical components, belt rim, controls and an optimistically named 'silencer'. The motor cycle builder supplied the frame, hubs, wheels and tyres, belt rim, brakes and seats – along with optional 'extras' such as lights and a horn, with many of these components being proprietary lines 'bought in'. It is possible that the only Shaw-built part of the Camden-made machines was the frame, with that likely to have been a strengthened version of his bicycle frame to accommodate the vibration of the engine.[140] In 1904, the Minerva 211cc single cylinder 1.5-horsepower engine was sufficient to allow a cruising speed of about 30 kph. Numerous engine sizes were in use at that time and the fact that Fred's motorcycles were of 1.5-horsepower strongly suggests they were the popular Minervas, the only engine then marketed in Australia of that exact size.

A c.1905 Adelaide-built Lewis Minerva motorcycle. It is certain that motorcycles built by Fred Shaw at Camden in 1908, with appropriate Etna livery, were similar in general appearance to this Lewis machine. [Lewis] motorcycles in the Molton Street [Adelaide] works, c.1905–6 at: http://earlymotor.com/lewis/articles/html/05wgbikes.htm

In the month prior to his marriage, Fred Shaw imported two eight-horsepower Phoenix cars direct from London. In praising Fred for 'placing himself in the position of being able to cater for requirements in the motor line' the *Camden News* noted that within hours of the arrival of the cars at his business premises 'Mr Shaw was on the road, his first trial trip was as far as the Carrington Hospital and the machine took the hills on the top gear, which as motorists know is an exceptional thing. These cars have already attracted much attention and doubtless Mr Shaw's venture will be a success'.[141]

And it *was* a success. Fred Shaw had become a motor dealer in addition to manufacturing, selling and repairing bicycles and motorcycles. Then, in 1912, two Camden businessmen purchased a large Vulcan car that had been owned by Dr West and appointed Fred Shaw to maintain it and manage its use as a hire car, with the *Camden News* noting that 'the experience of Mr Shaw in motoring will assure thorough competence' so the service may be relied upon.[142] Camden's demand for car hire services grew and in January 1914 the *Camden News* reported that Fred had acquired a large new and powerful car to keep up with the demands of his customers.[143] Within eighteen months, Fred added a second hire car to his business:

> Mr F. E. Shaw, motor expert of Camden, has added to his garage by purchasing the late Colonel Onslow Thompson's motor car [after its owner was killed in action in Europe]. This is a fine addition, and as it has been secured for the purpose of hiring to the public, it should be an acquisition to Mr Shaw's garage, for there is indeed pleasure in driving such a fine car such as Colonel Thompson had for his own personal convenience. Mr Shaw is a driver of the first order, and should have many demands on his time.[144]

In late 1918 Fred added a new Mitchell car to his hire fleet,[145] and he began operating an 18/20-seat bus, or 'passenger lorry', out of Camden from 1920. The bus was used to meet trains at Campbelltown (Camden was not on the main southern rail line), and ran a passenger service to the Narellan picture theatre on Friday and Saturday evenings. Services were provided to and from Campbelltown on Sunday mornings and to and from Menangle (for harness racing) on Tuesday evenings. The bus was also hired out for picnics and by clubs and sporting groups. In April 1923 Fred Shaw moved to establish a regular motor bus service between Camden and Campbelltown.[146]

The Camden Motor Garage

In 1914 Fred renamed and again relocated his business, now styled as the Camden Motor Garage (formerly Camden Bicycle Depot), to new premises a little further south at 47–49 Argyle Street.[147] His advertisements claimed this to be the 'most up-to-date motor garage within 100 miles of Sydney'. He sold and hired out cars, sold tyres, fuel and oil, garaged up to six cars at any one time for visitors to Camden and continued building bicycles. In that year he also enthusiastically became the Camden agent, often in association with the Machinery Department of Dalgety & Company of Sydney, for Buzacott Steam Pressure Canners, irrigation equipment and engines (kerosene and oil), Gane Milking Machines and Tangye pumping plants and engines.[148]

Fred Shaw's Camden Motor Garage, c.1923.
Shaw family archives

By 1915 Fred Shaw was Camden's 'Selling Agent for Buick and Ford Cars'[149] (the Ford cars and light trucks were the famous T-Models, 'Tin Lizzies' as they were famously called). His association with Ford as their Camden dealer continued over twelve years until late 1926. Buick cars were not mentioned in his later advertisements but by early 1921 he was selling Oakland[150] cars in addition to Fords and dealing in second-hand cars. His advertisements in the *Camden News* appeared, with little variation, on a more or less weekly basis. Fred had competitors selling bicycles and cars, and carrying out mechanical repairs in the limited Camden market that was estimated to have been about 2,000 people (with more living in small villages and on farms in the district) at this time.[151]

Ford vehicles sold in Australia combined mechanical components manufactured in Canada with non-standardised bodies of varying quality built in Australia, with this arrangement, Ford hoped, creating a 'British Empire image' for their products. Mechanical components were imported by state-based Ford agencies that arranged for the bodies to be built locally (more or less) to Ford Motor Company design and specifications. City and rural dealers then retailed and serviced the completed vehicles, supposedly with assistance and support from the state agents. By 1922–3 it was clear to Ford in both Canada and the United States that these procedures may be in need of review and in late 1923 two Ford Canada executives, Hubert French and Mel Brooks, were despatched to Australia to confer with Ford agents and dealers and to report their findings. Those findings were damning, especially of the primitive conditions under which their company's under-resourced and poorly supported rural dealers operated.

Fred Shaw's Ford dealership at his Camden Motor Garage did not escape criticism, although some of the blame was placed on the state agents, Davies & Davies, because of their lack of support. Hubert French's notes on his visit to Fred's dealership read:

> *Camden* is a small town with a population of less than 2,000 – Dealer has a store on the main street with a small display window showing lubrication oils, tyres, accessories, but very few Ford parts.
>
> Small repair shop, no showroom. Has been a Ford dealer for ten years, also has sold some Oakland and Essex. The dealer estimates the population of territory at 11,000.
>
> Has taken five cars, two trucks, and one tractor, during past four months. Claims that he will sell 16 cars in the year. Surrounding farm country only fair.
>
> Main road metalled and fairly good. Dealer has two or

> three spotters located throughout his territory from whom he gets the names of prospects and to whom he pays a small commission.
>
> No systematic selling effort of any description has been made. The dealer states that someone from Davies & Davies has called on him approximately every two months – duration of their visit has been very short – no attempt has been made on their part to give dealer selling help.
>
> His little premises showed unmistakable signs of being very recently cleaned up, probably as a result that we anticipated calling. I am not impressed with the dealer, although I find it hard to criticise him, in view of the fact he has had no instructions.[152]

Mel Brooks, whose expertise was in the servicing of Ford vehicles, wrote separate notes. The two sets of notes, along with those they wrote about other dealers and sundry general commentaries were brought together into the so-called French Report submitted to their Canadian bosses. That report set the scene for the establishment of Ford Australia with Hubert French as director and general manager. About Fred Shaw and his Camden Motor Garage, Brooks wrote:

> From there to the next stop, *Camden*, which is 8 miles, we travelled, and found the dealer F. E. Shaw, who has been established for a number of years.
>
> Mr Shaw has premises on the main street of Camden, which are covered with various signs, such as Mobiloil, with only one Ford sign, and that a poor attempt by a local painter, only visible from the street directly in front of the building.
>
> The part stock here is approximately 60/-/-, whereas it should have been 120/-/-, as the Ford cars in operation in the territory were 40. Here again no modern garage equipment was in use, and a very small premises.

> He claimed to be getting 75 per cent of the Ford Service work, although there are 4 other garages in the territory. These garages buy some of the parts from him at 15 per cent discount. He had no mechanic on the job, claiming he was away sick.[153]

Ford Motor controlled its Australia-wide advertising centrally. Authorised dealers were supplied with company-prepared advertising copy to which they added only their dealership name. A series of these illustrated display advertisements for Fordson tractors and Ford cars and trucks available through F. E. Shaw's Ford dealership appeared regularly in the *Camden News* from early 1923 until the end of 1926, just prior to Fred's departure from Camden.[154] In December 1926, the final advertisement for Fred's motor business was incorporated into advertising by Ashcroft Brothers of the nearby town of Picton, dealers for Cadillac, Vauxhall, Buick, Oakland, Oldsmobile and Chevrolet vehicles for General Motors (Australia) Pty. Ltd. Ashcroft Brothers of Picton described 'Mr Shaw' as their sub-agent in Camden,[155] and continued to do so in early 1927. By February 1927 Dunk Brothers, who had taken over Fred Shaw's Camden Motor Garage, were dealers for General Motors.[156]

Fred Shaw's departure from Camden prompted him to say something about his arrival 22 years earlier and his optimism about the opportunities the town offered for someone with a mechanic's expertise:

> It was raining the day I left Sydney … and I wondered what I'd struck on changing into the Camden tram at Campbelltown[157], and more so when with a heavy bump the engine stopped at Rudd's Gate, Kenny Hill, and Curran's Hill where at each place only one lone house was in sight. The scattered cottages and buildings at Narellan was a relief, but on arriving at Camden the prospects altered with a view of a busy town, then presenting a beauty not yet forgotten by the sun shining after a rain storm, and the street lined with

farmers' carts. At that time I had visions of the progress of the motor, although there were none then here in Camden. My experience with the Argyll cars and marine engines led me to believe that motorists would come along as they have done this past few years. Now that the time has arrived to think of leaving the regret is keenly felt, for I have made many friends here, and customers of 22 years standing.[158]

Return to Sydney and the end of the road

In 1927 Fred Shaw returned to live in Sydney after 22 years in Camden. He moved his family to 176 Wollongong Road, Arncliffe[159] and went into business as a motor mechanic at 115 Princes Highway, Arncliffe.[160] By 1931, he was renting a home at 3 Lansdowne Street, Arncliffe[161] just three doors from his sister and brother-in-law Mary and Brice Thomas. After three years there he moved briefly to nearby Rockdale[162] and by 1943 he and Rose were living at Yarran and Mulga Roads, Oatley.[163] Fred continued to earn a living as a motor mechanic.

What decided Fred to leave Camden is unknown. Maybe his decision was connected to the shake-up of Ford dealerships. Whatever the reason, Fred avoided the dealer problems caused worldwide by Henry Ford who, in May 1927 ceased production of the Ford Model T throwing 60,000 men out of work and creating havoc among his country's Ford dealerships, many of which were forced to close their doors. After a lapse of six months, during which his factories were re-tooled, Ford released his new Ford Model A but this was too late for the survival of many of his dealers.[164] The problems were felt in dealerships around the world, although less so in Australia because it was supplied from Canada. And then came the Great Depression. By 1928, Dunlop Motors (in no way associated with the Dunlop Rubber Company) was Camden's authorised Ford dealer.[165] By October 1929 Dunlop Motors was in liquidation.[166]

During his 22 years in Camden Fred was a popular and respected member of the community and he gave back to that community. He cycled competitively there and in the surrounding district of Picton, Cawdor, The Oaks and Thirlmere (falling in the 1906 Camden Wheel Race and breaking his collar-bone), donated generous cash and trophy prizes to the Camden Cycling Club, was elected Vice President of the Thirlmere Club and officiated as timekeeper, lapscorer, handicapper and judge at cycle race events. *Pro bono* he supported the Camden Cottage Hospital and was active in his Masonic Lodge. Always a sportsman, he was involved in the organisation of the Camden Aquatic Sports on the Nepean River in 1910 and 1911 and enjoyed marked success in rifle shooting competitions in 1911 and 1912.[167]

In something of a sea-change comeback, Fred skippered the 18-footer *Mele Bilo* on behalf of its owner in the 1930 Queen of the Harbour event, conducted by the Sydney Flying Squadron to raise money for the Royal Hospital for Women, Paddington. Before the race, the *Sydney Sportsman* reported that Fred had been busy recruiting his crew and that 'Big Joe Shankleton, the deaf mute, will be sheet hand; "Fringer" Thierlng, that great League footballer and boxer, will hoist the kites, and Aubrey Welch will do all the "shouting" – at the crew, not the bar'.[168] On a wild and squally day only ten of the 29 starters completed the course. *Mele Bilo* was not among them.

It is not clear how Fred Shaw came to skipper *Mele Bilo* in this race. The last mention found of him being in charge of a boat in a race in Sydney was for a race in 1905. After his 1904 move to Camden he continued to race occasionally in Sydney as time permitted but if he crewed on boats without skippering them his name did not appear in newspaper reports and has not been sighted in other records consulted.

Aged 71, Fred Shaw died in St George Hospital, Kogarah, Sydney, on 7 November 1947.[169] So ended the life that had seen the boy from Woolloomooloo excel at competitive cycling and sailing and then successfully carry forward his skills as a bicycle mechanic and builder to the early motorcycle and motor vehicle trade.

CHAPTER 6

Long-Distance Road Racer: Thomas John Shaw

Thomas John Shaw, the last of the nine Shaw children, was born to William Shaw and Mary Anne Shaw (née Inch) on 6 June 1878 at Woolloomooloo, Sydney.[1] Thomas was commonly known as Tom Shaw, T. Shaw or T. J. Shaw.

In Brisbane with brother Fred

The first known record of Tom Shaw's competitive bicycle racing career was just after his twentieth birthday when the Brisbane press announced handicaps for an Intercolonial Championship Carnival scheduled for 23 July 1898 at the Brisbane Cricket Ground, Woolloongabba (the 'Gabba').[2] Tom's handicaps of 50 yards for the Half-Mile Handicap, 70 yards for the One-Mile Handicap and 125 yards for the Three-Mile Handicap strongly suggest he had previous successful riding experience, possibly at club or country levels. For the Intercolonial Carnival he was also entered in the One-Mile Championship of Australia and he was shown in the announcement as riding for Queensland. As was often the case with cycle racing, entries and the issue of handicaps did not necessarily translate into starts as riders considered their handicaps and track conditions. Tom did not start in two of these events and was unplaced in the other two.[3]

It is possible that Tom travelled to Brisbane with his brother, maybe as a pacer for him, when Fred, who had raced in north Queensland the previous year, was taken to the northern capital, along with other southern cracks, to compete in the inaugural meeting of the League of Queensland Wheelmen in late June 1898. Whatever the story of Tom's arrival on the Brisbane bicycle-racing scene may be, it is clear that Fred mentored Tom in many matters related to cycling and worked closely with him in Brisbane and Camden over the years that followed.

A week after the League meeting, Tom was issued handicaps for races to be contested under the auspices of the Queensland Cyclists' Union at the Brisbane Cricket Ground at a Hospital Sports Carnival. Tom entered in all four of the handicap bicycle races at this mixed sports carnival, with these to be raced over half a mile, one mile, three miles and five miles. On the day, he raced, and without luck, in only the five-mile event.[4]

In November 1898, just after Fred Shaw had raced in a similar event over an almost identical course, Tom competed in a 40-mile road race from Brisbane to Cleveland and back conducted for amateurs by the Queensland Cyclists' Union. The race, known as the Austral-Swift Race was, for first place, a No. 1 Swift road racer, presented by the Austral Cycle Agency, and open orders for second, £8, third, £4, fourth, £2, fastest unplaced time, £3 and second fastest unplaced time, £2. Tom Shaw, off a handicap of 7 minutes and 30 seconds, was unplaced.[5]

While he almost certainly raced in club events that were not widely reported and for which records have not been located, in 1899 Tom Shaw was able to compete at higher levels in several community and charity events. In March he came third in his heat of the One-Mile Bicycle Handicap and then went on to take out second place in the final at a St Patrick's Day sports gathering at Brisbane's Exhibition Ground, for which 4,000 tickets had been sold. Tom's prize was £2.[6] He was allocated handicaps of 30 yards in the Half-Mile Handicap and 130 yards in the Three-Mile Handicap at the Ambulance Sports meeting to be held at the Brisbane Cricket Ground on 15 April. Those events were to be conducted by the Queensland Cyclists' Union for amateur riders. At the same meeting, Fred Shaw, Tom's brother, was set down to race in events conducted by the League of Queensland Wheelmen as a professional. Tom did not start in the half-mile event and was unplaced in the three-mile race.[7] Riding for the South Brisbane Cycling Club, Tom Shaw, with a time of 13 minutes and 30 seconds was placed third in a road race at Rocklea in mid-June, beating his brother Fred.[8] Over the same course in September, Tom was placed fourth in the South Brisbane Club's road race for a gold and opal medal. The race began at the Crown Hotel, Rocklea and finished at the Rockley Hotel. Tom was close to the gold and opal, with one report saying, 'The finish was most exciting, the first four being on top of each other'.[9]

Tom Shaw won the South Brisbane Cycling Club's Rocklea road race in May 1900 from over 100 riders who completed the seven-mile course. Racing for the Nissen medal, 'a very handsome piece of work', and with a handicap of just 1 minute and 20 seconds, he took out the medal by a machine's length.[10] Another road race followed for Tom when, from scratch, he rode the fastest time of 9 minutes and 5 seconds in the Redfern Gordon Club's four-mile race over a course from Northgate to Hamilton in Brisbane. In early June, in a three-mile road race conducted by the Brisbane Bicycle Club from Hamilton to Myrtletown, Tom was eliminated when a tyre punctured.[11]

Tom, reverting to path racing, won his heat of the One-Mile Bicycle Handicap conducted by the Queensland Cyclists' Union at the Hospital Sports Carnival held before between 3,000 and 4,000 spectators at the Brisbane Cricket Ground on 16 June but was unsuccessful in the final. Other bicycle events conducted at this charity sports meeting were a three-mile handicap and a Fancy Dress Parade (participant costumes and decorated bicycles) by members of the Queensland Cyclists' Union. A one-mile championship, with prizes of gold and silver medals, for boys aged under 18 attracted entrants from Brisbane Grammar School, Bowen House, and the Normal School. The carnival included 75 and 100 yard sprint races for boys as young as under ten, 220, 440 and 880 yard races, a pedestrian handicap of 880 yards, hurdles, a running high jump event and a 220 yard obstacle race. During the afternoon an abbreviated football match of two halves of ten minutes each was played between City and Merthyr (the latter a former Brisbane suburb, now part of the suburb of New Farm).[12]

Tom's South Brisbane Bicycle Agency, marriage, the loss of twin sons and insolvency

Tom followed his brother Fred into work as a bicycle mechanic and may have worked with him at the Goold Bicycle Company's works or stores in Brisbane building, repairing and selling Red Bird bicycles. When Fred left the Goold agency and joined the Cleveland Bicycle Company in Brisbane as a salesman in August 1900, the announcement of his appointment included that his brother, 'Mr Tom Shaw, is now sub-agent for the above high-class wheel at South Brisbane'.[13] Tom had commenced business in the bicycle trade as the sole proprietor of the South Brisbane Cycle Agency in Stanley Street.[14]

Thomas John Shaw married Wilhelmina (Minnie) Schultz on 27 March 1901 in Brisbane.[15] By May 1901, Tom's landlord, advertised two properties for sale in Stanley Street, South Brisbane, each of two storeys and each comprised of a shop and dwelling, and with one occupied, according to the real estate advertisement, by T. J. Shaw.[16] Twin boys, Leslie Hopetoun Shaw and William Leonard Shaw were born to Tom and Minnie in Brisbane on 19 September 1901 but, sadly, Leslie died on 6 November and William on 8 December.[17]

After the death of his twin sons, there is no further mention of Tom Shaw competing in cycling events in Queensland but within two months the Supreme Court of Queensland found Tom insolvent[18], in *forma pauperis*.[19] At that time he was recorded as living at Whynot Street, West End, South Brisbane.[20]

In February 1902, when Thomas John Shaw, mechanic, petitioned to be declared insolvent, he presented a Statement of Affairs to the Supreme Court of Queensland that showed he had no money at hand or at the bank, no property or furniture and nothing owing to him by creditors. His debts totalled £75/16/10. Tom's four major creditors were Thomas McKay of South Brisbane and the Brisbane businesses of James Smith and Sons (makers of Smith premier bicycles and suppliers of enamel parts, lamps and tyres), Messrs Smellie and Company (a hardware and engineering firm) and Skov and Campbell (pioneer Queensland bicycle builders and manufacturers of the Local brand bicycle). Lesser amounts were owed to Bosch, Barthel and Company (watchmakers and jewellers), A.J. Jackson (nickel-platers) and the Dunlop Tyre Company.[21] The nature of the debts incurred by Tom suggest that his small South Brisbane bicycle shop, typical of its type, traded in new and second hand bicycles and bicycle parts and accessories and that he carried out bicycle repairs.

Insolvency papers filed with the Supreme Court by Tom told that there were no books, papers or documents relating to the estate. 'Sickness and Deaths and out of Employment' were the reasons he gave for his insolvency.[22]

The Warrnambool to Melbourne road race (The Dunlop Road Race)

The Warrnambool to Melbourne road race, commonly known as the Dunlop Road Race or the Great Dunlop Road Race after its sponsor, the Dunlop Tyre Company, maker of bicycle tyres, was Australia's premier road race and the longest road race in the world at the turn of the twentieth century. The route followed for the race was from the south-western Victorian seaside town of Warrnambool via Terang, Camperdown, Colac, Winchelsea and Geelong to Melbourne,[23] a distance of 165 miles (265 km) along what is now known as the Princes Highway.

The inaugural Warrnambool to Melbourne road race took place in October 1895, inspired by a record-breaking run earlier that year by Daniel Charleston, an enterprising young bicycle shop owner.[24] Bicycle manufacturers and retailers quickly saw a commercial opportunity and so the race was born. With changes to the route and the starting and finishing points, the event has continued to the present day (although there have been 20 years in total where it was not run).[25] One account of the first race based on contemporary sources includes detail of the 3am start to take advantage of a full moon and the challenging road conditions encountered by participants along the way.[26]

This early flirtation with long-distance road racing developed alongside late colonial interest in what has been termed bicycle overlanding. In that separate, but related, branch of cycling lone riders on safety machines sometimes covered thousands of miles along crude bush 'roads' and tracks across sparsely settled outback country in search of adventure.[27]

A field of 101 riders contested the 1902 Warrnambool to Melbourne road race. The bicycle trade donated the race prizes, including bicycles and cash. First prize was £30 and a £5/5/- gold medal. Second prize was a Speedwell bicycle, third a made-to-order Albion bicycle and fourth a Charleston bicycle. The man riding the fastest time received a Massey-Harris machine.[28]

After overnight rain, the race began on a greasy and slippery road and it was not long before riders, 'carrying their damaged machines, and with skin and flesh off knee and elbow joints, returned to the starter's point with ruined hopes and doleful faces'. Heavy rain continued to fall over the 42 miles to Camperdown, by which point the mud-spattered field had been reduced to 70. By the time the racers reached Colac, 72 miles along the route, the field was further reduced to 45.[29] No pacing of any kind was allowed, 'except the assistance rendered by one contestant to another'.[30]

This type of racing, a severe test of fitness, strength, stamina and determination, was exhausting. As the *Ballarat Star* reported:

> [the winner] carried samples of all the 165 miles of the road on him. When he was helped off his machine he was as limp as a wet rag, and until a whisky and soda was poured down his throat he was unable to articulate. When he had slightly

> recovered, he was put in a cab and taken to the Melbourne baths where he went to sleep almost immediately.[31]

Stray dogs have been mentioned as a danger to racing cyclists. So, too, were work and farm animals, especially to road racers who, it must be said, were themselves a danger to the animals. Near Colac, a rider who collided with a blind horse was thrown on his head and rendered unconscious for over an hour. While no mention was made of the fate of the unfortunate horse, the Melbourne newspaper that reported the collision encouragingly speculated that the rider would be well enough to resume his journey to Melbourne by train the following day.[32]

The Dunlop Tyre Company spent £300 organising the race. From the finish line competitors were driven in cabs to the city baths, where hot baths were in readiness. A special van attached to the Warrnambool train brought the riders' spare clothing and personal effects to Melbourne, and with the assistance of telegraph operators, large maps were displayed in Melbourne throughout the day to show the progress of riders.[33] Another challenge for Dunlop was to feed and water the riders along the route. At Camperdown, each rider was handed a light food satchel and a pint tin of hot bread and milk, with the satchels being slung over shoulders so competitors could 'take it on the fly' and continue riding. At Mount Gellibrand the riders 'were again refreshed with a pint of sweetened milk' and at Winchelsea, the next checking and feeding station, riders received 'a pint of egg flip, containing a dash of kola'. At Geelong more hot bread and milk was dispensed and at Werribee the riders were fed with Bovril.[34] Dunlop must have been pleased with the publicity because, including the large crowd that assembled at the finish and those who turned out to watch the race along the road, it was estimated that 50,000 people followed the event[35] and scores of newspapers across the length and breadth of the country reported on it. Melbourne's *Punch* and *Weekly Times* published pages of photographs that captured aspects of the racing and details of the time and food stations along the route.[36] And within three weeks Dunlop gave away over 5,000 copies of a race souvenir in the form of a large pictorial poster depicting sixteen scenes from the race.[37]

Seven years later 312 riders started in the event. Increased interest in the race attracted a movie maker to film it. In these early days of silent movies, Messrs. Pathe Freres made a 'cinematograph picture' of the 1909 race. That film, which was widely screened in state capitals and large country towns, including at Geelong's His Majesty's Theatre,[38] within two weeks of the race, was '1800 feet long' and took '40 minutes to pass through the machine'. Confidently, but perhaps somewhat optimistically, the movie's makers claimed it to be 'the finest picture ever to be exhibited in Australia'.[39]

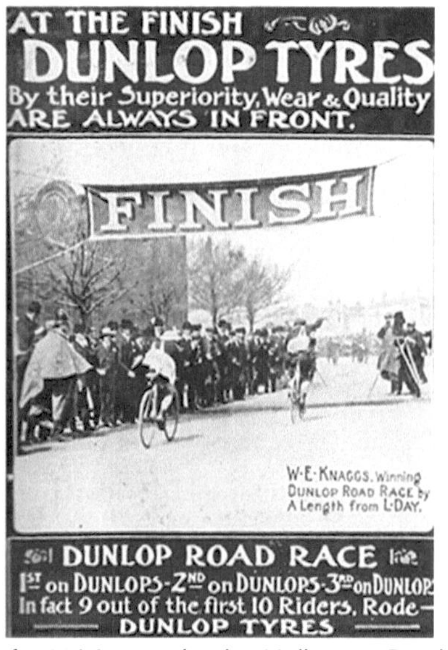

Finish of 1909 Warrnambool to Melbourne Road Race.
Dunlop Rubber Company advertising

Some idea of the scale of arrangements made by the sponsors of long distance road racing was provided by Launceston's *Daily Telegraph.* With an eye for detail, its account of the elaborate preparations made by the Dunlop Rubber Company for the 1909 race included that the official feeding stations along the course, to be manned by 50 Dunlop officials and hundreds of volunteers, would distribute gratis to riders '235 gallons of milk, 250 dozen bananas, 250 dozen oranges, 180 lbs Cailler's chocolate, 32 lbs of bread, 12 lb Bovril, 77 bundles of celery, 75 lb sugar, 35 dozen eggs, 100 lb Plasmon biscuits, 24 lb Plasmon cocoa and 120 lbs of meat jelly'. At Camperdown and Geelong 680 linen food bags (to be slung over the shoulder) were to be distributed along with 840 feeding tins for 'drinkables'.[40]

After a lapse of eleven years from 1911, the Warrnambool to Melbourne Road Race was revived in October 1922. A feature of the revival race was the large number of veteran riders attracted back to the competition, with 58 contestants from earlier 'Warrnambools' signed up a month before the race.

The 1902, 1909 and 1922 Warrnambool to Melbourne Dunlop road races are of particular interest because a T. J. Shaw was placed fifth in the 1902 race and recorded the fastest time among those riders with over a 20-minute start (handicap)[41] and was entered in all three races.[42] An exhaustive search of surviving race records has not revealed any identification of this man Shaw other than his initials.[43] Thomas John Shaw had the motivation to have been living and racing in Victoria in 1902 and 1909 (keeping a considerable distance away from his personal troubles in Brisbane, and attracted by the lure of the country's premier long-distance race, his preferred form of racing) – and to then to visit in 1922 to race as a veteran. However, there is insufficient evidence that this T. J. Shaw was the Thomas John Shaw who is the subject of this chapter. Indeed, in the course of this research a resident of Geelong – from an unrelated Shaw family – has offered photographs of three medals, one for the 1909 race but with no race or rider's name and no indication of whether it was a race prize or participation medal, one for an unidentified and undated road race won by a T. Shaw and one with just the initials T. J .S. engraved on its face. The medals come with a belief in her family that they were won in Dunlop road races by Thomas Joseph Shaw, a long-time resident of Geelong. The search for further information and clarification continues.

Tom's trouble with the law, and his mother-in-law

In December 1904, at the South Brisbane Police Court, Thomas John Shaw was charged with using threatening words to Elizabeth Schultz, his mother-in-law[44] and was released on bail. This charge was to herald another chapter in Tom's life that led him further into trouble with his wife, with whom he had another son, Ivan Conrad Victor Shaw, in 1904,[45] his mother-in-law and the legal system. Tom's cycling career was about to be interrupted and then led in new directions with the help of his brother Fred.

Tom Shaw headed south to Kempsey on the New South Wales north coast where he found work as the manager of the new Kempsey Cycle Depot, 'agent for B & B, Naumann and Triumph cycles and motors' in 1904. In his regular advertisements, Frederick Wagner, the owner of the business, described Tom as a skilled mechanic 'late of Sydney and Brisbane leading Houses'.[46] He raced at the Macksville Cycling Carnival at Easter and took first place and fastest time in an eight-mile road race in 1904,[47] but his year was dominated from September by a child desertion charge:

> Constable James Hanney deposed that about 4 o'clock on Monday afternoon, he went to Central Kempsey and arrested the accused at Mr Wagner's bicycle shop; he told the accused that there was a warrant out for his arrest for child desertion at South Brisbane; the name of the child was Ivan Conrad Victor Shaw; the accused told witness that he had never seen the child; he left Brisbane when he was hard up; he was out of work there and had no money; on returning home after looking for work all day, his wife and her mother refused to let him in; they handed his clothes over the fence and told him to get; he then had to tramp and seek work; witness said he then brought the accused to the station and charged him with child desertion; witness had known the accused for about 8 months during which time be had been working for Mr Neuhaus [a practical jeweller whose business

> incorporated a bicycle department], and (recently) with Mr Wagner; he had been very respectable and well conducted during the time witness had known him; he prayed for a remand of 8 days for the receipt of the warrant.

The P.M. (Police Magistrate) said this was the first case which had come before him, in which a person was brought up on a charge of the kind from another State. It was due to Federation, and as a policeman would have to come from Brisbane it meant great expense. He granted the remand.

The accused asked if bail could not be allowed and he would go and answer the charge. The P.M. said he was sorry under the circumstances that he had no power to grant bail. The accused had evidently conducted himself well here.[48]

Tom Shaw's woes were resolved, as it turned out only temporarily, when at the South Brisbane Police (Summons) Court, charged with desertion, he consented to an order being made to pay five shillings a week support, to enter into a surety of £13 for payment of the maintenance and to pay costs.[49]

Back in Kempsey in February 1905, Tom Shaw was dismissed by Frederick Wagner, his employer at the town's cycle agency over irregularities in the business accounts. Tom left the town for Sydney, where he was arrested and charged with two counts of embezzlement from Wagner.

In May, in Kempsey Court before the Police Magistrate, Frederick Wagner stated that Tom's work, as well as selling and repairing bicycles, included keeping the accounts of the business. Wagner claimed that after Tom travelled to Brisbane to face child desertion charges, he found discrepancies in the accounts that suggested dishonesty. The court ruled that the charge of embezzlement was not proved in this case. At the same hearing, however, Tom faced a second charge of embezzlement involving receiving money for goods sold but not showing receipt of that money in the firm's accounts. Found guilty of embezzlement, Tom Shaw was sentenced to one month in Kempsey Gaol.[50]

Sojourn in Camden, and a Camden to Sydney Road Race

After his release from Kempsey Gaol Tom Shaw moved to Camden, New South Wales, where his brother Fred had established the Camden Bicycle Depot in 1904. Under Fred's guidance and steady hand, Tom resumed his work as a cycle mechanic and a track and road racer. After Fred, racing in the Camden Wheel Race on New Year's Day 1906, broke his collarbone and suffered other severe injuries in a fall Tom stepped up and kept the Cycle Depot going throughout January.[51]

Tom rode in the Camden to Ashfield, Sydney, road race on 11 August 1906. Over a distance of 36 miles, for a first prize of £30, the race was conducted by the Camden Bicycle Club under the auspices of the New South Wales Cyclists' Union, the newly formed professional body for the sport. Exhausted after finishing 30th from 76 starters, Tom, described as a local [Camden] man, said he had 'quite enough, and like others enjoyed the glass of hot milk, etc, which was supplied by spectators between Minto and Liverpool'.[52]

Goulburn to Sydney Road Race

Tom Shaw, racing for the Parramatta club, and with a handicap of 50 minutes, was placed eleventh from a field of 93 starters and 43 who finished in the 1907 127-mile 'great road race', from Goulburn to Sydney, an event promoted by the Dunlop Rubber Company and conducted under the auspices of the League of New South Wales Wheelmen. First prize was £20 cash and a £5 gold medal presented by the Dunlop Rubber Company.[53] Estimates put spectator numbers at the Ashfield Town Hall finishing point at between 7,000 and 8,000.[54]

Conditions under which the riders contested the race were severe. The *Sydney Morning Herald* described the roughness of the course that in places was covered in new metal, and claimed that the heat, dust and a headwind made the long run irksome and monotonous. It went on to say that for long stretches there was not a soul in sight for miles but that it was the mountainous sections of the route, with gradients from 1 in 12 to 1 in 5 that posed the greatest challenges. These sections often caused riders to dismount, walk, and push their bicycles. The downgrades were equally challenging and required great skill and care to negotiate.[55] The old razorback road's gradients had challenged its users since the days of the bullock wagon in the 1830s and on race days it was now the turn of the cyclists to tackle its grades.[56]

To help offset the physical challenges of the race the Dunlop company supplied each rider with a satchel containing chocolate, raisins and fruit and supplied refreshments, including milk, at towns along the road. If they chose to, the racing men were able to eat and drink as they rode.

A rider in the 1907 Goulburn to Sydney road race being passed a refreshment satchel at Moss Vale. *Sydney Mail*, 11 September 1907, p. 678

Family matters, a bicycle business at Granville, bankruptcy and the T. J. S. bicycle

In March 1913, Wilhelmina Shaw proceeded against Thomas John Shaw, 'a thin, spare man, with a slight thatch of fair hair', in the South Brisbane Summons Court for maintenance. The Brisbane *Truth* reported at much length, and colourfully, on the hearing and described Wilhelmina as 'a brunette of prepossessing appearance above the ordinary, [who] was attired in an immaculate white summer costume, [and who] to keep up the general effect ... had donned a large hat to match it'. Her case made no mention of cruelty, drunkenness or desertion and she gave her husband, who she said was a cycle mechanic employed for 'about three quid a week', credit 'for all virtues he possessed, and to hear her giving evidence against her husband one would think he was a model man'. She did, however, allege he had a 'filthy habit' that she said made it impossible for her to live in the same house with him. She admitted that Tom was of 'most temperate habits' but claimed he 'used very bad language'. There had been strong disagreements between the couple, with interference from Tom's mother-in-law, about him disciplining their son and he left her in July 1912 after she refused to move to a Brisbane boarding house with him. The magistrate refused to make an order for Wilhelmina and deferred judgement on a maintenance allowance for their son.[57]

Wilhelmina Shaw petitioned for divorce on the ground of desertion and a decree nisi was granted in mid-1917, with that being made absolute in September 1918.[58] Just prior to the divorce being made absolute, Tom and Wilhelmina's son, Ivan Conrad Victor Shaw, aged fourteen, was accidentally drowned in a lagoon at Boggabilla, New South Wales.[59]

Thomas John Shaw applied at Victoria Barracks, Sydney in 1917, to enlist in the Australian Imperial Force (AIF). He signed the application 'Thos J Shaw' on 2 March and gave his address as 9 Australia Street, Croydon, Sydney. Tom stated his occupation as cycle mechanic. His age was recorded as 38 years 8 months and his height as 5 ft 4 and a quarter inches. After a preliminary medical examination he was declared unfit for service – the reason given being stated simply as 'Cardiac'. On 15 November 1917, Thomas John Shaw, now describing himself as a fitter, of 9 Australia Street, Croydon, Sydney, made a further application at Victoria Barracks to enlist in the AIF. His age was now recorded as 39 years and 5 months and his height as 5'5". In a margin of the application form it was recorded he was born in Sydney, that he weighed 150 lbs (68 kg) and was Presbyterian. Again, as a result of a preliminary medical examination, it was decided he was unfit for service – the reason given was 'Cardiac Apex displaced'. In March 1917 he is shown as married. In November 1917 he is shown as single. No other papers are on the military record of Thomas John Shaw.[60]

Thomas John Shaw, who stated his occupation as a motor fitter, married Alice Hutchings at Burwood in 1919.[61] At first the Shaws lived at Croydon, where a daughter was born in 1922. By early 1923 the family had bought property and moved to Merrylands, an outer Sydney suburb near Parramatta on the city's rural-urban fringe, where a son was born in that year.

Alice Shaw died, aged 35, on 24 September 1927[62] leaving Tom with two young children.

At the time of Alice's death Tom, who had been in business on his own account at Merrylands from about 1923, was proprietor of a bicycle shop in the nearby suburb of Granville. Following Tom's ownership of that business for a period approaching three years a sequestration order was made against him in the Supreme Court of New South Wales in Bankruptcy on 5 August 1927, just six weeks prior to his wife's death. The Sydney Novelty Company initiated the proceedings against him.

While aware of the death of Tom's wife shortly after his sequestration, the court did what it had to do and attempted to proceed quickly to deal with his bankrupt estate. That process did not occur with the level of co-operation from Tom that the court expected and the matter of winding up the estate was delayed. Public examinations of Tom before the Supreme Court's Registrar of Bankruptcy stretched through to November 1928 and revealed his poor record keeping, his continued failure to prepare an accurate statement of his affairs despite repeated and strong requests and that, at times, he was less than truthful with the court. He admitted that while he disputed some of the creditors' claims he could not produce evidence to support the stances he took about them. He also admitted that he accepted money from debtors after his sequestration and appropriated it for his own use, a practice the registrar suggested was stealing from his own estate.[63] The impression Tom gave was that he was naive, incompetent in financial matters and irresponsible.

Tom's Statement of Affairs was to summarise his assets and liabilities as at the date of his sequestration in August 1927. When he finally presented the statement in April 1928 it showed no cash in hand or at the bank and business debts of £215/18/3, all of which were 'bad debts' unlikely to be recovered. The statement listed 47 debtors who had bought new or used bicycles or parts and accessories (that he termed 'bicycle stuff') from him or who had him carry out repairs to their machines. Most were from Granville and Merrylands and the nearby suburbs of Auburn, Lidcombe, Harris Park, Wentworthville and Guildford.[64] Tom's business served a largely local clientele.

The Statement of Affairs also showed he owed money to a number of unsecured creditors. Bennett and Barkell, bicycle manufacturers and accessory suppliers, were owed £74 and £68 was due to the Sydney Novelty Company. Lesser amounts were owed for the supply of 250 calendars, lamps, and 30 cheap watches. Secured creditors were owed £118 on the Merrylands property, a small house and four blocks of land, for which Tom had paid £350 in December 1922, on household furniture and on business stock in trade.[65]

In late May 1928, the *Cumberland Argus and Fruitgrowers Advocate*, the principal Parramatta newspaper of the day, advertised that the family's furniture had been removed from the house and was for sale by auction.[66] In early November of that year the same newspaper carried an advertisement for the sale the Shaw property, detailing it as 'All That Parcel of Land, situate at Merrylands, having a frontage of about 60ft to Warialda St, by a depth through to Como Street of about 220ft, the frontage to Como Street being 20ft … Together with Weatherboard Cottage of three rooms erected thereon'.[67] In May 1929 a *New South Wales Government Gazette* notice referred to Thomas John Shaw, of Sydney Road, Granville, as a cycle manufacturer and notified his creditors that the first plan of distribution of his bankrupt estate showed payment of 'a dividend of threepence three-sixteenths of a penny in the £ on all proved concurrent claims'.[68]

At his Granville business premises Thomas John Shaw manufactured bicycles branded T. J. S.[69] in (at least) 1925 and 1926. While very little is known of this small-scale manufacturing venture, an advertisement placed by his 'Northern District Agent' at Woy Woy on the central coast of New South Wales in 1926 stated they were 'Built to Order – any shape or size'.[70] In some association he had with the Woy Woy bicycle club, Tom donated one of his T. J. S. bicycles as a road race prize in 1925. The prize was for the T. J. S. Bicycle Competition, which was unusual in that competitors rode in fifteen races, at weekly intervals and involving several central coast road racing courses ranging from twelve to 20 miles, but with only twelve of their rides counting in the competition. The race was run on a 'secret point score basis', with the results forwarded each Monday to the manager of the National Bank at Granville, with 'that gentleman … to decide the winner' in a way that was not explained.[71] In a further attempt to promote his bicycles, Tom donated a T. J. S. Bicycle as third prize in the 1926 Goulburn to Sydney amateur road race.[72]

The late 1920s were very difficult years for Tom but he recovered from his losses and continued his active association with the bicycle trade over the following decades. Electoral rolls recorded Tom as a cycle mechanic at addresses in Granville in the 1930s and at Homebush in 1943 and 1949.

After a life built around bicycles, Thomas John Shaw, aged 78, died at Homebush, Sydney in 1956.[73]

CHAPTER 7

The Brother-in-Law: Brice Heber Thomas

Mary Amelia Shaw and Brice Heber Thomas, c.1893.
Thomas family archives

Brice Heber Thomas was conceived on the Winburndale gold diggings, near Bathurst, New South Wales and, like his seven brothers and sisters, would have been born there in a tent or crude hut had his parents not separated. Brice's father, William Hinton Thomas, deserted his pregnant wife, Mary Sarah Thomas (née Corrie) and his seven children and headed for the new north Queensland diggings. Mary Sarah made her way to Sydney, where she had the support of her mother, Elizabeth Corrie (née Dawson).

Sadly, Mary Sarah's youngest child, not yet two years old, died in March 1874[1] in Glebe and then Brice Heber Thomas was born on 11 July[2] at Camperdown, Sydney. When Brice was six his mother remarried to Joseph Staples,[3] an ironworker, and the family lived at Redfern.[4] When Brice was thirteen, his stepfather died.[5]

After Brice finished his schooling, probably at the age of about fourteen, he began work with a tailor and in 1890, when he was sixteen, was awarded an honours pass in tailors' cutting in examinations conducted by Sydney Technical College.[6] Later in 1890 he won a Grade 1 Honours award in examinations at the college that year.[7] Brice Thomas was employed as a tailor's cutter, and then as a manager for a tailoring firm, for most of his working life and operated a small grocery store for some years before his retirement.

'To Mary from Brice'

Mary Amelia Shaw, who was born on 16 July 1874 at Riley Street, Woolloomooloo,[8] was the youngest of the three daughters of William Shaw and Mary Anne Shaw (née Inch), and youngest sister of the five cycling Shaw brothers. Brice and Mary knew one another at least as early as 1889 when they were both fifteen and when Brice was bold enough to give Mary a sparsely worded Christmas and New Year card simply inscribed 'To Mary from Brice'.[9] Thus Brice, from an early age, was acquainted with all of the Shaw brothers who then or later raced bicycles. Six years later he became their brother-in-law.

Brice and his bicycles

Like many other young men of his age, Brice adopted the bicycle as his means of personal transport and then raced bicycles as a sport. Some of his very early riding was on ordinaries or penny farthings and he retained a heavy iron-framed one into the 1940s,[10] apparently for sentimental reasons. Men did become very attached to their ordinaries even long after they moved on to more modern machines.

Most, if not all, of Brice's competition riding was on safety bicycles. Although he is likely to have ridden in minor club competition events beforehand, perhaps sometimes on ordinaries, the first record of his racing that has been located is for a one-mile race, held under the auspices of the newly-formed Austral Bicycle Club at the Drummoyne Park Fete and Garden Party in June 1892, as he approached his eighteenth birthday. Like other charity events hoping to draw large spectator crowds, this fete, as it was called, offered a wide range of attractions, 'a great programme of sport', that included bicycle, pedestrian and boat racing as well as a tug-of-war between teams of cyclists. Sideshows and refreshment stalls were on hand to widen the appeal for those that travelled to the sports day by ferry from the city.

Just as the Drummoyne Fete was a mixed sports day so, too, was its one-mile bicycle race a mixed event. At this time, when ordinaries had almost disappeared from competition, they were permitted to race against safety bicycles in this event. And as tyre technology was rapidly changing, cycles with the old solid tyres, others with cushion tyres and still others with the newer pneumatic tyres were all allowed. Twenty-six riders were listed to start. Brice Thomas, riding a safety bicycle with cushion tyres, was allocated a handicap of 70 yards, while Sam Shaw, as mentioned in Chapter 3, on an ordinary cycle with solid tyres was to ride off 165 yards. Neither Brice nor Sam was placed.[11]

Also in June 1892, Brice, along with William and Sam Shaw, rode in the Suburban Bicycle Club's Open Road Race over the ten-mile Botany course off a handicap of 5 minutes and 45 seconds. While Brice raced on cushion tyres, William and Sam's machines were shod with the older style solid tyres. Brice Thomas was unplaced.[12]

In September 1892, Brice, now eighteen, raced at the Sydney Bicycle Club's 11th Annual Amateur Race Meeting at the Association Cricket Ground, Moore Park. Riding on the grass track for the Crusaders' Bicycle Club, and sporting silks of dark and light blue, Brice raced in a field of eight roadsters in his heat of the One-Mile Maiden Scratch Race ('four times round') but was unplaced. The afternoon's events, which also saw Sam Shaw race in the Three-Mile Open Handicap ('for the Ladies Bracelets') comprised nineteen events run off between 2.30pm and 5pm.[13] Brice saw a lot of racing on the day that was likely his first as a competitor on what was to become the Sydney Cricket Ground.

At that meeting, at which riders from the Crusaders', Sydney, Speedwell, Eclipse, Suburban and Redfern clubs raced, rain fell throughout the afternoon, making conditions uncomfortable for the riders and the grass track 'treacherous and dangerous'. One newspaper reported that, 'Nearly 20 falls occurred, and the damage done to machines represents a large amount of money. Some are almost unmendable while others are badly buckled and twisted'[14] and went on to say that one rider fell three times, each time breaking a different machine. The meeting was followed by a smoke concert at Quong Tart's tea rooms.

Brice next entered the Austral Bicycle Club's Open Road Race, for £7, £3 and £2 on 17 September. His handicap was 4 minutes 30 seconds, while that of William Nathaniel Shaw, a much more experienced rider on the racetrack, was allocated a handicap of 2 minutes and 45 seconds. Given that the race was run over the Botany course (but slightly shortened to under ten miles), the small difference in starts strongly suggested that the handicappers held a high opinion of Brice and his chances of being among the leaders at the finish. Thirty riders raced, one on an unusual pneumatic ordinary. Neither Brice nor William took home a prize in the club's first cash prize road race, described as 'the club's maiden effort to cater for those riders who prefer cash to trophies'[15] following leads from Victorian clubs. Brice had chosen the professional path.

The Speedwell Bicycle Club held its annual road race for members, again for £7, £3 and £2, over the Botany course in late May 1893. One report of the race provided information about Brice's handicap and those of both William and Henry Shaw that showed where each started in relation to one another and the race's other riders, as well as race conditions, that pacers were used, and outcomes:

> There was a very strong northerly wind, and the road, which had just been watered, was very treacherous in parts. The following were the handicaps: – P. E. Wootten scratch, A. Hawken, J. M 'Innes 45sec., E. D. Smith 1min. 30sec., W. F. Phelan 1min. 50sec., E. E. Debelle, F. Rathgen 2min. 40sec., W. L. Lancaster 3min. 5sec., W. W. [*sic*] Shaw 3min. 25sec., B. A. Simmonds, J. B. Buck 4min., D. Exland 4min.15sec., H. S. Cusack 4min. 20sec., C. Neilson 4min. 25sec., E. Howson 4min. 40sec., B. Thomas 5min., H. Shaw 6min., F. W. Thompson 7min. Punctually at 3.30 the limit was sent away, and the rest got well away to their allotted times. The strong northerly wind gave them an excellent lead to Botany, but the road in some parts was very slippery, and consequently some of the men fell, including Thompson and the scratch man, P. Wootten. Neilson, who was riding exceedingly well, took up the lead before reaching Botany, with Buck lying second. M'Innes and Hawken, both riding well, were not, however, able to catch the front men. Coming up to the cross-roads the hill told on Neilson with his high gear, but he got up all right. Buck and Cusack came up in splendid style, the former looking the freshest of any of the men. The various pace makers took the men along at a good pace, but the wind now was dead against them, and the pace slackened down considerably. Neilson was, however, too good. The following are the results and the actual times of riding: – C. Neilson, 33min. 6sec., 1; J. Buck, 34min. 11sec.,

> 2; F. Ruthgen, 33min. 54sec., 3; M'Innes, 32min, 31sec.; Hawken, 33min. 6sec.; Smith, 33min. 15sec.; Debelle, 34min. 1sec.; Phelan, 34min. 16sec.; Wooten, 34min. 41 3-5sec. The others finished at long intervals …[16]

However, despite its detail the race article leaves the reader none the wiser about whether Brice and the two Shaw brothers were among those who fell or whether they were among the others who 'finished at long intervals' or, indeed, the order in which the three men reached the finish.

40 races at Lillie Bridge

After mid-1893, Brice Thomas turned his attention to racing at the Lillie Bridge bicycle and pony race meetings, many of which were held at night (including week nights, when Mondays, Wednesdays and Thursdays were favoured) under electric light.

Between August 1893 and May 1895, Brice raced on at least 40 occasions at the Lillie Bridge night meetings, an arrangement that fitted well with his day job as a tailor's cutter in the city. The mixed-programmes for these meetings 'for ponies and cyclists' invariably comprised several pony races and one bicycle race, with the bicycle race usually being the first event of the night. The bicycle races were conducted variously over half a mile, one mile, one and a half miles, two miles and three miles with there being no apparent pattern to that arrangement. All races were handicap events, the winner sometimes receiving £20. When races were postponed because of bad weather they were rescheduled and run off within a matter of days.

It is difficult to be precise about the number of races conducted at Lillie Bridge and their outcomes. No official records that may have been kept of these privately sponsored meetings have been located so that information about the racing is entirely dependent on newspaper reports. No one newspaper, however, published comprehensive coverage but information published before and after races can be learned from a range of papers. Prior to meetings, often on the day they were to be held, details of the handicaps that had been declared was made available for the cyclists and for possible spectators who may have wished to consider their betting options. On the day after races a more restricted range of newspapers than had publicised handicaps published the results but often only naming the winner and with no details of the running of the race.

Nevertheless, much useful information about Brice's participation in bicycle racing at Lillie Bridge over an almost two-year period to May 1895 can be gleaned from the newspaper reports that are available. Starters in races numbered from six or seven through to 20, and occasionally more. Brice's best-known competitors, usually racing from scratch or thereabouts, included champions of the day such as Joe Megson, Bob Lewis and W.F. Phelan. They also often included William Shaw, sometimes included Henry Shaw and, on at least one occasion, Sam Shaw. The starts allotted to Brice generally decreased over time with this signalling that the handicappers were aware he was improving his riding times over the various distances.

There is only one report of Brice winning at Lillie Bridge. On 5 December 1894 he won the One-Mile Handicap by ten yards in a time of 2 minutes 56¾ seconds. Shortly afterwards, on two other occasions in January 1895, he was placed second in races over one mile, with this only being known from the newspapers when they reported that the winners had beaten Thomas by so many yards. Betting was part and parcel of the Lillie Bridge experience and, on occasions, the press published details of the odds. In a January 1894 race that Joe Megson won odds laid between pairs of riders showed 'Thomas 10 to 1 v. Megson' and in the race Brice won on 5 December 1894 the odds were 5 to 1 against him.[17]

The Young Harry *and the* Regina

As was the case with Fred Shaw, and to a lesser extent Henry Tait Shaw, Brice Thomas combined competitive sailing with competitive cycling in his sporting calendar. He did not own his own boat but served as a working hand on boats owned by others.

Brice sailed as a crewmember on the 24-foot dinghy sailboat *Young Harry* in competitions in Sydney Harbour in 1893 and 1894 with much of this activity dovetailed with his Lillie Bridge racing programme. He is shown in a group photograph captioned 'Young Harry Sailing Crew 1893' as a nineteen-year-old leisure sailor.[18] The photograph of sixteen men also showed Henry Tait Shaw, Brice's future brother-in-law, and George Robert Parrett, the skipper, brother of Will[iam] Parrett, who was also later to be a brother-in-law of Brice Thomas when he married Christina (Teenie) Shaw in 1895.

George Parrett, who by 1901 had become vice-president of the Sydney Flying Squadron, skippered the 24-foot *Young Harry* in races at least 21 times between 7 November 1892 and 1 April 1895 (the actual number is likely to have considerably exceeded this because sometimes the skipper's name was not mentioned in newspaper coverage). The boat contested events sponsored by the Johnstone's Bay, Port Jackson, East Sydney, North Sydney and Port Hacking sailing clubs, the Double Bay, Anniversary, Balmain, and Sydney Flying Squadron regattas, and the NSW v Queensland Intercolonial Sailing Carnival. It is impossible to learn from the various newspaper sources of this data those sailings in which Brice Thomas participated because, with rare exceptions, only the skipper's name appeared in newspaper race reports.

Just as members of cycling clubs organised social events to build cohesion and to include lady friends and families so, too, did sailing clubs and the owners of sailboats. In May 1894 the *Sydney Morning Herald* carried an account of an excursion and sailing club picnic sponsored by George Parrett:

> A successful outing was carried through by the members of the Young Harry sailing crew on Saturday last. The picnic was arranged to celebrate the closing of the sailing season. About 25 couples left Double Bay pier about 10 a.m. in the

> steamer Reliance, which conveyed the party some distance up Middle Harbour, after which a return was made to Pearl Bay, where all landed. Various forms of amusement were then indulged in, dancing finding most favour, to the strains of Toni's band. At 2 o'clock the party were invited to an excellent luncheon, served by Mr Moon. Mr J. Pringle occupied the chair. Toasts were proposed, amongst which were – 'The Skipper,' 'Success to Sailing,' 'Vice-Skipper,' 'The Ladies,' 'The Secretary,' 'Working Hands,' 'Our Visitors,' and 'The Press,' each of which was responded to. During the proceedings, Mr R. F. Jones was the recipient of a beautifully illuminated address from the members of the crew, the work of Mr R. Pringle. A large photo of the Young Harry, nicely framed, was also presented to the skipper, Mr George Parrett, by Mr F. Chapman.[19]

In a similar account of the crew's 1894 picnic day, the *Australian Star* added that this was this crew's sixth annual picnic day together under George Parrett and that the six years had involved the 24-footers *Our Jack* (two seasons), *Our Tom* (one season), *Regina* (one season) and *Young Harry* (two seasons). The account also said that the expenses of the season were defrayed by the season's winnings and that 'the whole of the present members' had signified their intention of continuing for the next season.[20]

In a rare published listing, Brice was shown as a crewmember aboard the 24-foot dinghy sailing boat *Regina* to contest the Australian Anniversary Handicap on 26 January 1892 against 20 other sailboats. Prizes were £25 and a champion gold medal to the captain, £10 and £5. The Sydney Harbour course was from a line between the starter's boat and the flagship, around Fort Denison, around the lightship and Sow and Pigs [reef] around Shark Island, back to the flagship and finishing between the flagship and Clark Island. George Parrett skippered the boat and the 20-man crew included Brice Thomas, William Shaw, Sam Shaw and Henry Tait Shaw.[21] *Regina* finished the course but was unplaced.

While George Parrett clearly trained and retained a crew across several summer sailing seasons, it is inevitable that some changes to membership took place over the six years referred to. Nevertheless, this information suggests the possibility that Brice Thomas and some of the Shaw brothers sailed together on the very demanding 24-footers on Sydney Harbour from as early as 1889, the year Brice met Mary Shaw, his future wife.

A gold medal from a win at Goulburn?

Gold medal presented to Brice Thomas by the League of New South Wales Wheelmen. Thomas family archives

The Goulburn branch was one of the first established after the League of New South Wales Wheelmen was formed in September 1893. Brice Thomas participated in their two major race carnivals in 1894, one in May and the other in November.

Goulburn's Olympic Ground was the venue for the first meeting, held on 24 May to celebrate the Queen's birthday. A large crowd of spectators turned out on a bitterly cold day to watch the racing on the ground's cinder track. Brice Thomas, riding a 32 lb machine off a handicap of 55 yards, won the first heat of the One-Mile Novice Handicap and 'rode well' to win the final by ten yards, the prize for which was £4.[22] Twenty riders contested the event. It is likely that the prize was the gold medallion valued at £4 that Brice wore on a chain throughout his entire life. Of the numerous photographs of Brice in Thomas and Shaw family albums, showing him formally dressed (including at his 50th and 60th wedding anniversaries) and informally on picnics and camping trips, it is rare to find him not wearing the medal. It is clear he was immensely proud of it.

At the same meeting, at which William and Sam Shaw also raced, Brice was entered in the One-Mile Handicap, off 85 yards, and the Two-Mile Handicap, off 355 yards. He did not start in the one-mile event. In the two-mile race, he was placed fourth in his heat but was not successful in the final.

The cycling carnival was a highlight of the Queen's Birthday celebrations for the people of Goulburn. A local paper reported:

> The most successful cycling event, and one of the most exciting and pleasant day's amusement ever held in Goulburn took place on the Olympic Ground yesterday in the presence of about 800 spectators, amongst whom was noticed a large number of ladies, whose bright faces and neat costumes gave a very pleasing effect to the oval, and shows that the ladies are not going to be left out when there is a good day's sport to be enjoyed …
>
> Mr Magee of the Post-office hotel had a booth on the ground and appeared to be well patronised. A fruit-stall by Mrs Bigwood of Eastgrove was also liberally attended. A dressing-tent for the competitors had been erected under the shed at the western and of the ground, and the men were well sheltered from the wind. The track, which is laid down in cinders, was in splendid condition, and the riders

> expressed themselves as well satisfied with it, which speaks well for those who had the matter in hand. All the riders wore jockey costumes, which had a very pleasing effect. Most of the competitors rode racing machines specially brought from Sydney for the occasion …
>
> The final contest for the Two-mile Handicap caused a vast amount of excitement. Men cried themselves hoarse and threw their hats in the air; ladies clapped their hands, and without doubt the majority seemed to have only one thought and wish, and that was that the local favourite should win. The excitement reached the climax when Everett passed the post some ten or fifteen yards in front of Shaw. On dismounting, the winner was carried shoulder-high to the dressing tent.[23]

The second Goulburn cycling carnival for 1894, the 'Grand Carnival' as it was described, was set down for 9 and 10 November and again Brice Thomas, this time with Sam and Henry Shaw, made the journey by train to participate. Brice entered for the Half-Mile Handicap, off 80 yards, the One-Mile handicap, off 190 yards, and the Two-Mile Handicap, The Goulburn Wheel Race, off 380 yards. Based on their experience with the League carnival earlier in the year, the Goulburn organisers offered the public and the riders an event to dominate the town's weekend. A report on the first day's racing in the *Goulburn Herald* summarised the event's attractions:

> A two-days' cycling carnival, under the auspices of the Goulburn branch of the New South Wales League of Wheelmen, was commenced on the Olympic Ground to-day, and will be continued to-morrow. It is undoubtedly the best cycling ever held in Goulburn, and the fact that the ten-mile championship of New South Wales is included in the second day's programme adds greatly to its importance.

For this event, which is timed to start at half-past four to-morrow, there are no less than fourteen entries, including the Melbourne men D. Walker and L. Scharp, and J. Megson, R. W. Lewis, and J. McInroe, the Sydney cracks, besides other good riders [including Sam Shaw] of less repute.

The weather on the first day was fine, with a strong wind blowing, which very greatly interfered with fast riding, but the gathering was thoroughly successful, over two thousand persons being present. A special reserve was set apart and provided with seats for ladies, of whom a goodly number were present. The track, four laps of which go to a mile, is composed of cinders, and is all that could be desired for racing purposes. …

Mr O'Halloran of the Cooma Hotel had the publican's booth, and the cake and fruit stall was in the hands of Mr T. Byrne. Both appeared to be doing fairly well.

Prior to the starting of the sports a procession of cyclists was formed at the corner of Auburn and Goldsmith streets and proceeded to the ground. About twenty-five cyclists took part, the procession being headed by one of the old-fashioned 'bone-shakers.'

At one o'clock several members of the City Band marched to the ground, playing on the way, and they contributed several selections throughout the afternoon.

For the first day's racing nine events were down on the programme, the principal being the Goulburn Wheel Race of two miles, for which thirty-four entries were received. Much interest was also centred in the half-mile open handicap and the three miles race. Proceedings commenced at twelve o'clock with the first heat of the half-mile open handicap, for which thirty entries had been received.[24]

Brice Thomas, racing for £5, £2, £1, looked good in his heat of the half-mile race. In what was described 'a grand contest' Brice led to within 150 yards from home in his heat but was beaten by Joe Megson. In the Goulburn Wheel Race, for £30, £6, £2 and £1 plus £1 for the winners of each heat, Brice was placed second in his heat but was unplaced in the final.

On the second day of the carnival Brice led in his heat of the One-Mile Handicap, for £10, £3 and £1, until about 100 yards before the finish but was beaten to the line by others who 'carried too many guns'. He also started in the last race of the day, the Beaten Stakes Handicap, for £2, £1 and 10/-, a consolation race for all who had not won a first prize during the meeting. While he led during the second lap, Brice was unplaced in the race. In the manner of the day, as reported by the press, as this race concluded the proceedings, the band struck up God Save the Queen.[25]

Marriage, a family, tailoring, managing, a mixed business and an Etna connection

Brice Heber Thomas, tailor's cutter, married Mary Amelia Shaw at Woollahra, Sydney on 18 December 1895[26], five months after they both turned 21. No record has been located that suggests Brice cycled or sailed competitively after that date. It reads almost as if Brice's cessation of sporting competition was a condition of the marriage since Mary was said to have been concerned about injuries and that competition, along with the training to prepare for it, was time consuming and potentially detrimental to family life, especially at a time when the working week stretched through to midday on Saturdays.

Brice and his growing family lived at Woollahra, Enfield, Leichhardt, Waverley and Arncliffe[27] in Sydney and he continued in employment as a tailor's cutter, eventually working his way up to a management position with the city tailoring firm of Palmers. A photograph of Palmers' employees in the early 1900s shows Brice, James Shaw and Henry Tait Shaw all worked for this same firm at that time.[28] After 1933, with his wife Mary,

Brice conducted a mixed business and grocery store at Stoney Creek Road, Bexley, Sydney. He had a long association with Masonic lodges, including in senior roles, and in 1908 and 1909 chaired meetings of the Leichhardt, Petersham and Annandale Starr-Bowkett Society.[29]

In November 1920, Brice joined with George Christopher Bellingham to form the Etna Plate Polish Company to manufacture and wholesale a polish for cleaning silver plating.[30] The company was registered at 67 Alt Street, Waverley, Brice's home address, but it is unlikely he gave up his day job in favour of this venture. George Christopher Bellingham, of Parramatta Road, Annandale and William Street, Sydney, was a manufacturing confectioner with machinery able to manufacture and package the product, that was made in blocks the size of a cake of soap and packaged in a branded cardboard box, an example of which, with its contents, has survived.[31] While the product was intended for use in polishing household EPNS (electro plated nickel silver) items such as teapots and serving trays and for silverware, brass and copper, it may also have had an outlet in the bicycle trade for use in polishing EPNS, brass and copper bicycle parts and may have first been made for that use. While no record has been found of the period over which Etna Plate Polish was produced by Brice Thomas and George Bellingham, it is clear that it was manufactured in quantity: one saleroom offered 100 dozen boxes of the polish at a city auction in 1923.[32] Adoption of the brand name Etna, a name previously favoured by Fred Shaw for his 14-footer dinghy sailboat, and for the bicycles and motorcycles he manufactured at Newtown and Camden, suggests the possibility that the product originated with him.

Brice Thomas died, aged 84, on 29 November 1958.[33] Mary Amelia Thomas (née Shaw) died, aged 85, on 5 June 1960.[34]

Notes

1 – Backstories: Bicycling, the Shaw Family and Woolloomooloo

1 Jim Fitzpatrick, *Wheeling Matilda: The Story of Australian Cycling*, Kilcoy, Queensland, Star Hill Studio, 2013, p. 3.

2 See Paul Farren, 'The Cycle Industry in the Australian Colonies During the 1880s', in Claire Simpson (ed.), *Scorchers, Ramblers and Rovers: Australian Cycling Histories*, Melbourne, Australian Society for Sports History, 2006.

3 Jim Fitzpatrick, 'Cycling', in Wray Vamplew et al. (eds.), *The Oxford Companion to Australian Sport*, Melbourne, Oxford University Press, 1997, p. 129.

4 Ibid.

5 Ibid.

6 Charles Spencer, *The Bicycle Road Book*, cited in Frederick Alderson, *Bicycling: A History*, Newton Abbott, David & Charles, 1972, p. 28, emphasis added.

7 Paul Smethurst, *The Bicycle: Towards a Global History*, Basingstoke, Hampshire, Palgrave Macmillan, 2015, p. 39.

8 See David Herlihy, *Bicycle: The History*, New Haven, Yale University Press, 2004 for a rich and marvellously illustrated exposition of high wheelers or ordinaries and the subtle differences between different makes and models.

9 Smethurst, *The Bicycle*, p. 40.

10 R. A. Buchanan, *The Power of the Machine: The Impact of Technology from 1700 to the Present Day*, London, Penguin, p. 147.

11 Jim Fitzpatrick, 'The Spectrum of Australian Bicycle Racing: 1890–1900', in Richard Cashman and Michael McKernan (eds.), *Sport in History: The Making of Modern Sporting History*, Brisbane, University of Queensland Press, 1979, p. 326.

12 Fitzpatrick, *Wheeling Matilda*, p. 5.

13 H. Graves, George Lacey Hillier and Susan, Countess of Malmesbury, *Cycling*, London, Lawrence and Bullen, 1898.

14 Fiona Kinsey, 'Stamina, Speed and Adventure: Australian Women and Competitive Cycling in the 1890s', *The International Journal of the History of Sport*, 28, 10, 2011, pp. 1376–9.

15 Ibid., pp. 1379–82.

16 Ibid., pp. 1382–3.

17 Sydney Cricket Ground Museum, *Celebrating 120 Years of the Ladies Pavilion*, Sydney, 2016.

18 Fiona Kinsey, 'Australian Women Cyclists in the 1890s', in Claire Simpson (ed.), *Scorchers, Ramblers and Rovers: Australian Cycling Histories*, Melbourne, Australian Society for Sports History, 2006, p. 87.

19 Kinsey, 'Australian Women Cyclists', p. 87.

20 'A Prominent Lady Cyclist: Miss Eta Todd', *Cycling Gazette,* 19 November 1895, p. 13.

21 *Cycling Gazette,* 19 November 1895, p. 15.

22 *Cycling Gazette,* 16 January 1897, p. 3.

23 Marc Rerceretnam, 'Cycling Communities: Bicycle Clubs in Australia with an Emphasis on Sydney, c.1860s–2000s', *Journal of the Royal Australian Historical Society,* 103, 2, pp. 154–80; *Sydney Bicycle Club, Twelfth Annual Report,* 21 October 1891.

24 Fitzpatrick, '*Cycling*', p. 129.

25 F.G. Chippendale Hanslow (ed.), *Australian Cycling Annual: A Complete Record of Australian Cycling and Other Interesting Information*, Sydney, George Robertson & Co., 1897, pp. 78–98. This hefty 'annual' saw only one issue published, 1897.

26 See *Australian Star,* 19 May 1896, p. 3; *Sunday Times,* 31 May 1896, p. 5; and 'Society Doings in Sydney', *Australasian,* 10 July 1897, p. 42.

27 Hanslow, *Australian Cycling Annual,* pp. 131–2.

28 *Sydney Bicycle Club, Rules 1890* (including Library Rules approved August 1899), Fry Family, Papers of James Arthur Barrett Fry 1860–1926, Box 2, Mitchell Library, Sydney. See also *Sydney Bicycle Club, Ninth Annual Race Meeting, Official Programme,* 30 August 1890, Association Ground, Moore Park.

29 Original invitation card preserved in W. H. Kavanagh, *Album Collection of News Cuttings, Tickets, Invitations, Business Cards and Other Memorabilia Related to Australian Cycling 1886–1912*, State Library of New South Wales, unpaginated.

30 Michael Hutchinson, *Re: Cyclists: 200 Years on Two Wheels*, London, Bloomsbury, 2017.

31 *Speedwell Bicycle Club, Third Annual Report and Balance Sheet,* 1890, pp. 1–2.

32 *Sydney Bicycle Club, Twentieth Annual Report,* 3 January 1900, Fry Family, Papers of James Arthur Barrett Fry 1860–1926, Box 2, Mitchell Library, Sydney.

33 Original invitation card preserved in Kavanagh, *Album Collection.*

34 *Sydney Wheelman,* 22 August 1895, p. 17.

35 Original invitation card preserved in Kavanagh, *Album Collection.*

36 Craig Fry, 'Cycling', in Dave Nadel and Graeme Ryan (eds.), *Sport in Victoria: A History,* Melbourne, Ryan Publishing and Australian Society for Sports History, 2015, p. 73.

37 *New South Wales Cyclists' Union, Seventeenth Annual Report,* 28 March 1900, pp. 9–10.

38 *Handbook, New South Wales Cyclists' Touring Union,* 1898, Powerhouse Museum, Sydney, Object No. 90/542.

39 See, for example, 'Street Scorchers', *Sydney Wheelman,* 5 September 1895, p. 31.

40 'The World 'A Wheel', *Sydney Mail*, 25 July 1896, p. 176.

41 *Cycling Gazette*, 19 November 1896, p. 13.

42 *Cycling Gazette*, 30 January 1897, p. 147.

43 *Official Programme, First Meeting of the Darlinghurst Harriers Amateur Athletics Club*, Association Cricket Ground, Sydney, 25 July 1891.

44 Joannah Luetjens, 'Cycling Through the History of Melbourne', *Agora*, 48, 1, 2013, p. 24.

45 The Australian Natives' Association (ANA) was a Melbourne-based friendly society whose membership was restricted to white men born in Australia.

46 Fitzpatrick, *Wheeling Matilda*, p. 135.

47 Keith Dunstan, *Sports*, Melbourne, Cassell, 1973, p. 206.

48 Dunstan, *Sports*, p. 207.

49 Sydney High School, *Official Programme for Amateur Athletic Club, 3rd Annual Sports Meeting*, Association Cricket Ground, Moore Park, 9 May 1888.

50 Sydney High School, *Official Programme*.

51 H. ('Curly') Grivell, *Australian Cycling in the Golden Days*, Adelaide, Courier Press, 1952, p. 14.

52 Hanslow, *Australian Cycling Annual*, p. 121.

53 *Sydney Wheelman*, 19 September 1895, p. 64.

54 Hanslow, *Australian Cycling Annual*, p. 300.

55 *Redfern Bicycle Club – Rules 1899*, p. 2.

56 *West Australian Wheelman*, 31 December 1897, p. 2.

57 Robert Smith, *A Social History of the Bicycle: Its Life and Times in America*, New York, American Heritage Press, 1972, p. 161.

58 Kavanagh, *Album Collection*. See also *The Australian Cyclist*, 5 July 1900, p. 22.

59 Dunstan, *Sports*, p. 212.

60 Hanslow, *Australian Cycling Annual*, pp. 398–9.

61 *Sydney Wheelman*, 12 September 1895, p. 50.

62 *League of New South Wales Wheelmen, Second Annual Report*, 17 April 1895, p. 1.

63 *League of New South Wales Wheelmen, Third Annual Report*, 19 April 1896, p. 1.

64 Ibid., p. 5.

65 Advertising card issued by the Newcastle Branch, League of New South Wales Wheelmen to promote their forthcoming Easter Race Meeting, 1898, Kavanagh, *Album Collection*.

66 *Programme, Bourke Branch, League of New South Wales Wheelmen, Bicycle Carnival*, Bourke Show Ground, Good Friday, 8 April 1898.

67 *Daily Telegraph* (Sydney), 10 September 1900, p. 3.

68 Fitzpatrick, '*The Spectrum*', p. 331.

69 Those consulted for this work are held in the State Library of New South Wales/ Mitchell Library in the Davis Sporting Collection, the E. S. Marks Collection, the Fry Family Papers and the 1886–1912 cycling memorabilia album collection

of W.H. Kavanagh who began racing for smaller clubs and subsequently rode in events conducted by the League of New South Wales Wheelmen and then became an official of the League.

70 For example a bound volume, H. A. Fry, *Interclub Race Meetings 1884–1893*, Sydney, 1927, likely a one-off album, was auctioned from a private collection in Queensland. It is not in any Australian library and now is probably in a private collection. According to auction notes, the volume contains a copy of a pamphlet, W. R. George, *A Short Sketch of the History of the Sydney Bicycle Club*, 1896, and about 25 cycle race programmes.

71 *Suburban Bicycle Club, Grand Amateur Race Meeting, Official Programme,* Association Cricket Ground, Moore Park, 17 May 1890.

72 *Speedwell Bicycle Club, Grand Amateur Autumn Race Meeting, Official Programme,* Lillie Bridge Ground, Forest Lodge, 30 May 1890.

73 Advertisement for Jaye and Freeman, Keppel Street, Bathurst, *Official Programme, Occidental Bicycle Club, Bathurst, Fourth Annual Amateur Race Meeting,* Bathurst Cricket Ground, Prince of Wales' Birthday, Friday, 9 November 1888, p. 17, Fry Family, Papers of James Arthur Barrett Fry 1860–1926, Box 3, Mitchell Library, Sydney.

74 *Official Programme, League of New South Wales Wheelmen, Monster Cycling Carnival,* Agricultural Ground, First Day, Saturday 7 October 1899, Fry Family, Papers of James Arthur Barrett Fry 1860–1926, Box 3, Mitchell Library, Sydney.

75 Grivell, *Australian Cycling,* pp. 10–11.

76 'A Cycle Bookmaker's Confession', *Australian Cyclist and Motor-Car World*, 13 June 1901, p. 28.

77 'Reminiscences of a Bookmaker: Cycle Racing Not Profitable', *Australian Cyclist and Motor-Car World*, 18 July 1901, p. 1.

78 Jim Fitzpatrick, *The Bicycle and the Bush: Man and Machine in Rural Australia*, Melbourne, Oxford University Press, 1980, p. 245.

79 *Sydney Wheelman*, 15 August 1895, p. 1; 12 September 1895, p. 49.

80 *Cycling Gazette,* 11 September 1897, p. 93.

81 For example, *Sands Directory*, 1867, 1868, 1869, 1870, 1873; *Sydney Morning Herald*, 24 March 1871, p. 11.

82 Shaw family archives.

83 Ibid. See also 1861 Census of Scotland.

84 1851 Census of Scotland entry for Mary Anne Inch.

85 Extract of an entry in a Register of Marriages, District of Govan, County of Lanark, Scotland, *Glasgow Herald*, 14 June 1861, p. 5.

86 Shaw family archives.

87 Eileen Johnson, *They Came Direct: 'Light Brigade' 1863*, Tinana, Queensland, Eileen Johnson, 2005.

88 Thomas Keneally, *Australians: From Eureka to the Diggers*, Sydney, Allen & Unwin, 2011, p. 85.

89 Supreme Court of New South Wales, Ecclesiastical Jurisdiction, *Probate Packet*

for Tait Pitkethly. Document 2–133, 1873–1867. State Archives and Records NSW. Note: numerous spellings of the name Pitkethly were used, sometimes on one page of the same document.

90 Letter from Samuel Shaw to his brothers written in March 1878 from Sydney. Retained with Samuel Shaw's diary 1877–78, MS 2829, National Library of Australia, Canberra.

91 Letter from Samuel Shaw to his parents written on 26 March 1878 from Sydney. Retained with Samuel Shaw's diary 1877–78, MS 2829, National Library of Australia, Canberra.

92 Shirley Fitzgerald, 'Woolloomooloo', *Dictionary of Sydney*, 2008, http://dictionaryofsydney.org/entry/woolloomooloo, viewed 12 Jul 2017.

93 Andrew Garran (ed.), *Picturesque Atlas of Australasia*, Sydney and Melbourne, The Picturesque Atlas Publishing Co., 1886, p. 80.

94 'House Poison', *Sydney Morning Herald*, 31 August 1878, p. 18.

95 Death registration for Mary Anne Shaw, New South Wales BDM 1879/1635. See also *Sydney Morning Herald*, 30 September 1879, p. 10; 1 October 1879, p. 16; 4 October 1879, p. 1.

96 Ian Hoskins, *Sydney Harbour: A History*, Sydney, UNSW Press, 2009, pp. 185, 188.

2 – On Your Marks: William Nathaniel Shaw

1 Birth registration for W. N. Shaw, New South Wales BDM 469/1864; Shaw family archives.

2 Attestation Papers for William Nathaniel Shaw, NAA: B2455, 2 June 1916, National Archives of Australia.

3 The Zoological Gardens, also known as the Billy Goat Swamp Zoo, was on land at Moore Park now occupied by Sydney Boys High School and Sydney Girls High School.

4 *Evening News*, 18 August 1887, p. 5, 26 August 1887, p. 8; *Sydney Mail*, 27 August 1887, p. 462; *Sydney Morning Herald*, 31 August 1887, p. 11; *Australian Town and Country Journal*, 3 September 1887, p. 40.

5 Marriage registration for William Nathaniel Shaw and Mary King, New South Wales BDM 787/1888.

6 *Australian Star*, 2 May 1888, p. 2; *Australian Town and Country Journal*, 5 May 1888, p. 39; *Daily Telegraph*, 7 May 1888, p. 6.

7 *Australian Star*, 7 May 1888, p. 3.

8 *Sydney Morning Herald*, 7 May 1888, p. 5.

9 *Sydney Bicycle Club, Twelfth Annual Report*, 21 October 1891, p. 4.

10 *Sydney Morning Herald*, 5 June 1892, p. 8, 20 June 1892, p. 3; *Daily Telegraph*, 15 June 1892, p. 6.

11 *Referee*, 10 August 1892, p. 6.

12 *Official Programme, Sydney Bicycle Club, 11th Annual Amateur Race Meeting*, Association Cricket Ground, Moore Park, Saturday 3rd September 1892, Box

18, Davis Sporting Collection, Mitchell Library, Sydney; *Daily Telegraph*, 1 September 1892, p. 3, 5 September, p. 6; *Sydney Mail*, 5 September 1892, p. 9; *Australian Star*, 5 September 1892, p. 7.

13 *Daily Telegraph*, 5 September 1892, p. 6.

14 Margaret Tart, *The Life of Quong Tart*, A digital text sponsored by the New South Wales Centenary of Federation Committee, University of Sydney Library, 2001, p. 12, http://setis.library.usyd.edu.au/ozlit/pdf/fed0048.pdf

15 See also Sophie Couchman, 'Riding with the Best of Them: Chinese Australians and Cycling in Australia', in Claire Simpson (ed.), *Scorchers, Ramblers and Rovers: Australian Cycling Histories*, Melbourne, Australian Society for Sports History, 2006.

16 *Referee*, 21 September 1892, p. 8.

17 F.G. Chippendale Hanslow (ed.), *Australian Cycling Annual: A Complete Record of Australian Cycling and Other Interesting Information*, Sydney, George Robertson & Co., 1897, p. 399.

18 *Newcastle Morning Herald and Miners' Advocate*, 3 October 1892, p. 3.

19 *Australian Town and Country Journal*, 8 October 1892, p. 39.

20 *Sydney Morning Herald*, 8 November 1892, p. 2; *Daily Telegraph*, 10 November 1892, p. 6.

21 *Sydney Mail*, 17 December 1892, p. 1377.

22 *Bird O' Freedom*, 10 December 1892, p. 8.

23 'The Intercolonial Carnival. Abandoned Through Rain. The Summer Cup Undecided', *Referee*, 21 December 1892, p. 3.

24 The track was later further developed and renamed the Harold Park Paceway. It closed in 2010 and by 2016 had been transformed into an area of large multi-storey apartment towers.

25 'The Lillie Bridge Grounds', *Sydney Mail*, 4 January 1890, p. 4.

26 'Sporting Opinion', *The Dead Bird*, 15 February 1890, p. 6.

27 'Speedwell Club Sports', *Referee*, 30 May 1891, p. 1.

28 Wayne Peake, *Sydney's Pony Racecourses: An Alternative Racing History*, Sydney, Walla Walla Press, 2006, pp. 6–9; John O'Hara, *A Mug's Game: A History of Gaming and Betting in Australia*, Sydney, New South Wales University Press, 1988.

29 *Australian Star*, 30 May 1891, p. 1.

30 While bicycle races were traditionally named according to their distances and whether they were handicap or scratch races, pony races followed either standard horse racing conventions such as being named after the suburbs of Glebe or Forest Lodge or the ground's lighting technology (The Electric Handicap) or reflected the fact that ponies were involved in many races – hence the Midget Handicap, the Tom Thumb Handicap, the Dwarf Handicap and the Lilliputian Handicap.

31 Analysis of in excess of 70 newspaper announcements and articles, *Evening News*, 4 January 1893 to 28 December 1893; *Australian Star*, 4 January 1893 to 22 November 1893; *Daily Telegraph*, 6 January 1893 to 29 November 1893.

32 *Sydney Morning Herald*, 29 May 1893, p. 3; *Daily Telegraph*, 29 May 1893, p. 3.

33 *Sydney Mail*, 29 July 1893, p. 248. See also *Evening News*, 18 July 1893, p. 5.

34 *Sydney Mail*, 3 September 1893, p. 550.

35 *Daily Telegraph*, 21 September 1893, p. 6; *Evening News*, 3 October 1893, p. 6.

36 *Goulburn Herald*, 25 May 1894, p. 2; *Goulburn Evening Penny Post*, 26 May 1894, p. 4.

37 Divorce records for William Nathaniel Shaw and Mary Shaw, NSW 1401, July 1894, State Archives and Records NSW.

38 'Shaw v. Shaw', *Daily Telegraph*, 18 August 1894, p. 11. See also *New South Wales Government Gazette*, 20 July 1894, p. 4704.

39 Marriage registration for William N. Shaw, and Rachel Inglethorpe, New South Wales BDM 469/1864; Shaw family archives.

40 Bankruptcy papers for William Nathaniel Shaw, 1911, Supreme Court of New South Wales, Document 18977, State Archives and Records NSW. See also *New South Wales Government Gazette*, 18 October 1911, p. 5635.

41 Bankruptcy papers for William Nathaniel Shaw, 1911.

42 Death registration for William Nathaniel Shaw, New South Wales BDM 5340/1956.

3 – 'One of the Fastest Sprinters': Samuel Robinson Shaw

1 Birth registration for Samuel R. Shaw, New South Wales BDM 1813/1870; Transcription, registration of birth for Samuel Robinson Shaw, 12 August 1870; Shaw family archives.

2 *Sands Directory*, 1870; *City of Sydney Assessments*, 1870; Sheet 11, Ryegate and West's Plans of Sydney, 1887, *Historical Atlas of Sydney*.

3 Birth registration for James Shaw, New South Wales BDM 1389/1866; Transcription, registration of birth for James Shaw, 23 July 1866; Shaw family archives.

4 See *Freeman's Journal*, 4 February 1905, p. 26.

5 See, for example, a series of advertisements in the *Watchman*, 26 September 1903 to 27 February 1904.

6 *New South Wales/Sydney Telephone Directory*, 1912, 1913, 1914, 1916, 1917, 1918, 1919 and all years 1932 to his death in 1935.

7 Annotated copy of the *Official Programme of the Sydney Bicycle Club, Tenth Annual Championship Race Meeting*, Association Ground, Moore Park, 22 August 1891, Box 18, Davis Sporting Collection, Mitchell Library, Sydney.

8 *Official Programme, Suburban Bicycle Club, Sixth Grand Amateur Championship Race Meeting*, Association Cricket Ground, Moore Park, Saturday 26 September 1891, Box 18, Davis Sporting Collection, Mitchell Library, Sydney; 'Suburban Bicycle Club Sports', *Evening News*, 28 September 1891, p. 6; *Referee*, 30 September 1891, p. 8.

9 *Sydney Morning Herald*, 18 June 1892, p. 2; 21 June 1892, p. 6.

10 *Daily Telegraph*, 22 June 1892, p. 6.

11 *Evening News*, 8 August 1892, p. 6; *Referee*, 10 August 1892, p. 6.

12 *Official Programme, Sydney Bicycle Club, 11th Annual Amateur Race Meeting*, Association Cricket Ground, Moore Park, Saturday 3rd September 1892, Box 18, Davis Sporting Collection, Mitchell Library, Sydney.

13 *Referee*, 14 September 1892, p. 8.

14 *Australasian*, 17 September 1892, p. 28.

15 *Australian Star*, 3 October 1892, p. 6. See also *Newcastle Morning Herald & Miners' Advocate*, 3 October 1892, p. 3; *Referee*, 5 October 1892, p. 8; *Australian Town and Country Journal*, 8 October 1892, p. 39.

16 *Daily Telegraph*, 10 November 1892, p. 6.

17 *Newcastle Morning Herald & Miners' Advocate*, 19 November 1892, p. 11.

18 *Referee*, 25 January 1893, p. 8; 1 February 1893, p. 6.

19 *Australian Town and Country Journal*, 1 April 1893, p. 39; *Australian Star*, 22 March 1893, p. 8.

20 *Newcastle Morning Herald & Miners' Advocate*, 6 May 1893, p. 11.

21 *Maitland Mercury*, 7 November 1893, p. 4.

22 *Maitland Mercury*, 11 November 1893, p. 2.

23 *Programme of Sports, Twenty-Sixth Highland Gathering*, New Year's Day, 1894, Association Cricket Ground, Moore Park, Fry Family, Papers of James Arthur Barrett Fry 1860–1926, Box 3, Mitchell Library, Sydney; *Evening News*, 2 January 1894, p. 5; *Australian Star*, 2 January 1894, p. 6.

24 *Maitland Daily Mercury*, 26 March 1894, p. 2.

25 Slow races, novelty events common at cycling carnivals, involved competitors travelling as slowly as they could manage without losing balance and falling. The last rider cycling was declared the winner.

26 *Sydney Morning Herald*, 5 May 1894, p. 7, 7 May 1894, p. 3.

27 *Goulburn Herald*, 25 May 1894, p. 2.

28 *Referee*, 15 August 1894, p. 3. See also *Newcastle Morning Herald & Miners' Advocate*, 18 August 1894, p. 11.

29 *Australian Star*, 24 September 1894, p. 6.

30 *Goulburn Penny Post*, 6 November 1894, p. 3.

31 Bone-shakers were velocipedes that preceded high wheelers. Early machines had wooden wheels and iron tyres along with a heavy cast iron frame.

32 *Goulburn Herald*, 7 November 1894, p. 2, 9 November 1894, p. 2, 12 November 1894, p. 2; *Truth*, 11 November 1894, p. 7.

33 *Sydney Mail*, 5 January 1895, p. 41.

34 *Sydney Morning Herald*, 14 January 1895, p. 3.

35 See *Daily Telegraph*, 31 January 1895, p. 6; *Sydney Mail*, 4 May 1895, p. 925; *Australian Town and Country Journal*, 27 April 1895, p. 43; *Evening News*, 2 July 1895, p. 2.

36 W. H. Kavanagh, *Album Collection of News Cuttings, Tickets, Invitations, Business Cards and Other Memorabilia Related to Australian Cycling 1886–1912*, State Library of New South Wales, unpaginated.

37 *Australian Town and Country Journal*, 6 April 1895, p. 42.

38 *Bird O' Freedom*, 13 April 1895, p. 6.

39 *Australian Town and Country Journal*, 18 May 1895, p. 43. See also *Sunday Times*, 12 May 1895, p. 7; *Referee*, 15 May 1895, p. 8.

40 *Australian Star*, 3 June 1895, p. 6.

41 *Truth*, 7 July 1895, p. 6; *The Australian Star*, 8 July 1895, p. 8. *The Cumberland Argus and Fruitgrowers Advocate*, the principal Parramatta newspaper, also ran the story of the win by Sam Shaw, presumably because he had a following there resulting from his support for the formation of the Parramatta Branch of the League of New South Wales Wheelmen.

42 *Newcastle Morning Herald & Miners' Advocate*, 13 July 1895, p. 11.

43 *Referee*, 24 July 1895, p. 3.

44 Marriage registration for Samuel R. Shaw, New South Wales BDM 8148/1896.

45 *Sydney Mail*, 11 October 1896, p. 11.

46 For example, *Australian Star*, 1 January 1896, p. 6; *Evening News*, 13 December 1895, p. 2, 11 May 1897, p. 2; *Sydney Morning Herald*, 23 March 1896, p. 6; *Australian Town and Country Journal*, 22 August 1896, p. 2, 10 October 1896, p. 41; F. G. Chippendale Hanslow (ed.), *Australian Cycling Annual: A Complete Record of Australian Cycling and Other Interesting Information*, Sydney, George Robertson & Co., 1897, p. 110.

47 Wheelman, 'League of New South Wales Wheelmen', *Sydney Mail*, 25 July 1896, pp. 181, 188.

48 *Australian Town and Country Journal*, 10 October 1896, p. 41; *Evening News*, 9 November 1896, p. 5.

49 *Australian Star*, 4 February 1897, p. 7.

50 *Bowral Free Press and Berrima District Intelligencer*, 17 April 1897, p. 2, 21 April 1897, p. 4.

51 *Referee*, 9 June 1897, p. 6. See also *Australian Town and Country Journal*, 12 June 1897, p. 39.

52 *Australian Star*, 21 May 1897, p. 7.

53 *Sands Directory*, 1898. See also 1899, 1900.

54 *Town and Country Journal*, 3 June 1899, p. 52; *Woollahra Council Assessment Books*, Woollahra Library, Local History Centre, Double Bay, Sydney.

55 A billy run was essentially a picnic run where riders took along food and a billy (a billy can or bucket-shaped container used for boiling water over a campfire) to make pots of tea.

56 See, for example, *Sydney Morning Herald*, 20 June 1899, p. 5, 1 July 1899, p. 7, 5 July 1897, p. 10, 8 August 1899, p. 6; *Evening News*, 11 July 1899, p. 2

57 *Sydney Morning Herald*, 8 September 1900, p. 9; *Evening News*, 10 September 1900, p. 2.

58 1901 Census of Australia (taken 31 March 1901).

59 Catherine Warne, *Pictorial History: Lower North Shore*, Sydney, Kingsclear Books, 2005, p. 69.

60 *Index to Registers of Firms*, State Archives and Records NSW, Packet number: 06973, Item number: [2/8531], 1903, p. 487.

61 Birth registration for Donald S. E. Shaw, New South Wales BDM 26256/1902; Kate Riseley, Archivist, The Sydney Church of England Grammar School (Shore), personal correspondence, 3 August 2012.

62 Twenty-three issues of the *New South Wales/Sydney Telephone Directory*, 1909–1939.

63 Twenty-two issues of *Sands Directory*, 1904 to 1932–1923 and numerous newspaper advertisements.

64 *Sydney Sportsman*, 17 April 1907, p. 10; *Sydney Morning Herald*, 7 August 1908, p. 10.

65 *Sunday Sun*, 4 September 1904, p. 6.

66 *Sydney Sportsman*, 9 September 1908, p. 3; *Referee*, 4 November 1908, p. 10; *Arrow*, 4 June 1910, p. 5.

67 *Sydney Morning Herald*, 29 August 1924, p. 7, 25 June 1934, p. 15; *Sunday Times*, 5 April 1925, p. 1.

68 *Sands Directories.*

69 *Referee*, 4 November 1908, p. 10; *Evening News*, 30 October 1908, p. 2.

70 *Arrow*, 24 October 1919, p. 4, 14 November 1919, p. 4.

71 *Arrow*, 12 December 1919, p. 3.

72 *Evening News*, 23 July 1920, p. 8.

73 *Referee*, 18 August 1920, p. 11, 17 November 1920, p. 15; *Sunday Times*, 18 September 1921, p. 8; *Commercial News and Shipping List*, 21 September 1921, p. 8S; *Arrow*, 16 March 1923, p. 5.

74 Death registration for Samuel Robinson Shaw, New South Wales BDM 25409/1939; Shaw family archives.

75 *The Torch-Bearer*, Magazine of The Sydney Church of England Grammar School [Shore], No.4, Vol. XX11, April 1917, p. 11.

76 *The Torch-Bearer*, Magazine of The Sydney Church of England Grammar School [Shore], No.4. Vol. XX1V, June 1919, p. 160.

77 *Arrow*, 12 September 1919, p. 4.

78 *Arrow*, 17 October 1919, p. 4.

79 Personal interview with Don's daughter, Margaret Leask, Sydney, 30 July 2012.

80 *Sydney Morning Herald*, 17 February 1922, p. 13.

81 *Arrow*, 20 October 1922, p. 15.

82 *Sydney Morning Herald*, 23 February 1923, p. 12, 5 November 1923, p. 12, 3 December 1923, p. 11.

83 *Sydney Morning Herald*, 19 October 1925, p. 15.

84 *Sydney Morning Herald*, 19 May 1926, p. 17.

85 *Sydney Morning Herald*, 19 October 1936, p. 15, 13 May 1937, p. 19.

86 Personal interview with Don's daughter, Margaret Leask, Sydney, 30 July 2012.

87 Probate Packet, Item number 353 250, Donald Samuel Ewart Shaw, Archives of New South Wales.

4 – Soldiering On: Henry Tait Shaw

1 Birth registration for Tait Ewart Shaw, New South Wales BDM 2008/1872; Transcription, registration of birth for Tait Ewart Shaw, 7 August 1872, showing amendment of name to Henry Tait Shaw on 15 September 1872 when he was baptised.

2 *Sydney Morning Herald*, 27 October 1904, p. 4.

3 *Official Programme of the Speedwell Bicycle Club, Grand Amateur Autumn Race Meeting*, Lillie Bridge Ground, Forest Lodge, 30 May 1891, Fry Family, Papers of James Arthur Barrett Fry 1860–1926, Box 3, Mitchell Library, Sydney; 'Speedwell Club Sports', *Referee*, 30 May 1891, p. 1.

4 *Official Programme, St Leonard's Bicycle Club, Grand Amateur Championship Race Meeting*, Saturday 18th July 1891, St Leonard's Park Oval, North Sydney, Box 18, Davis Sporting Collection, Mitchell Library, Sydney.

5 *Official Programme, Sydney Bicycle Club, Tenth Annual Amateur Championship Race Meeting*, Association Ground, Moore Park, Saturday 22 August 1891, Box 18, Davis Sporting Collection, Mitchell Library, Sydney.

6 *Official Programme, Suburban Bicycle Club, Sixth Grand Amateur Championship Race Meeting*, Association Cricket Ground, Moore Park, Saturday 26 September 1891, Box 18, Davis Sporting Collection, Mitchell Library, Sydney.

7 *Referee*, 21 December 1892, p. 3, 28 December 1892, p. 3.

8 *Australian Star*, 23 January 1892, p. 3.

9 Marriage registration for William J. Parrett and Christina Shaw, New South Wales BDM 7596/1895.

10 *Maitland Mercury*, 7 November 1893, p. 4. See also *Sydney Morning Herald*, 4 November 1893, p. 7.

11 *Newcastle Morning Herald & Miners' Advocate*, 30 December 1893; See also *Australian Star*, 21 December 1893, p. 8.

12 *Programme of Sports, Twenty-Sixth Highland Gathering*, New Year's Day, 1894, Association Cricket Ground, Moore Park, Fry Family, Papers of James Arthur Barrett Fry 1860–1926, Box 3, Mitchell Library, Sydney.

13 *Australian Town and Country Journal*, 22 September 1894, p. 40.

14 Various issues of the *Referee*, *Australian Town and Country Journal*, *Evening News*, *Sydney Morning Herald*, *Sydney Mail*, *Newcastle Morning Herald & Miner's Advocate*, and *Goulburn Herald*.

15 *Australian Star*, 6 March 1895, p. 8, 8 April 1895, p. 6; *Sydney Morning Herald*, 16 March 1895, pp. 2 and 12, 6 April 1895, p. 12; *Evening News*, 1 April 1895, p. 2; *Sunday Times*, 7 April 1895, p. 6; *Newcastle Morning Herald & Miners'*

Advocate, 8 April 1895, p. 3; *Referee*, 10 April 1895, p. 6.

16 *Sydney Morning Herald*, 16 March 1895, p. 12.

17 *Australian Star*, 27 March 1895, p. 7.

18 R. J. Mecredy and A. J. Wilson, *The Art and Pastime of Cycling*, London, Archbald Constable & Co., 1897, p. 149.

19 Mecredy and Wilson, *The Art and Pastime of Cycling*, p. 151.

20 *Wheelman*, 9 November 1895, p. 7.

21 H. ('Curly) Grivell, *Australian Cycling in the Golden Days*, Adelaide, Courier Press, 1952, p. 14.

22 *Sydney Wheelman*, 12 September 1895, p. 50.

23 *Daily Telegraph*, 26 October 1895, p. 11; *Sydney Mail*, 2 November 1895, p. 922.

24 *Official Programme of the International Championship Bicycle Race Meeting '95*, Sydney Cricket Ground, First Day, 16 November 1895, Box 18, Davis Sporting Collection, Mitchell Library, Sydney.

25 *Sydney Mail*, 23 November 1895, p. 1077.

26 *Official Programme of the International Championship Bicycle Race Meeting '95.*

27 See, for example, *Evening News*, 24 May 1895, p. 2, 22 August 1895, p. 5; *Sydney Mail*, 1 June 1895, p. 1131; *Sydney Morning Herald*, 17 June 1895, p. 3; *Truth*, 21 July 1895, p. 7; *Australian Town and Country Journal*, 28 September 1895, p. 42.

28 *Wheelman*, 15 February 1896, p. 14.

29 *Wheelman*, 29 February 1896, p. 9.

30 *Australian Star*, 20 February 1896, p. 8.

31 *Sydney Morning Herald*, 7 March 1896, p. 2.

32 *Daily Telegraph*, 16 March 1896, p. 5.

33 *Evening News*, 23 March 1896, p. 5. See also *Wheelman*, 28 March 1896, p. 12.

34 *Wheelman*, 28 March 1896, p. 18.

35 *Wheelman*, 11 April 1896, p. 12.

36 *Armidale Chronicle*, 29 April 1896, p. 3.

37 *Sportsman*, 28 April 1896, p. 7; *Newcastle Morning Herald & Miners' Advocate*, 27 April 1896, p. 8.

38 Marriage registration for Henry T. Shaw and Emily A. Breakwell, New South Wales BDM 407/1897; *Sydney Morning Herald*, 3 April 1897, p. 1.

39 *Australian Star*, 9 July 1897, p. 6.

40 *Sydney Morning Herald*, 18 September 1899, p. 4.

41 *Evening News*, 11 August 1899, p. 8.

42 Bankruptcy papers for Henry Tait Shaw, 1903, Supreme Court of New South Wales, Document 15791, State Archives and Records NSW.

43 *Sydney Morning Herald*, 25 May 1901, p. 18, 26 November 1901, p. 10.

44 Bankruptcy papers for Henry Tait Shaw, 1903, Supreme Court of New South Wales, Document 15791.

45 Bankruptcy papers for Henry Tait Shaw, 1903, Supreme Court of New South Wales, Document 15791.

46 *Sydney Morning Herald*, 27 October 1904, p. 4.

47 Henry Tait Shaw, Australia, Electoral Rolls, 1903–1980, Wynnum, Oxley, Brisbane, Queensland, 1913, 1914.

48 Henry Taite (*sic*) Shaw and Emily Agnes Shaw, Australia, Electoral Rolls, 1903–1980, Parramatta, New South Wales, 1913.

49 World War 1 service records for Henry Tait Shaw (SN 906), 1 September 1915–30 August 1917, National Archives of Australia.

50 World War 1 service records for Henry Tait Shaw (SN 906), 16 November 1917–19 November 1918, National Archives of Australia.

51 Service records for Henry Tait Shaw (SN 906), 24 June 1919–Unknown discharge date, National Archives of Australia.

52 Death registration for Henry T. Shaw, New South Wales BDM 12498/1921; *Sydney Morning Herald*, 5 September 1921, p. 8.

53 *Newcastle Morning Herald & Miners' Advocate*, 28 December 1916, p. 5.

54 *Newcastle Morning Herald & Miners' Advocate*, 29 January 1917, p. 3.

5 – 'A Man of Great Determination': Frederick Ewart Shaw

1 Birth registration for Frederick Ewart Shaw, New South Wales BDM 2319/1876; Shaw family archives.

2 *Evening News*, various issues, 29 October 1890 to 11 May 1895. See also *Sydney Mail*, 7 March 1891, p. 545, 28 March 1891, p. 719, 30 May 1891, p. 1124.

3 For example, *Australian Star*, 22 March 1904, p. 6; *Camden News*, 20 December 1906, p. 4, 30 December 1909, p. 6, 9 April 1914, p. 6.

4 The Crusaders' Bicycle Club held its meetings at the Grand View Hotel, Paddington, and served as the club for that suburb and surrounds.

5 *Evening News*, 4 July 1894, p. 3; *Australian Star*, 5 July 1894, p. 8.

6 *Official Programme, Suburban Bicycle Club and Darlinghurst Harriers, Australasian Bicycle and Athletic Carnival*, Sydney Cricket Ground, Saturday 1 September 1894, Fry Family, Papers of James Arthur Barrett Fry 1860–1926, Box 3, Mitchell Library, Sydney.

7 *Newcastle Morning Herald & Miners' Advocate*, 17 September 1894, p. 3. See also *Sydney Morning Herald*, 16 July 1894, p. 7; *Referee*, 29 August 1894, p. 6, 26 September 1894, p. 3.

8 *Official Programme of the International Championship Bicycle Race Meeting, '95*, Sydney Cricket Ground, Second Day, 23 November 1895, Box 18, Davis Sporting Collection, Mitchell Library, Sydney. See also *Evening News*, 11 March 1895, p. 2, 7 April 1895, p. 6, 25 November 1895, p. 5.

9 *Wheelman*, 28 March 1896, pp. 9 and 12.

10 *Sportsman*, 28 April 1896, p. 7; *Newcastle Morning Herald & Miners' Advocate*, 27 April 1896, p. 8.

11 'The Megson–Lewis Benefit,' *Truth*, 27 April 1896, p. 7.

12 Named in honour of Lord Hampden, Governor of the Colony of New South Wales 1895–1899.

13 See 'A League Handicap', *Sunday Times*, 28 June 1896, p. 7; 'League of Wheelmen. F. Shaw Wins the Half-mile', *Australian Star*, 30 June 1896, p. 8; *Australian Town and Country Journal*, 4 July 1896, p. 41.

14 See, for example, *Sydney Mail*, 1 August 1896, p. 252.

15 'Smoke Concert (or Smoker)', *Australian Star*, 17 August 1896, p. 2.

16 *Truth*, 23 August 1896, p. 7. See also *Australian Star*, 17 August 1896, p. 2, 24 August 1896, p. 2; *Sunday Times*, 23 August 1896, p. 7; *Evening News*, 24 August 1896, p. 5; *Goulburn Herald*, 24 August 1896, p. 2 and *Newcastle Morning Herald & Miners' Advocate*, 24 August 1896, p. 3.

17 *Sydney Morning Herald*, 28 September 1896; *Newcastle Morning Herald & Miners' Advocate*, 28 September 1896, p. 3, 3 October 1896, p. 11.

18 *Goulburn Herald*, 9 November 1896, p. 3; *Evening News*, 10 November 1896, p. 2.

19 *Goulburn Herald*, 27 January 1897, p. 2.

20 See 'Those Wonderful Wheelmen' (Chapter 7), in Philip Derriman, *The Grand Old Ground; A History of the Sydney Cricket Ground*, Sydney, Cassell, 1981, pp. 45–51.

21 *Australian Star*, 27 February 1897, p. 11.

22 *Evening News*, 27 February1897, p. 4.

23 *Australian Star*, 4 March 1897, p. 3.

24 *Newcastle Morning Herald & Miners' Advocate*, 3 April 1897, p. 11.

25 *Sunday Times*, 28 March 1897, p. 7.

26 Advertisement for Cleveland cycles placed by The Sydney Cycle Co., Ltd, 'Riding School and Showrooms', George Street, Sydney, in, for example, *Sunday Times*, 28 March 1897, p. 7; *Sydney Morning Herald*, 31 March 1897, p. 10.

27 *Newcastle Morning Herald & Miners' Advocate*, 3 April 1897, p. 11.

28 *Bowral Free Press and Berrima District Intelligencer*, 21 April 1897, p. 4. See also the same paper of 17 April 1897, p. 2.

29 See, for example, *Sunday Times*, 23 May 1897, p. 7, 30 May 1897, p. 7, 27 June 1897, p. 7, 15 August 1897, p. 7; *Sydney Mail*, 5 June 1897, p. 1208, 4 September 1897, p. 511; *Australian Star*, 23 July 1897, p. 8; *Wagga Wagga Express*, 3 August 1897, p. 7; *Australian Town and Country Journal*, 4 September 1897, p. 40.

30 *Australian Star*, 30 August 1897, p. 6.

31 *Wheelman*, 11 April 1896, p. 12.

32 *Australasian*, 20 March 1897, p. 18.

33 For example, a two-piece cartoon in the *Wheelman*, 21 March 1896, pp. 5 and 7. The first of the two parts showed riders, officials and spectators being frightened by a bulky, four-wheeled steam pacer at speed. The title of the second part, 'The Pacer All Broke Up', tells its own story.

34 *Newcastle Morning Herald & Miners' Advocate*, 4 September 1897, p. 12.

35 *Maitland Daily Mercury*, 6 September 1897, p. 4.

36 *Wagga Wagga Express*, 30 September 1897. p. 2; *Cootamundra Herald*, 2 October 1897, p. 6.

37 *Sunday Times*, 2 October 1898, p. 4.

38 *Northern Miner*, 29 April 1897, p. 3.

39 *Newcastle Morning Herald & Miners' Advocate*, 25 October 1897, p. 6.

40 *Sydney Mail*, 6 November 1897, p. 990; *Goulburn Herald*, 10 November 1897, p. 2.

41 See, for example, *Age*, 5 November 1897, p. 6; *Australasian*, 13 November 1897, p. 23; *Sportsman*, 7 December 1897, p. 3.

42 *Age*, 25 January 1898, p. 5. See also, *Age*, 3 January 1898, p. 6, 27 January 1898, p. 6.

43 Second prize in this ANA Art Union was a gold vase valued at £150. There were also 128 cash prizes ranging from £1 to £60.

44 'The Visiting Cyclists. An Official Welcome', *Brisbane Courier*, 10 June 1898, p. 7. See also 'Champion Cyclists. Arrival in Brisbane', *Telegraph*, 10 June 1898, p. 2.

45 'League of Wheelmen Carnival. The First Day's Sport', *Queenslander*, 25 June 1898, p. 1212.

46 *Brisbane Courier*, 20 June 1898, p. 6, 27 June 1898, p. 5; *Telegraph*, 20 June 1898, p. 6; *Week*, 24 June 1898, p. 9; *Queenslander*, 2 July 1898, p. 19.

47 *Brisbane Courier*, 4 July 1898, p. 7.

48 *Maryborough Chronicle, Wide Bay and Burnett Advertiser*, 17 September 1898, p. 4; 19 September 1898, p. 6; 22 September 1898, p. 3; 26 September 1898, p. 3; *Brisbane Courier*, 28 September 1898, p. 7.

49 *Referee*, 5 October 1898, p. 4.

50 'Swift Road Race. To Cleveland and Back' *Telegraph*, 18 October 1898, p. 2.

51 *Western Star and Roma Advertiser*, 12 November 1898, p. 2.

52 *Maryborough Chronicle, Wide Bay and Burnett Advertiser*, 13 December 1898, p. 2. See also the *Referee*, 14 December 1898, p. 6.

53 *Referee*, 14 December 1898, p. 6.

54 *Sunday Times*, 1 January 1899, p. 4.

55 *Newcastle Morning Herald & Miners' Advocate*, 7 January1899, p. 11.

56 *Wyalong Star and Temora and Barmedman Advertiser*, 13 January 1899, p. 3.

57 'What a Champion Cyclist Earns: Facts and Figures Worth Pondering Over', *The Australian Cyclist*, 24 November 1898, p. 7.

58 An alternative spelling of the word 'dinghy' that was in common use at the time.

59 *Telegraph*, 18 November 1898, p. 6, 9 December 1898, p. 3, 'Fourteen-Footers Championship', 9 January 1899, *Brisbane Courier*, 6 January 1899, p. 7, 9 January 1899, p. 7.

60 Anonymous, 'Sailing and yachting', in Wray Vamplew et al. (eds.), *The Oxford Companion to Australian Sport*, Melbourne, Oxford University Press, 1997, p. 372.

61 Carlin de Montfort, 'Centreboards and Sails: The Rise of Open-Boat Racing in Sydney During the 1890s', *The International Journal of the History of Sport*, 30, 2, 2013, pp. 146–50.

62 Bob Ross, *The Sailing Australians*, London, Robert Hale and Company, 1974, p. 50.

63 *Telegraph*, 13 January 1899, p. 6.

64 The term 'some pumpkins' was American slang meaning a person of consequence, someone special or impressive, a 'big deal'.

65 *Brisbane Courier*, 16 January 1899, p. 7.

66 'Intercolonial Sailing. Anniversary Regatta Yesterday ... Queensland Boats Unplaced', *Brisbane Courier*, 27 January 1899, p. 6; 'Anniversary Regatta. A Splendid Aquatic Carnival', *Sydney Mail*, 4 February 1899, p. 263–7.

67 *Brisbane Courier*, 14 July 1899, p. 8.

68 John Ferguson (ed.), *The Amateurs: The Second Century Begins 1972–1992*, Sydney, Maritime Heritage Press, 1976, pp. 1–6.

69 Ian Hoskins, *Sydney Harbour: A History*, Sydney, UNSW Press, 2009, p. 163.

70 Ross, *The Sailing Australians*, p. 50.

71 *Queenslander*, 25 February 1899, p. 342.

72 *Brisbane Courier*, 18 March 1899, p. 11.

73 'Ambulance Sports, Cycling Events', *Telegraph*, 17 April 1899, p. 3. See also *Referee*, 19 April 1899, p. 7; *Queenslander*, 22 April 1899, p. 728.

74 *Brisbane Courier*, 2 May 1899, p. 5. See also *Queenslander*, 6 May 1899, p. 823.

75 *Brisbane Courier*, 29 May 1899, p. 7.

76 *Queenslander*, 3 June 1899, p. 1015, 'Road Racing at Rocklea. Large Attendance', 17 June 1899, p. 1140; *Brisbane Courier*, 12 June 1899, p. 7.

77 'L.Q.W. Cycling Carnival' *Telegraph*, 25 August 1899, p. 5; *Evening News*, 28 August 1899, p. 6; *Australian Town and Country Journal*, 2 September 1899, p. 53.

78 *Brisbane Courier*, 9 October 1899, p. 5; *Queenslander*, 21 October 1899, p. 803; 28 October 1899, pp. 851–2; *Gympie Times and Mary River Mining Gazette*, 11 November 1899, p. 3.

79 *Brisbane Courier*, 13 September 1899, p. 4, 27 October 1899, p. 7, 7 November 1899, p. 7, 13 November 1899, p. 7; 11 December 1899, p. 6; *Telegraph*, 20 November 1899, p. 3.

80 *Brisbane Courier*, 2 January 1900, p. 3, 5 February 1900, p. 7, 3 March 1900, p. 7, 12 March 1900, p. 5, 9 April 1900, p. 7.

81 *Telegraph*, 26 March 1900, p. 7; *Brisbane Courier*, 26 March 1900, p. 7.

82 de Montfort, 'Centreboards and Sails', p. 145.

83 *Brisbane Courier*, 15 January 1900, p. 7.

84 *Referee*, 4 July 1900, p. 6, 1 August 1900, p. 6; *Sunday Times*, 1 July 1900, p. 4; *Brisbane Courier*, 16 July 1900, p. 7; *Table Talk*, 19 July 1900, p. 20; *Evening News*, 19 July 1900, p. 20; *Australasian*, 21 July 1900, p. 22; *Queenslander*, 21 July 1900, p. 110; *Telegraph*, 27 July 1900, p. 2, 30 July 1900, p. 7; *Punch*, 2 August 1900, p. 26.

85 Peter Nye, *Hearts of Lions: The History of American Bicycle Racing*, New York, W. W. Norton & Co., 1988, p. 72.

86 'A Death in Eaglehawk: The Charles Mayman story, Part 1', *Serpolette's Tricycle:*

The Early Motor in Australia, May 2012, p. 12.

87 'A Death in Eaglehawk', p. 12.

88 *Telegraph*, 26 July 1900, p. 3.

89 'Through the Drought-Stricken West', *Western Champion and General Advertiser for the Central-Western District*, 1 May 1900, p. 14; *Queenslander*, 12 May 1900, p. 907S, 23 June 1900, p. 1172, 11 August 1900, p. 245.

90 Robert A. Smith, *A Social History of the Bicycle: Its Early Life and Times in America,* New York, American Heritage Press, 1972 p. 148.

91 *Brisbane Courier*, 18 February 1899, p. 11, 1 March 1899, p. 3, 13 March 1899, p. 8, 18 March 1899, p. 3; *Queenslander*, 11 March 1899, p. 437.

92 'Cycling Carnival. L.Q.W. Second Day. Series of Exciting Contests', *Telegraph*, 28 August 1899, p. 2. See also *Telegraph*, 23 August 1899, p. 3, 23 August 1899, p. 5.

93 *Queenslander*, 2 September 1899, pp. 466–7.

94 *Brisbane Courier*, 12 September 1899, p. 9.

95 'A Novel Challenge', *Referee,* 16 January 1901, p. 6.

96 *Queenslander*, 21 September 1901, p. 578S, 26 October 1901, p. 817S; *Brisbane Courier*, 23 September 1901, p. 7, 'The Shaw-Rickards Match', 30 September 1901, p. 7; *Northern Miner,* 30 September1901, p. 3; 'F. Shaw v. F. Rickards', *Referee*, 2 October 1901, p. 6; *Telegraph*, 10 October 1901, p. 5.

97 'Horse v. Cycle', *Telegraph*, 6 February 1900, p. 4, 'Horse v. Cycle Race', 9 February 1900, p. 3, 10 February 1900, p. 6, 14 February 1900, p. 6; *Brisbane Courier*, 8 February 1900, p. 2, 'Horses v. Cycle', 12 February 1900, p. 7; 'Horse v. Cycle Contests. The Bike Wins all Round', *Darling Downs Gazette*, 12 February 1900, p. 3; *Referee*, 14 February 1900, p. 6.

98 'Cycling. News from all Corners', *Sydney Sportsman*, 16 April 1902, p. 2.

99 No longer were these intercolonial events following the Federation of Australia and the formation of the Commonwealth of Australia on 1 January 1901.

100 *Sydney Morning Herald*, 30 January 1901, p. 4; *Evening News*, 31 January 1901, p. 2; *Referee*, 6 February 1901, p. 4; *Sydney Sportsman*, 6 February 1901, p. 7.

101 *Telegraph*, 27 March 1901, p. 6; *Referee*, 27 March 1901, p. 6.

102 *Brisbane Courier*, 7 May 1901, p. 7.

103 *Telegraph*, 29 July 1901, p. 7; *Referee*, 31 July 1901, p. 6.

104 *Australian Star*, 25 October 1901, p. 7; *Sunday Times*, 3 November 1901, p. 4; *Sydney Sportsman*, 6 November 1901, p. 7, 1 January 1902, p. 7; *Brisbane Courier*, 30 December 1901, p. 7.

105 *The Yachtsman's Guide to Sydney Harbour*, 1898, cited in Ross, *The Sailing Australians*, p. 50.

106 *North Queensland Register*, 6 January 1902, p. 39.

107 *Northern Miner*, 29 March 1902, pp. 6–7, 9 June 1902, p. 3; *Evening News*, 24 September 1902, p. 2, 16 October 1902, p. 7; *The Age*, 11 November 1902, p. 7; *Sydney Sportsman*, 19 November 1902, p. 8.

108 Various issues of the *Sydney Sportsman*, *Sunday Times*, *Sydney Morning Herald*,

Evening News and *Australian Star.*

109 *Sydney Sportsman*, 17 February 1904, p. 8. See also *Sunday Times*, 14 February 1904, p. 8.

110 *Sunday Times*, 5 February 1905, p. 8, 2 April 1905, p. 10; *Sydney Sportsman*, 8 March 1905, p. 3.

111 *Sydney Morning Herald*, 12 November 1905, p. 7.

112 For example, *New South Wales Cyclist and Motor Review*, 3 May 1902, p. 11.

113 *Australian Cyclist*, 1 December 1898, p. 7. Advertisement placed by James Trahair.

114 *Index to Registers of Firms*, State Archives and Records NSW, Packet number: 06973, Item number: [2/8531], 1903, p. 487.

115 'Shaw Bros. Trophy', *Australian Star*, 26 February 1904, p. 2. See also *Daily Telegraph*, 26 March 1904, p. 14.

116 Ian Willis, *Pictorial History of Camden and District*, Sydney, Kingsclear, 2015, p. 48.

117 *Sands Directories* (Country), 1906–1915; *Camden Council Rates Book 1907*, Camden Museum.

118 'Bicycle Extraordinary', *Camden News*, 14 February 1907, p. 11.

119 *Campbelltown Herald*, 27 February 1907, p. 1.

120 *Camden News*, 21 June 1906, p. 1.

121 'Camden Show 1907', *Camden News*, 28 March 1907, p. 3.

122 Tom Fitzpatrick, 'Back Pedalling on District Cycling', *The Biz*, 16 August 1951, p. 11.

123 'Etna cycles run easy', *Camden News*, 17 January 1907, p. 3.

124 For example, *Camden News*, 12 October 1905, p. 1, 4 January 1906, p. 1, 26 September 1907, p. 4, 16 July 1908, p. 1, 2 November 1908, p. 10, 4 September 1913, p. 3, 12 March 1914, p. 6.

125 *Camden News*, 7 February 1907, p. 3.

126 *Australian Star*, 10 August 1904, p. 2.

127 *Official Programme of the Diavolo Cycling Carnival held under the auspices of the New South Wales Cyclist's Union*, 26 November 1904, Box 18, Davis Sporting Collection, Mitchell Library, Sydney.

128 'Diavolo, the Looper', *Referee*, 23 November 1904, p. 6.

129 'Cycling. League of Wheelmen', *Sydney Morning Herald*, 28 June 1906, p. 6.

130 'Camden to Queensland by Motor', *Camden News*, 17 October 1907, p. 5; 'The Queensland Motor Trip (Continued)', *Camden News*, 31 October 1907, p. 7.

131 An extremely steep hill between Camden and Picton, the road over which was notorious for bringing early motor vehicles (and cyclists) to a standstill (or worse).

132 *Camden News*, 28 November 1907, p. 4.

133 Marriage registration for Frederick E. Shaw and Rosa M. Smith, New South Wales BDM 10501/1908; Camden Area Family History Society Inc. (2008), *Camden Pioneer Register 1800–1920*, Third Edition, p. 238.

134 Personal conversation with Janice Johnson, Secretary, Camden Museum and St John's Anglican Church, Camden, 2014.

135 The house name Wandeen was the same as the name of the 14-footer sailboat Fred had previously raced in Sydney.

136 'Wedding Bells', *Camden News*, 29 October 1908, p. 3.

137 'Etna Bicycles Still Scoring', *Camden News*, 9 January 1908, p. 7.

138 'The Holiday. Camden Cycling Club's Sports', *Camden News*, 11 June 1908, p. 1.

139 See *Harley and the Davidsons*, three-part TV mini-series, Discovery Channel (also available on DVD), 2016. See also Internet Movie Database (IMDb) (Amazon).

140 See 'Attaching Motors to Bicycles', *Australian Cyclist and Motor Car World*, 18 April 1901, p. 19.

141 'Motors', *Camden News*, 1 October 1908, p. 3.

142 *Camden News*, 2 May 1912, p. 6.

143 *Camden News*, 8 January 1914, p. 1.

144 *Camden News*, 21 October 1915, p. 6.

145 'Mitchell Movements', *Sun*, 23 November 1918, p. 2.

146 'A New Motor Bus', *Camden News*, 11 November 1920, p. 2; 'Motor Bus', 18 November 1920, p. 4, 25 November 1920, p. 9, 'Motor Bus', 2 December 1920, p. 4, 15 September 1921, p. 5, 19 April 1923, p. 3.

147 Dr Ian Willis, 4 September 2017.

148 'Buzacott Steam Pressure Canner', *Camden News*, 22 January 1914, p. 8, 'Farmers, Irrigate Your Land!', 12 March 1914, p. 10, 'Gane Milking Machines', 29 October 1914, p. 2, 'Tangye Pumping Plant', 17 December 1914, p. 2.

149 'Phone 52. Camden Motor Garage', *Camden News*, 22 July 1915, p. 1.

150 *Camden News*, 17 February 1921, p. 9.

151 J. Wrigley, *Camden Population Numbers*, Camden Historical Society, 2000.

152 Hubert French, Notes on the Ford dealership of F. E. Shaw, Camden, New South Wales, 26 November 1923, Ford Canada Archives. Transcribed by Peter Kable for Ian Irwin, June 2017.

153 Mel Brooks, Notes on the Ford dealership of F. E. Shaw, Camden, New South Wales, 26 November 1923, Ford Canada Archives. Transcribed by Peter Kable for Ian Irwin, June 2017.

154 For example, 'Ford: The Universal Car', *Camden News*, 28 March 1923, p. 9, 'Tractor [Fordson] Production', 23 August 1923, p. 4, 'Yes! the Ford is a Wonderful Car', 29 May 1924, p. 7, 'Ford The Country Car', 26 June 1924, p. 6, 'Your harvest is close at hand', 25 September 1924, p. 8, 'Ford. A British Empire Production', 11 December 1924, p. 7, 'Ford Price Reductions', 5 March 1925, p. 8.

155 *Camden News*, 25 November 1926, p. 9.

156 'Camden Motor Garage. Dunk Bros. (Late F. E Shaw)', *Camden News*, 13 January 1927, p. 9.

157 The so-called Camden Tram was a small steam train that operated on a thirteen-kilometre light gauge rail that connected Campbelltown, on the main southern railway line, with Camden.

158 'Mr Shaw Leaving Camden', *Camden News*, 16 December 1926, p. 1.

159 *Sands Directory*, 1928–1931.

160 *Camden News*, 21 April 1927, p. 3.

161 *Sands Directory*, 1932–1933; Frederick Ewart Shaw, Electoral Rolls 1903–1980, Arncliffe, Lang, New South Wales, 1931, 1934, 1935, 1936.

162 Frederick Ewart Shaw, Electoral Rolls 1903–1980, Rockdale, Barton, New South Wales, 1937.

163 Frederick Ewart Shaw, Electoral Rolls 1903–1980, Peakhurst, Barton, New South Wales, 1943.

164 Robert Lacey, *Ford: The Men and the Machine*, London, Pan, 1987, pp. 360–3. See also Bill Bryson, *One Summer: America 1927*, London, Doubleday, 2013, pp. 276–8.

165 'Have You Ridden in the New Ford Yet?', *Motor Life*, 15 December 1928, p. 40. The 'New Ford' was the Model A, released in 1928.

166 'Notice to Creditors [Dunlop Motors, Camden]', *Camden News*, 31 October 1929, p. 7.

167 *Camden News*, 16 November 1905, p. 4, 'Cycling Sports in Camden', 4 January 1906, p. 1, 30 August 1906, p. 1, 4 October 1906, p. 6, 8 July 1909, p. 4, 1 July 1910, p. 2, 'Camden Aquatic Sports', 21 January 1909, p. 3, 11 March 1909, p. 4, 3 August 1911, p. 10; 'Thirlmere Bicycle Club', *Picton Post*, 23 December 1908, p. 4, 'Camden Rifle Club', 20 September 1911, p. 4; *Evening News*, 2 August 1906, p. 2, 1 July 1910, p. 2; 'Cycle and Motor', *Sydney Mail*, 17 August 1910, p. 56. For photographs of the Aquatic Sports on the Nepean River, Camden, see *Camden Images – Past and Present.* Online, Camden Historical Society, 2014, Images CHS1\CHS 1225, CHS0\CHS 0108 and CHS0\CHS 0110, photographed by O. V. Coleman, Camden, about 1910.

168 'Sailing Splashes', *Sydney Sportsman*, 4 February 1930, p. 13, 18 February 1930, p. 13, 'The Jolly Crew of the Mele Bilo', 25 February 1930, p. 16.

169 Death registration for Frederick Ewart Shaw, New South Wales BDM 25435/1947.

6 – Long-Distance Road Racer: Thomas John Shaw

1 Birth registration for Thomas John Shaw, New South Wales BDM 2069/1878; Shaw family archives.

2 *Brisbane Courier*, 18 July 1898, p. 7, 'Amateur Sports Carnival', 25 July 1898, p. 6; 'Cycling and Athletics. Championship Carnival', *Telegraph*, 18 July 1898, p. 4; 'Intercolonial Championship Carnival', *Queenslander*, 23 July 1898, p. 159.

3 *Brisbane Courier*, 25 July 1898, p. 6.

4 'Hospital Sports Carnival', *Brisbane Courier*, 27 July 1898, p. 67; *Telegraph*, 27 July 1898, p. 3; *Queenslander*, 6 August 1898, p. 253.

5 *Telegraph*, 7 November 1898, p. 4; *Referee*, 9 November 1898, p. 6.

6 *Brisbane Courier*, 18 March 1899, p. 1; *Telegraph*, 18 March 1899, p. 8.

7 *Telegraph,* 10 April 1899, p. 2.'Ambulance Sports', *Brisbane Courier*, 17 April 1889, p. 6.

8 'Road Racing at Rocklea', *Queenslander*, 17 June 1899, p. 1140S.

9 *Brisbane Courier*, 11 September 1899, p. 7. See also *Telegraph*, 12 June 1899, p. 6.

10 *Brisbane Courier*, 7 May 1900, p. 7; *Queenslander*, 12 May 1900, p. 907S.

11 'Redfern Gordon Club', *Brisbane Courier*, 14 May 1900, p. 4, 4 June 1900, p. 7; 'Road Races. Along Hamilton Road', *Telegraph*, 4 June 1900, p. 7.

12 *Telegraph*, 18 June 1900, p. 2; 'Queensland Cycling', *Referee*, 20 June 1900, p. 7; 'Hospital Sports', *The Week*, 22 June 1900, p. 29.

13 *Brisbane Courier*, 3 November 1900, p. 10.

14 *Queensland Post Office Directory* (Wise's), South Brisbane Directory, 1902, p. 1068. The same directory, p. 182, listed Thomas J. Shaw living at Belmore Cottage, Wynot Street, South Brisbane, the same address as his mother-in-law, Elizabeth Schultz.

15 Australian Marriage Index 1788–1950. 1901/B936. See also 'Shaw v Shaw', *Sydney Morning Herald*, 12 June 1917, p. 4.

16 'Splendid Business Property in Stanley Street, South Brisbane', *Brisbane Courier*, 7 May 1901, p. 8.

17 Australian Birth Index 1788–1922. For both boys deaths were recorded with the birth entries.

18 'In the Supreme Court of Queensland. In Insolvency', *Queensland Figaro*, 27 February 1902, p. 1.

19 Latin: 'in the form of a pauper', without the funds to pursue the normal costs of a lawsuit and allowed to proceed to court without payment of the usual fees.

20 'New Insolvent', *Brisbane Courier*, 1 March 1902, p. 11.

21 *Insolvency Papers for Thomas John Shaw 1902*, Supreme Court of Queensland in Insolvency, February–June, ID 1062165, Queensland State Archives.

22 *Insolvency Papers for Thomas John Shaw 1902.*

23 'Dunlop Road Route. Warrnambool to Melbourne', *Australian Cyclist and Motor-Car World*, 18 July 1901, p. 15.

24 John Craven, *The 'Warrnambool': A Fascinating and Colourful Insight Into One of the World's Greatest and Oldest Bike Races*, Dromana, Victoria, Bas Publishing, 2015, p. 29.

25 Craven, *The 'Warrnambool',* pp. 195–214. The years the race was not run were 1912–1921 (inclusive), 1927 and 1928, 1934 and 1940–1946.

26 Craven, *The 'Warrnambool',* pp. 30–9.

27 Georgine Clarsen, 'Pedaling Power: Bicycles, Subjectivities and Landscapes in a Settler Colonial Society', *Mobilities*, 10, 5, 2015, pp. 706, 709–10.

28 'Dunlop Road Race', *Australian Star*, 1 September 1902, p. 6.

29 'The Great Dunlop Road Race. Warrnambool to Melbourne', *New South Wales*

Cyclist, 13 September 1902, p. 5.

30 'Dunlop Road Route. Warrnambool to Melbourne', p. 15.

31 *Ballarat Star*, 1 September 1902, p. 4.

32 'The Dunlop Road Race. A Competitor Injured', *Argus*, 1 September 1902, p. 7.

33 'The Great Dunlop Road Race', p. 6.

34 'The Great Dunlop Road Race', pp. 5–6.

35 'The Great Dunlop Road Race', p. 5.

36 'Road Race. Warrnambool to Melbourne', *Punch*, 4 September 1902, pp. 12–14; 'One Hundred and Sixty-Five Miles in Nine Hours', *Weekly Times*, 6 September 1902, p. 9S.

37 *Punch*, 18 September 1902, p. 34.

38 Rod Charles, *A Whirr of Many Wheels: Cycling in Geelong, a Chronicle from 1869 to 1914*, Volume 1, Manifold Heights, Victoria, Charles & Co., p. 451.

39 'Dunlop Road Race Picture', *Hamilton Spectator*, 13 October 1909, p. 4.

40 'Motoring and Cycling', *Daily Telegraph*, 2 October 1909, p. 5.

41 'Warrnambool-Melbourne Road Race', *Age*, 1 September 1902, p. 6; 'The Big Road Race', *Sportsman*, 3 September 1902, p. 2.

42 'Motoring and Cycling World. Big Road Race Discussed', *Weekly Times*, 16 September 1922, p. 92. See also 'Warrnambool to Melbourne', *Sydney Morning Herald*, 13 September 1922, p. 13; 'Dunlop Road Race', *Sydney Sportsman*, 3 October 1922, p. 9.

43 For bicycle racing records such as lists of entrants, acceptances, handicaps and results it was the practice of clubs, race promoters, newspapers and cycling magazines to show only a rider's initials – or the first initial only.

44 *Brisbane Courier*, 5 December 1903, p. 7.

45 Queensland Birth Registrations, 1904 B7748. The B denotes Brisbane.

46 For example, *Macleay Argus*, 20 August 1904, p. 12.

47 *Macleay Argus*, 6 August 1904, p. 5.

48 *Macleay Chronicle*, 22 September 1904, p. 4. See also 'Apprehensions', *New South Wales Police Gazette*, 16 November 1904, p. 459.

49 'Deserting a Child', *Telegraph*, 4 October 1904, p. 2.

50 'Kempsey Court', *Macleay Chronicle*, 11 May 1905, p. 6.

51 *Camden News*, 4 January 1906, p. 1, 11 January 1906, p. 4, 18 January 1906, p. 8.

52 *Camden News*, 16 August 1906, p. 8. See also *Sydney Sportsman*, 12 September 1906, p. 8; 'Cycle and Motor', *Sydney Mail*, 1 August 1906, p. 313; *Sunday Sun*, 12 August 1906, p. 7; 'Camden-Ashfield Road Race', *Sydney Morning Herald*, 13 August 1906, p. 11.

53 John Hepher and John Drummond, *Goulburn to Sydney: A Narrative of Ninety Years of a Cycling Classic 1902–1992*, Queenstown, Tasmania, Penghana Press, 2007, p. 99.

54 'Cycling Race from Goulburn to Sydney', *Sunday Sun*, 8 September 1907, p. 3; 'Long-Distance Cycling', *Daily Telegraph*, 9 September 1907, p. 6; 'Cycling

Chatter', *Sydney Sportsman*, 11 September 1907, p. 4.

55 'Great Road Race', *Sydney Morning Herald*, 9 September 1907, p. 11.

56 Elizabeth Villy, *The Old Razorback Road; Life on the Great South Road Between Camden and Picton 1830–1930*, Sydney, Rosenberg, 2011.

57 *Truth*, 30 March 1913, p. 11.

58 *Sydney Morning Herald*, 12 June 1917, p. 4, 2 September 1918, p. 5.

59 'Boy drowned in Lagoon', *Brisbane Courier*, 21 January 1918, p. 6. See also *Darling Downs Gazette*, 21 January 1918, p. 4; *Armidale Express and New England General Advertiser*, 25 January 1918, p. 3.

60 Applications to Enlist in the Australian Imperial Force, Thos. J. Shaw/Thomas John Shaw, 2 March and 15 November 1917, National Archives of Australia.

61 Marriage registration for Thomas J. Shaw and Alice E. Hutchings, New South Wales BDM 14763/1919; Transcription, registration of marriage for Thomas John Shaw and Alice Eleanor Hutchings, 27 December 1919.

62 Death registration for Alice E. Shaw, New South Wales BDM 12239/1927; *Sydney Morning Herald*, 29 September 1927, p. 10.

63 *Bankruptcy Papers for Thomas John Shaw 1927–1928*, Supreme Court of New South Wales in Bankruptcy, Item 26637, Box 10/24305, State Archives and Records NSW.

64 *Bankruptcy Papers for Thomas John Shaw 1927–1928.*

65 *Bankruptcy Papers for Thomas John Shaw 1927–1928.*

66 'Without Reserve ... In the Estate of T. J. Shaw, of Merrylands, in Bankruptcy', *Cumberland Argus and Fruitgrowers Advocate*, 25 May 1928, p. 5.

67 'In the Estate of T. J. Shaw, in Bankruptcy', *Cumberland Argus and Fruitgrowers Advocate*, 8 November 1928, p. 5.

68 'In Bankruptcy'. *New South Wales Government Gazette*, 3 May 1929, p. 1973.

69 *Bankruptcy Papers for Thomas John Shaw 1927–1928.*

70 'T. J. S. Cycles. Speedy and Reliable', *Gosford Times and Wyong District Advocate*, 14 October 1926, p. 11.

71 *Gosford Times and Wyong District Advocate*, 9 July 1925, p. 12, 17 September 1925, p. 12, 22 October 1925, p. 15, 3 December 1925, p. 15.

72 'Goulburn–Sydney Race', *Newcastle Sun*, 14 August 1926, p. 6.

73 Death registration for Thomas John Shaw, New South Wales BDM 18706/1956

7 – The Brother-in-Law: Brice Heber Thomas

1 Death registration for Herbert Charles Thomas, New South Wales BDM 2314/1874.

2 Birth registration for Brice Heber Thomas, New South Wales BDM 4198/1874.

3 Marriage registration for Joseph Staples and Mary Sarah Thomas, New South Wales BDM 1267/1880.

4 *City of Sydney Assessments*, Cook Ward, 1882 for four-roomed house at 6 East Street, Redfern occupied by Joseph Staples; *Sands Directory*, 1886, 1887, 1889.

5 Death registration for Joseph Staples, New South Wales BDM 1389/1887.

6 *Daily Telegraph*, 21 January 1890, p. 6.

7 Certificate No. 708 issued by the New South Wales Department of Public Instruction, Technical Education Branch, Sydney Technical College, 4 December 1890.

8 Birth registration for Mary Amelia Shaw, New South Wales BDM 2057/1894.

9 The card has survived, Shaw family archives.

10 Thomas family archives.

11 *Sydney Morning Herald*, 18 June 1892, p. 2, 21 June 1892, p. 6; Daily *Telegraph*, 22 June 1892, p. 6; *Newcastle Morning Herald and Miners' Advocate*, 2 July 1892, p. 11.

12 *Evening News*, 22 June 1892, p. 5; *Referee*, 22 June 1892, p. 3; *Sydney Mail*, 25 June 1892, p. 1471.

13 *Official Programme, Sydney Bicycle Club, 11th Annual Amateur Race Meeting*, Association Cricket Ground, Moore Park, Saturday 3rd September 1892, Box 18, Davis Sporting Collection, Mitchell Library, Sydney.

14 'The Sydney Bicycle Club Sports', *Daily Telegraph*, 5 September 1892, p. 6.

15 'Cycling Notes … The Austral Bicycle Club. First Road Race.', *Referee,* 21 September 1892, p. 8. See also *Sydney Morning Herald*, 15 September 1892, p. 6; *Daily Telegraph,* 15 September 1892, p. 3; *Australian Town and Country Journal*, 24 September 1892, p. 41.

16 'Cycling. Speedwell Club', *Daily Telegraph*, 29 May 1893, p. 3.

17 Analysis of over 300 reports on bicycle racing at Lillie Bridge in the *Referee*, *Evening News*, *Daily Telegraph*, *Australian Star*, *Sunday Times* and *Sydney Morning Herald*, August 1893 to May 1895.

18 Photograph captioned 'Young Harry Sailing Crew 1893', Thomas family archives.

19 'Young Harry Sailing Club Picnic', *Sydney Morning Herald*, 8 May 1894, p. 8.

20 'Young Harry Sailing Crew', *Australian Star*, 9 May 1894, p. 8.

21 *Australian Star*, 23 January 1892, p. 3.

22 *Referee*, 16 May 1894, p. 3, 'The Goulburn Cycling Carnival', 30 May 1894, p. 7; *Goulburn Herald*, 16 May 1894, p. 2, 'Cycling Carnival, 25 May 1894, p. 2; *Australian Star*, 25 May 1894, p. 4; 'Cycling Meeting at Goulburn', *Sydney Morning Herald*, 25 May 1894, p. 3; 'Cycling Carnival', *Goulburn Evening Penny Post*, 26 May 1894, p. 4; *Sydney Mail*, 2 June 1894, p. 1132.

23 'Cycling Carnival', *Goulburn Herald*, 25 May 1894, p. 2.

24 'League of New South Wales Wheelmen. Champion Cycling Carnival', *Goulburn Herald*, 9 November 1894, p. 2. See also *Evening News*, 10 November 1894, p. 5.

25 'League of New South Wales Wheelmen. Champion Cycling Carnival', *Goulburn Herald*, 12 November 1894, p. 2. See also *Sydney Morning Herald*, 12 November 1894, p. 6;

26 Certificate of Marriage between Brice Heber Thomas, 86 Arthur Street, Surry Hills and Mary Amelia Thomas, 103 Point Piper Road, Woollahra, 18 December 1895; Marriage registration for Brice H. Thomas and Mary Shaw, New South Wales BDM 7992/1895.

27 Thomas family archives, based on entries in Electoral Rolls and various issues of *Sands Directories*.

28 Thomas family archives.

29 *Sunday Times*, 12 April 1908, p. 4, 28 November 1909, p. 3.

30 Index to Register of Firms, State Archives and Records NSW, 37443 [2/8551], 3 November 1920.

31 Thomas family archives.

32 Advertisement by Valentine and Company, General Auctioneers, *Sydney Morning Herald*, 5 July 1923, p. 13.

33 Death registration for Brice Heber Thomas, New South Wales BDM 30138/1958; Thomas family archives.

34 Death registration for Mary Amelia Thomas, New South Wales BDM 14897/1960; Thomas family archives.

Select Bibliography

Alderson, Frederick, *Bicycling: A History*, Newton Abbott, David & Charles, 1972.

Aplin, Graham and Storey, John, *Waterfront Sydney 1860–1920*, Sydney, Allen & Unwin, 1984.

Barnard, Edwin, *Emporium: Selling the Dream in Colonial Australia*, Canberra, National Library of Australia, 2015.

Brodsky, Isadore, *Sydney's Little World of Woolloomooloo*, Sydney, Old Sydney Free Press, 1967.

Buchanan, R. A., *The Power of the Machine: The Impact of Technology from 1700 to the Present Day*, London, Penguin, p. 147.

Bryson, Bill, *One Summer: America 1927*, London, Doubleday, 2013.

Cashman, Richard and McKernan, Michael (eds.), *Sport in History: The Making of Modern Sporting History*, Brisbane, University of Queensland Press, 1979.

Charles, Rod, *A Whirr of Many Wheels: Cycling in Geelong, a Chronicle from 1869 to 1914, Volume 1*, Manifold Heights, Victoria, Charles & Co., 2013.

Craven, John, *The 'Warrnambool': A Fascinating and Colourful Insight Into One of the World's Greatest and Oldest Bike Races*, Dromana, Victoria, Bas Publishing, 2015.

de Montfort, Carlin, 'Centreboards and Sails: The Rise of Open-Boat Racing in Sydney During the 1890s', *The International Journal of the History of Sport*, 30, 2, 2013, 145–61.

Derriman, Philip, *The Grand Old Ground; A History of the Sydney Cricket Ground*, Sydney, Cassell, 1981.

Dunstan, Keith, *Sports*, Melbourne, Cassell, 1973.

Ferguson, John, (ed.), *The Amateurs: The Second Century Begins 1972–1992*, Sydney, Maritime Heritage Press, 1976.

Fitzpatrick, Jim, *Major Taylor in Australia*, Kilcoy, Queensland, Star Hill Studio, 2011.

Fitzpatrick, Jim, *Wheeling Matilda: The Story of Australian Cycling*, Kilcoy, Queensland, Star Hill Studio, 2013.

Fitzpatrick, Jim, *The Bicycle and the Bush: Man and Machine in Rural Australia*, Melbourne, Oxford University Press, 1980.

Fotheringham, William, *Cyclopedia: It's All About the Bike,* Chicago, Review Press, 2015.

Garran, Andrew (ed.), *Picturesque Atlas of Australasia*, Sydney and Melbourne, The Picturesque Atlas Publishing Co., 1886.

Graves, H, George Lacey Hillier and Susan, Countess of Malmesbury, *Cycling*, London, Lawrence and Bullen, 1898.

Grivell, H. ('Curly'), *Australian Cycling in the Golden Days*, Adelaide, Courier Press, 1952.

Hanslow, F.G. Chippendale (ed.), *Australian Cycling Annual: A Complete Record of Australian Cycling and Other Interesting Information*, Sydney, George Robertson & Co., 1897.

Henslow, Leonard, *Cycling: The Sport and the Pastime*, Melbourne, Martin, 1897.

Hepher, Jack and Drummond, John, *Goulburn to Sydney: A Narrative of Ninety Years of a Cycling Classic 1902–1992*, Queenstown, Tasmania, Penghana Press, 2007.

Herlihy, David, *Bicycle: The History*, New Haven, Yale University Press, 2004.

Hoskins, Ian, *Sydney Harbour: A History*, Sydney, UNSW Press, 2009.

Hutchinson, Michael, *Re: Cyclists: 200 Years on Two Wheels*, London, Bloomsbury, 2017.

Inglis, Gordon, *Sport and Pastime in Australia*, London, Methuen, 1912.

James, Bill and James, Jean, *Queensland Cycling: The First Hundred Years*, Brisbane, Cyclists Association, 1993.

Johnson, Eileen, *They Came Direct; 'Light Brigade' 1863*, Tinana, Queensland, Eileen Johnson, 2005.

Kavanagh, W. H., *Album Collection of News Cuttings, Tickets, Invitations, Business Cards and Other Memorabilia Related to Australian Cycling 1886–1912*, State Library of New South Wales.

Keneally, Thomas, *Australians: From Eureka to the Diggers*, Sydney, Allen & Unwin, 2011.

Lacey, Robert, *Ford: The Men and the Machine*, London, Pan, 1987.

Lazarus, Geraldine, *Development of the Motor Car Industry in Australia*, Unpublished PhD thesis, Monash University, 1981.

Luetiens, Joannah, 'Cycling Through the History of Melbourne', *Agora*, 48, 1, 2013.

Mallon, B. and Heijams, J., *Historical Dictionary of Cycling*, Lantham, Md., Scarecrow Press, 2011.

Mecredy, R. J. and Wilson, A. J., *The Art and Pastime of Cycling*, London, Archbald Constable & Co., 1897.

Nadel, Dave and Ryan, Graeme (eds.), *Sport in Victoria: A History*, Melbourne, Ryan Publishing and Australian Society for Sports History, 2015.

Nowra, Louis, *Woolloomooloo: A Biography*, Sydney, New South Publishing, 2017.

Nye, Peter, *Hearts of Lions: The History of American Bicycle Racing*, New York, W. W. Norton & Co., 1988.

O'Hara, John, *A Mug's Game: A History of Gaming and Betting in Australia*, Sydney, New South Wales University Press, 1988.

Peake, Wayne, *Sydney's Pony Racecourses: An Alternative Racing History*, Sydney, Walla Walla Press, 2006.

Ritchie, Andrew, *King of the Road: An Illustrated History of Cycling*, London, Wildwood House, 1975.

Ross, Bob, *The Sailing Australians*, Adelaide, Rigby, 1973.

Simpson, Claire (ed.), *Scorchers, Ramblers and Rovers: Australian Cycling Histories*, Melbourne, Australian Society for Sports History, 2006.

Sloane, E., *The Complete Book of Cycling*, New York, Simon and Schuster, 1988.

Smethurst, Paul, *The Bicycle: Towards a Global History*, Basingstoke, Hampshire, Palgrave Macmillan, 2015.

Smith, Robert, *A Social History of the Bicycle: Its Life and Times in America*, New York, American Heritage Press, 1972.

Stannard, Bruce, *The Bluewater Bushmen: The Colourful Story of Australia's Best and Boldest Boatmen*, Sydney, Angus and Robertson, 1981.

Sydney Cricket Ground Museum, *Celebrating 120 Years of the Ladies Pavilion*, Sydney, 2016.

Sydney Amateur Sailing Club Historical Committee, *The Amateurs: A Documentation of the First 100 Years of Sailing on Sydney Harbour*, Sydney, Sydney Amateur Sailing Club, 1972.

The London Library, *Cycling: The Craze of the Hour*, London, Pushkin Press, 2016.

Vamplew, Wray et al. (eds.), *The Oxford Companion to Australian Sport*, Melbourne, Oxford University Press, 1997.

Villy, Elizabeth, *The Old Razorback Road; Life on the Great South Road Between Camden and Picton 1830–1930*, Sydney, Rosenberg, 2011.

Warne, Catherine, *Pictorial History: Lower North Shore*, Sydney, Kingsclear Books, 2005.

Willis, Ian, *Pictorial History of Camden and District*, Sydney, Kingsclear Books, 2015.

Index

Adelaide Oval 14
Albion Ground 57, 84
AJS (motorcycle) 79
amateur 17–20, 37, 42–4, 52, 55, 59, 65, 71, 98, 124, 142, 156, 171
Amilcar (car) 79
ANZAC 94–5
Ariel (bicycle) 118
Argyll (car) 75, 153
Arncliffe 153, 185
Austral Bicycle Club 39, 52, 91, 174–5
Austral-Swift Race 156
Austral Wheel Race 17–18, 113
Australian Cycling Union 19
Australian Motor Yacht Squadron 80
Ayer's Sarsaparilla 134

Ballarat 42
Balmain 93–5, 102, 137, 179
Beeston Humber (bicycle) 103, 118
betting, *see* gambling
Bondi Junction 72
Bowral 68, 108
Bowral Wheel Race 68, 108
Botany 13, 37–9, 41, 46, 53, 57, 62–3, 83–4, 101, 137, 174–6
Bourke 21
Brisbane Cricket Ground/ Woolloongabba/'Gabba' 14, 115, 123–4, 127–8, 132–3, 135, 155–7
Brisbane Dinghey Club 120–1
Brisbane Exhibition Ground 123, 125, 136, 156
Brisbane River 29, 35, 120, 125–6, 136, 139
Brisbane Wheel Race 116, 127
Buick (car) 75, 79, 149, 152
Bundaberg 115, 117, 130

Camden 13, 139–54, 156, 166, 186
Camden Aquatic Sports 154
Camden Bicycle Depot 139, 149, 166
Camden Cottage Hospital 154
Camden Cycling Club 145, 154
Camden Motor Garage 149–52
Camden to Sydney Road Race 142, 166
Camden Wheel Race 145, 154, 166
Campbelltown 140, 148, 152
Century Run 6, 70
Charleston, Daniel 159
Charmant 137
Charters Towers 28, 113, 117, 130, 136–7
Chinese 39, 108–10
Cleveland Cycle Company 129, 158
Colac 159–61
Corrie, Elizabeth (née Dawson) 173
Crows Nest 72, 78
Crows Nest Bicycle Club 74
Crusaders' Bicycle Club 9, 16, 41, 52–3, 82, 98, 175

Dalgety & Company 149
De Dion 128, 144
Dee Shaw 80
Diavolo 143
dinghy/dinghey/dingy 35, 39, 119–20, 126, 136, 179–80, 186

Dubbo 8, 20, 41, 49, 55
Duck, Fred 140
Dunlop 13, 23, 101, 108, 112, 127–8, 145, 153, 159, 161–3, 166–7
Dwyer, Con 18

Eastern Suburbs Bicycle Club 71
electric light 12, 43–5, 105–6, 121, 177
Etna (sailboat) 120–1, 125–6, 132, 135–7, 139–40, 186
Etna (bicycles and motorcycles) 139–43, 145–6, 186
Etna Cycle Works, Camden 140
Etna Plate Polish Company 186
Excelsior (motorcycle) 78–9

Ford (car) 80, 149–53
Fordson (tractor) 152

gambling 12, 21, 23–4, 41–2, 44–5, 100, 119, 122, 126, 129, 178
Goold Bicycle Company 119, 124, 128, 139, 142, 158
Goulburn 13, 20, 41, 47, 58–9, 78, 84–5, 87, 101, 103–5, 113, 142, 181–5
Goulburn to Sydney Road Race 13, 101, 142, 166, 171
Granville 94–5, 168–71
Gympie 115, 117, 125

Hampden Track 100, 106
Hampden Wheel Race 103
Hamilton, Isabella 'Bell' 64
Healy, Mick 125, 130–1, 133
high wheelers/penny farthings/ ordinaries 1, 3–6, 8, 14, 33, 35–7, 40, 47, 50, 52–6, 69, 168, 174–5
Highland Gathering 14, 56, 67, 84, 104
Homebush 10, 171
Hudson (car) 75

Inch, Mary Anne, *see* Shaw, Mary Anne
Inch, Nathaniel 30
Inglethorpe, Rachel 48
Irex 136

James Challenge Cup 124, 136
Johnstone's Bay Sailing Club 121, 136–7, 179
Junee Wheel Race 113

Kempsey Cycle Depot 164
Kempsey Gaol 165–6
Knowles-Darracq (car) 143

League of New South Wales Wheelmen 9–11, 14, 17, 19–21, 23, 26, 39, 46–7, 56–7, 59, 62, 64–5, 68, 71, 84–5, 88, 90, 93, 99, 101–2, 105, 108, 113, 143, 166, 181
League of Queensland Wheelmen 14, 115, 117, 124, 127–30, 135–7, 156–7
League of Victorian Wheelmen 11, 14, 19
Lewis, Bob 86, 90–1, 99, 178, 184
Light Brigade 30, 34
Lillie Bridge Grounds 13, 23, 42–7, 54–5, 66, 82, 84, 98, 177–9
Long Reef 76

Mademoiselle Serpolette 6
Maitland 20, 28, 41, 56–7, 84, 87, 99, 144
Maryborough 116–19
Massey Harris (bicycle) 118, 160
mechanic 100, 140, 142–5, 152–4, 158, 164, 166, 168, 171
Megson, Joseph 'Joe' 57, 60–1, 66, 68, 77, 82, 84–7, 90–1, 99, 108, 115, 135, 178, 184–5
Mele Bilo 154
Melbourne 3, 6–7, 13–14, 25–8, 39, 41–2, 85, 105, 111, 113, 115, 117, 159–61, 163, 184
Melbourne Bicycle Club 8, 15, 18, 113
Melbourne Exhibition Ground 114
Melbourne Cricket Ground 14, 113

Merrylands 169–70
Minerva (car) 146–7
Mitchell (car) 148
Moore Park 22, 37, 39, 46, 52, 54, 56, 60, 82, 143, 175
Moss Vale 68, 108
moto-cycle/motocycle 90–2, 100, 111
motorcycle 15, 56, 75–80, 100, 127–8, 144–8, 154, 186
Motor Cyclists' Association of New South Wales 77
Mount Gellibrand 161
multicycle 20, 105–6, 116, 125

New South Wales Cyclists' Union 7, 11, 16, 71, 166
Newcastle 20–1, 28, 40–1, 50, 54–6, 63, 85, 87, 96, 107, 112–13, 127
Newcastle Wheel Race 107, 112
Newport/Newport Beach 74, 78
Newtown 116, 138, 140, 186
North Sydney 13, 48, 50, 71–2, 74, 77–8, 80, 138, 179
North Sydney Reserve 53–4
Northern Suburbs Motor Club 77, 79
Northern Suburbs Motorcycle Club 75–6, 78–9

Olympic Ground 58–9, 181–3
Our Own 125–6
overlanding 160

Pacific Highway 80
Paddington 11, 69–72, 93–5, 154
Paddington Bicycle Club 69, 71, 93
Parramatta 10, 20, 46, 62, 64, 70, 76, 87, 94, 144, 166, 169–70, 186
Parrett, George 83, 179–81
Parrett, William 29, 83, 179
Pathe Freres 162
pedestrianism 13, 21, 23, 29, 44, 97, 136, 157, 174
Phoenix (car) 147
Picton 87, 142, 144, 152, 154
Pitkethly, Tait 31–2, 51
professional 19–22, 26, 42, 47, 64, 124, 128, 157, 166, 175

quads 105, 112
Queensland Cyclists' Union 156–7
Quong Tart 23, 39, 52, 110, 175
quints 105, 115–16

Red Bird (bicycle) 113, 117–19, 123–4, 128–9, 132, 158
Redfern 13, 51, 59, 61, 84, 98, 157, 173
Redfern Bicycle Club 9–10, 17, 61–2, 175
Regina 83, 178, 180
Rickards, Fred 'Freddy' 132, 136
rinking night 9–10
road race/racing 10, 12–13, 15, 27–8, 36–41, 46, 53, 57, 71, 74, 83–4, 93, 101, 117, 122, 124, 126, 141–2, 145, 156–7, 159–64, 166, 171, 175–6
Rockhampton 28, 113, 115, 117, 128
Roma 117, 119
Royal Agricultural Society 48, 66
Royal Enfield (motorcycle) 80
Rudge (bicycle) 38, 53

St Leonards 13, 16, 41, 53, 64, 82
St Patrick's Day 123, 135, 156
safety bicycle/safeties 1, 3–6, 14, 22, 33, 35–6, 38, 40, 50, 52–4, 56, 145–6, 160, 174
sailboat/sailboating 29, 35, 119–23, 126, 132, 139–40, 179–80, 186
Shaw, Alice (née Hutchings) 169
Shaw Brothers 72, 80, 138
Shaw, Christina 'Teenie' 29, 83, 179
Shaw, Donald Samuel Ewart Shaw 'Don' 72, 74, 76–80, 138
Shaw, Frederick Ewart 'Fred/Freddy/Freddie/F. E.' 29, 68, 72, 84, 86, 88, 91–2, 96–101, 103–8, 112–21, 123–58, 164, 166, 178, 186
Shaw, Henry Tait 'Harry/H. T./Hy'

29, 38, 44–5, 56–7, 81–5, 87–8, 90–6, 98–9, 176, 178–80, 183, 185
Shaw, James 29, 51–2, 81, 185
Shaw, Janet 'Jessie' (née Pitkethly) 29–30
Shaw, Mary Amelia 29, 173, 185–6
Shaw, Mary Anne (née Inch) 29–32, 34–6, 51, 69, 81, 97, 155, 173
Shaw, Samuel John 32
Shaw, Samuel Robinson 'Sam/Sammy/S. R.' 29, 38–40, 45–7, 51–64, 67–72, 74–7, 79, 82–4, 91–2, 96, 98–9, 108, 132, 138, 174–5, 178, 180, 182–4
Shaw, Thomas John 'Tom/T. J.' 29, 88, 129, 132, 155–9, 163–6, 168–71
Shaw, Wilhelmina 'Minnie' (née Schultz) 158, 168
Shaw, William 29–32, 34–6, 51, 81, 97, 155, 173
Shaw, William Nathaniel 'W. N.' 29, 36–42, 44–51, 54, 56, 58, 81, 83, 174–6, 178, 180, 182
Sir Joseph Banks Grounds 63
smoke concert/smoker 9–10, 39, 67, 71, 74, 77, 102–3, 107, 116–17, 127, 137, 175
South Australia 8, 14, 28, 85, 87, 135
South Brisbane Bicycle Club 124, 157
South Brisbane Bicycle Agency 158
Speedwell Bicycle Club 10, 23, 41, 43, 46, 55, 65, 82–3, 160, 175–6
Staples, Joseph 173
Stearns/Stearns Yellow Fellow (bicycle) 128, 133
Suburban Bicycle Club 9, 16, 22–3, 38, 52–3, 82, 84, 98, 174
Sydney Bicycle Club 8–10, 16, 37–8, 42, 46, 52–3, 82, 175
Sydney Cricket Ground/Association Cricket Ground 7, 10, 14, 16, 19, 22, 39, 41, 46, 52–3, 55, 57, 59–60, 62–6, 68–9, 82, 84–5, 87–8, 98–9, 105–6, 143, 175
Sydney Flying Squadron 154, 179
Summer Hill Bicycle Club 10, 16

tandems 15, 27, 85, 91, 101, 105, 108, 111–12, 116, 123, 125, 127–8
Texas Jack 133–4
The Oaks 154
Thomas, Brice Heber 29, 39, 45–7, 57–8, 83–4, 153, 172–83, 185–6
Thomas, Mary Amelia *see* Shaw, Mary Amelia
Thomas, Mary Sarah (née Corrie) 173
Thomas, William Hinton 173
Thirlmere Club 154
T.J.S. bicycle 168, 171
Toowoomba 123, 132, 136, 144
Townsville 137
track race/track racing 9, 12–13, 16, 29, 38, 45
triplets 105, 112, 116, 133

Victoria Wheel Race 69
Vulcan (car) 148

Wandeen 137
Warrnambool 13, 159–61, 163
Warrnambool to Melbourne Road Race 13, 159–61, 163
Wee Dash 80
Werribee 161
West, Dr Francis 143–4, 148
Willoughby Bicycle Club 74, 78
Winchelsea 159, 161
Wollstonecraft 74, 77, 80
Woollahra 69, 72, 185
Woolloomooloo/The 'Loo 1, 29–35, 50–1, 69, 77, 81, 93–4, 97, 122, 128, 154–5, 173
Woy Woy 171

Young Harry 178–80

Zephyr 137
Zimmerman, Arthur 14, 66, 87, 109

www.ingramcontent.com/pod-product-compliance
Ingram Content Group UK Ltd.
Pitfield, Milton Keynes, MK11 3LW, UK
UKHW041637190726
13854UKWH00006B/2539

9 781925 801521